MUSIC IN PROTESTANT WORSHIP

Dwight Steere has held music posts at colleges in Iowa, Ohio, and the Carolinas. Since 1945, he has headed the department of music at Centre College of Kentucky and conducted the college choir.

A native of Michigan, Steere received most of his musical training at the University of Michigan, where he studied organ under Earl V. Moore and Palmer Christian. After graduate study there, he took additional training at the Christiansen Choral School.

Throughout his teaching years, Steere has served as organist and choirmaster in many churches of different sizes and denominations. An Associate of the American Guild of Organists, he is the author of *Music for the Protestant Church Choir*.

MUSIC
IN
PROTESTANT
WORSHIP

Dwight Steere

JOHN KNOX PRESS
RICHMOND, VIRGINIA

Library of Congress Catalog Card Number: 60-15657

Preface

This book is written first of all for ministers. Of course, quantities of books on worship have been written for ministers by ministers. Some of these have dealt briefly with music in worship. On the other hand, quantities of books have been written for church musicians by church musicians. But between the two categories there has been something of a chasm. This is one of the few books written for ministers by a church musician.

No matter how well equipped he may feel himself to be to face the world, the young minister is not long out of seminary before he becomes aware of gaps or weaknesses in his training. Frequently the seminary is in no way to blame. It may have done all it could do within the three years available to it. Three years are not enough. Therefore some things must be neglected in order that the main foundations may be well laid. Many seminaries would probably agree with many ministers in the field that music in worship has been one of the branches too often neglected.

Whether the seminary is large or small, if the seminarian gets any music at all, it is apt to be little more than a course in hymnology, with perhaps some fundamentals of music thrown in. He is fortunate indeed if his preparation has included precise and practical information on how to make use of the musical resources he has at hand. Yet he may need to furnish the guidance for the building of a new church, or the rebuilding of an old one, and may have to meet the problems of organ selection and choir location head-on. His church may look to him for leadership in organizing the musical life of his church. Although he may not "know one note from another," he may be obliged to take command of the music in the small churches he serves. Ultimately, he *must* determine how music is actually to be used in his worship services.

Yet the minister, young or older, will not easily find the prac-

5

tical help he may need on his musical problems. Some of it is scattered widely in technical books. Some of it is not in books at all. Tied as he is to one church at a time, he is not often able to travel and to compare his problems with those of other ministers. To all of these, this book is addressed.

This book is also written for church musicians, present and future. I do not speak as one having authority. I have deliberately avoided the use of technical information on these pages. The musician will already possess that. I have tried rather to throw light on those areas which are not normally covered by the usual college or training school courses on church music. This information falls largely under that loose category known as varied experience. Curiosity concerning the worship practices in all sizes and types of churches has brought me much. Persistence has brought more.

The word "Protestant" in the title of this book is used in its broadest sense. Its first concern is with non-liturgical churches; their worship practices tend to be less prescribed. There should, however, be much here that is useful for certain Episcopal and Lutheran churches, particularly those in smaller communities.

I would not have the boldness to address both the clergy and musicians without having sought and received much help from those wiser than I. Being a layman, I particularly needed guidance from able ministers. The first of these is Dr. Donald E. Bartlett, now of Lake Forest College, with whom I was associated for years on the faculty of Centre College of Kentucky. There is also Dr. Harry G. Goodykoontz, Professor of Christian Education of Louisville Presbyterian Seminary, who took time from a busy schedule to counsel me. My former pastor, Dr. John R. Gosney, now Field Director of Christian Education to the Synod of New Jersey of the United Presbyterian Church in the United States of America, brought to my aid his great knowledge of the worship of many denominations. The Rev. George E. Calvert, pastor of the Church of the Son of Man, on East 104th Street, one of the churches of East Harlem Protestant Parish in New York City, shared his insights on the problems of the inner-city church. I also owe much to my son, the Rev. David Steere, of the faculty of Louisville Presbyterian Seminary, who not only brought me much knowledge concerning the rural church, but also spent many hours reading and criticizing the manuscript.

I am grateful to a number of musicians who checked my knowledge at many points: Mr. Frederick L. Swann, one of the two organists of Riverside Church in New York City; Mr. W. Raymond Randall, organist and choirmaster of the First Presbyterian Church of Stamford, Connecticut; Mr. David W. McCormick, Supervisor of Field Work of the School of Sacred Music of Union Theological Seminary of New York City, who also spent many hours reviewing and criticizing the manuscript; and Dr. W. Lawrence Curry, Music Editor of Westminster Press and Music Consultant to the United Presbyterian Church in the United States of America. His wife, Mrs. Louise H. Curry, gave valuable aid in regard to the speech choir.

I could not have written on the organ safely without the generous help of the following officials in four organ companies: Mr. M. A. Gariepy of the Aeolian-Skinner Organ Company; Mr. R. L. Hillgreen of Hillgreen, Lane & Co.; Mr. Martin M. Wick of the Wicks Organ Company; and Mr. William E. Pilcher, Jr., of M. P. Möller, Inc. I am also grateful to the various electronic organ companies for all the materials furnished me. Finally, I would not forget those unsung heroes who staff the various libraries I have visited, and who cheerfully satisfied my wishes.

This book was made possible in part throught grants-in-aid allocated by the Board of Christian Education of the Presbyterian Church in the United States, and by the Research Fund of Centre College of Kentucky. The author, however, is solely responsible for the contents.

Centre College of Kentucky, in Danville

Contents

Introduction

The time is at hand to re-establish worship
at the center of the church.[1]

"Preacher," said a member to his pastor at the close of a rural
church service, "it took you thirty-five minutes today to get rid
of the preliminaries!" To this church member—I did not say
worshiper—the only significant part of the service he had attended
was the sermon. He is not alone. There are still many laymen and
not a few ministers who would call morning worship the "preaching service."

This belief in the primacy of preaching is not a strange thing.
It lies at the center of Protestant thought. The Protestant Reformation was a movement of preaching and teaching. Yet it must
not be supposed that worship was neglected. When Luther and
Archbishop Cranmer sought to give the Mass to the people they
were certainly not destroying worship, but changing it, so as to involve the people in it. Although Calvin, as he looked at Roman
Catholic ritual practices, wrote that "numerous ceremonies have no
other use than to stupefy the people, instead of instructing them,"[2]
he prescribed an order of worship which made considerable use of
stated prayers, as well as other fixed items of worship.

With the advent in the British Isles and later in America of
what may loosely be called Puritanism, the emphasis changed.
The exposition of the Scriptures and the sermon, then frequently
two parts of the same meeting, were greatly expanded. The extempore prayer replaced all use of materials from *The Book of
Common Prayer*. Churches of the Reformed tradition tended to
forget the ordered worship planned by Calvin. American Methodists early rejected the Anglican ritualism recommended to them by
Wesley. The use of creeds, the Lord's Prayer, the Lord's Supper,
and all congregational and choral responses ceased in many of

our churches. The tendency, particularly in America, was to stress the informal aspects of worship.

The past few years, however, have witnessed a change in the current Protestant thought and practice. Preaching and teaching are not enough to keep the Church vigorous and devout. This we lack: an emphasis on corporate worship. This need is reflected in the titles of three books that have been written during this century: *Restoring Worship, The Recovery of Worship,* and *Reality in Worship*.[3] Many other books on worship have been published during the past few years. Several denominations have set up commissions which have published materials aimed at the enrichment of devotional life within the churches. In our church colleges, theological seminaries, and training schools, worship is claiming a somewhat greater portion of our attention.

Yet "the conduct of public worship is probably the weakest point in the ordinary protestant church," writes Dr. A. W. Palmer.[4] It is still possible for a seminary student to complete his curriculum and receive ordination with very little training in the conduct of public worship. It is possible for a minister to spend his life driven by ever-recurring sermon deadlines, harried by countless demands on his time and sympathy, without ever acquiring the use of those rich agencies of worship which could make his ministry more vital. If a minister cannot command the various resources of corporate worship, how can he summon them from those who assist him in worship? How can he transmit them to his congregation?

> If it be true, in the words of E. R. Micklem, that "in order that she shall accomplish anything the Church must live, and her life depends on her worship," then no part of a minister's training, and no part of his work, is so important as the preparation to lead the worship of his people.[5]

What Do You Mean—Worship?

Worship has been described in various ways: one writer calls it celebration; another says that it consists in appreciation, offering, and communion; another defines it as the recognition of the worth-ship of God. We recognize that it exists in at least four relationships or levels: that of private prayer, that of family devotions, that of such less formal groups as the Sunday school class or the youth fellowship, and that of public worship within the Church. The four levels are interrelated and interdependent; it is hard for a Christian's spiritual life to be healthy unless all four levels of devotion are active. It is likewise difficult for the Church's spiritual life to be sound unless the devotional life of its membership is active on all four levels.

It follows, I believe, that it would be difficult for individuals to maintain a consistent closeness to God if their only contacts with Him were in terms of personal and family devotions. On the other hand, we should not expect to experience deeply the presence of God in corporate worship unless that experience grows out of our personal and family devotions. We discuss worship hereafter at the upper two levels, but not because we regard the lower two as being less important. It is rather that music has less significance in personal and family devotions but may exert a profound influence on worship within the Church.

We speak of the Church in three common relationships:

> We build a church.
> We belong to a church.
> We go to church.

But whether we speak of the Church as a building, as a fellowship, or as the practice of corporate worship, we are speaking inevitably of the same thing, for we as Christians must relate ourselves to the Church in all three ways. *We are the Church*; we cannot live successfully separated from that Body of which we are a part.

For the purposes of this study, let us define worship in this way: Worship is the practice of communion with God within the Christian fellowship. It is a two-way conversation. He speaks to us, and we to Him. We speak to Him through our adoration in prayer and praise; through our confessions and petitions; through our hymns, anthems, responses, and organ music; through our offering of self and substance. He speaks to us through the beauty, dignity, and majesty of the house we have built for Him; through His Word; through the messages of His servants in pulpit and choir; through the sacraments; through the silence within the sanctuary, in which He can speak most freely.

A deep sense of communion with God is not easy to achieve. It is not that God is either far from us or unwilling to talk with us. It is rather that we, through ignorance, indifference, or hostility, have generated within ourselves so much spiritual static that it is difficult for us to speak to Him, and we can hear Him speak scarcely at all. For "God is a Spirit," and we must worship Him in spirit. If as we approach His presence we cannot be divested of our selfishness, or freed from the anxieties and burdens of our daily lives, we cannot enter freely into the life of His Spirit, nor can we clearly feel His presence.

The goal of our corporate worship should be the perfect experience of the presence of God. How is this experience to be achieved? The design of its achievement is twofold: On the one hand, the Church should provide those physical and spiritual conditions which give to the worshiper direct, easy, and continuing access to God's presence. On the other hand, the Church should shut out all those influences and associations which suggest to the worshiper the life of the world outside. The church building is the house of God, and should not remind those who enter it of an auditorium or an assembly hall. The attitude of those entering it should be that of reverence and awed expectancy, and not that of those who seek human fellowship, or even knowledge. The words uttered and the music sounded should draw the worshiper into the world of the spirit, and hold him there. Even the sermon, which must inevitably deal with the job of everyday living, must detach itself sufficiently from this daily life to obtain the perspective of spiritual judgment.

Worship in the Church should not be primarily for human fellowship, although one can scarcely worship without a warm fellow feeling for those who share his experience. Worship should not be, first of all, the occasion for one to escape his burdens and perplexities, although worship should bring him cleansing and relief. The worshiper should not seek knowledge above all, although new insight will usually come with worship. Worship will bring all these things, and more. Its most precious gift is the experience itself, the presence of God. From this experience should also come guidance and power for living. Perhaps the greatest task of the Church is to provide for those who seek it these regular periods of spiritual withdrawal, refreshing, and retooling. This is the heart of corporate worship.

Enter Music

No attempt needs to be made in this day to justify the use of music in church. We have moved a long distance from Calvin's limitation of music in church to metrical psalms. After bitter controversy the hymn, the organ, and the choir have won almost universal acceptance as aids to divine worship. Who in Christendom would still question the value of music in worship? But where few would shut music out of worship, there are very many who would admit it without asking themselves why or to what end.

I have found only one writer who frankly states that music attracts congregations. Yet many of our city churches have used music as a promotional device. Their music committees have hired the best-known soloists and most brilliant organists available, and have advertised this fact by press and bulletin board. Yet such promotional use of church music is self-defeating. No longer can the church hope to compete, on a musical basis, with the concert stage, radio, television, and the hi-fi set. Corporate worship is notoriously bad entertainment, and efforts to improve it in this direction are unprofitable. One does not wisely go to church for entertainment.

Likewise futile is the open competition that exists in some of our cities as to which of the churches may furnish the most spectacular musical organization and program. Such attempts are vanity. It is hard to see how they could be pleasing to the Lord.

"Music prepares the way, mood and atmosphere for true sermonizing," writes Dr. Harper.[6] And so it does. But is that all it does? If the service is little more than the sermon, that is all we should ask of it. In such a situation the music would be part of the "preliminaries." Worship is, however, far more than the sermon. Music will prepare both the minister and the congregation for "true sermonizing," but it should do much more than that.

Today a common use of music might be termed the escape from silence. We Americans dread silence in the same way nature traditionally abhors a vacuum. A person upon entering a restaurant will feed the jukebox before he orders his own meal. A college boy cannot study unless his radio is on. Likewise the movie devotee knows that a person marooned on a desert island is really not alone; near at hand is a symphony orchestra to keep him company. In like manner the organist feels called upon to fill every interval of time not actually occupied by minister, choir, or congregation. Of course the organist must "cover" the seating of latecomers. But must he also accompany the movement of the minister from pulpit to communion table, and all periods of "silent" prayer?

Some Protestant churches use music during the worship service in somewhat the same way the Roman Catholic Church uses incense during High Mass. The organist, when he is not otherwise occupied, continues to weave a fine fabric of sound which quietly envelops every spoken word, reluctantly ceasing for not much more than the sermon. It is all quite soothing and beautiful, but does it not lead our thoughts astray? Does it not cloud, rather than illumine, our contemplation of God?

If music should primarily serve none of these purposes, what purposes should it serve? Since this question has been answered repeatedly and at length, a brief restatement of what has been said will suffice. First of all, music speaks directly and immediately through the ear to the emotions. As the worshiper enters the church, the music of the organ should at once perform that act within him which separates him from the world he is leaving for a period. As music speaks through the ear, the beauty and symbolic meaning of God's house speak through the eye. Thus through the two senses by which man receives most of his impressions of the world, his spirit is prepared for that richest experience he may have in, but not of, the world.

"It is supremely in the hymn of praise that we unite with the universal Church, in heaven and on earth, to magnify the grace and glory of God," writes K. L. Parry.[7] Because most of us can sing after a fashion, and enjoy doing so, the hymn has become a most natural and characteristic expression of our worship together. The fact that we also express our praise in prayer, and that many of our hymns are prayers rather than praise, changes this thesis very little. The essence of our thought is that we as Christians *unite* our hearts with our voices in the expression of our inmost responses toward God, our Father.

"Music stimulates and reinforces the ideas and emotions with which it is associated," writes S. Arthur Devan.[8] Words set to music may take wings of power, beauty, and significance which they did not possess when they were simply spoken. Let us give the following words to a Charles Laughton, and ask him to deliver them with all the conviction available to his great personality and voice:

"Hallelujah! For the Lord God Omnipotent reigneth,
      and He shall reign forever and ever. Hallelujah!"

Then give the same words to a fine choir, and let them be sung as Handel set them down in the Hallelujah Chorus. Mr. Laughton, with all his gifts and skill, cannot approach the power these words assume by their expression through music.

Music in church is, finally, an offering we make to God. This is true from two aspects. As a congregation silently enters into an affirmation of the prayers of the minister, so it may and should enter into the words sung by the choir. Minister and choir together make their offerings in behalf of, and speaking for, the congregation. In a higher sense, the congregation makes its self-offering in its direct expressions of praise and adoration through music.

In a personal and profound sense, music in church should be the self-offering of those who, week after week, present it in His name. For many years this service was not highly regarded because it was so casually offered. Organists, soloists, quartets were hired on an annual basis to perform specific tasks; little personal dedication was asked or tendered. Yet the "volunteer" choir is not necessarily an improvement; it is easy to volunteer one's service only when personal preference and convenience dictate such service. Now a change is taking place. As we seek in these days to lift the quality of our worship, we see clearly the increased importance of our worship music, and of our church musicians. It is not sufficient that they sing well; they must sing well to the glory of God. Their singing is an offering to Him, and they are blessed in their giving of it.

Self-offering in worship is not only a quality of it; it should also be a yardstick by which we measure all our acts of worship. What Dr. Milligan said to the young ministers of Scotland deserves this broader application:

> It is going to make all the difference in the tone and character of the Ministry which you are looking forward to exercise whether you accustom yourself to think of the Church service as something you prepare for man, or an offering which in the name and in the spirit of Jesus Christ you lay upon the altar of God.[9]

PART ONE

We Build a Church

THE PLACE OF WORSHIP

THE CHOIR

THE ORGAN

MUSICAL ACCESSORIES

I

THE PLACE OF WORSHIP

> A principle of good taste is that a building should express
> the idea behind its erection and fulfill its function with singleness
> of purpose. . . . Everything about it should suggest its devotion
> to one end.[1]

With these words Dr. Henry Sloane Coffin begins his brief
description, not of the whole church building, but of the room
dedicated to worship. His statement bears the quality of axio-
matic truth. But what is the "one end" to which it should be
devoted, the correct "idea behind its erection"?

"The sanctuary designed for common worship should have that
as its sole aim."[2] Dr. Coffin here has not only indicated the "one
end," but has also named the place of worship the *sanctuary*. The
purist may object, however, that the word "sanctuary" should apply to the holiest place in the church, near the altar, and should
not include the whole room. Yet it can be argued that the sanctuary in its limited sense departed from the nonliturgical church
with the going of clerical vestments and the high altar. We belong to the "priesthood of all believers." No longer is worship
performed before our eyes by a separated priestly class. All of us
participate in "common worship" and the room in which all of us
worship is the *sanctuary*. The dictionary definition of the sanctuary
as a "consecrated place" is admirable for our purpose.

Yet we still find the place of worship frequently called the "auditorium." The word identifies the place, but it far too often also describes its function. Fleeting reference should be made here to
the departing, but not extinct, Akron Plan auditorium. The pulpit

is in a corner of the room, the hub of curving pews on a sloping floor. When a sliding partition is opened, the Sunday school assembly room and radiating classrooms are added to the other room, with a consequent increase in seating capacity. This not only provides the needed space for Christmas and Easter services, but takes care of other "community" needs. With the opening of the partition, the pulpit level becomes a stage. With a little moving of the ecclesiastical stage properties, the room will do very nicely for a lecture, concert, play, or other "entertainment." Of course, it becomes difficult for a churchgoer on Sunday morning to put out of his mind thoughts of the comedian or the magician who, during the preceding evening, stood on the same spot now occupied by the minister of the Lord. Ultimately the very flexibility of this church plan was its undoing. Although churches of this type are still being used, no new ones are appearing, to my knowledge.

The "standard" arrangement of the sanctuary in the non-liturgical church, unless it has adopted the divided chancel, still has the pulpit at its focal point. Whereas the Akron Plan placed the choir and organ on one side, in the "standard" plan they usually share the central position with pulpit and minister. The implications and results of this arrangement are far-reaching, particularly to the music of the church. Dr. Hedley describes it well, although strangely he speaks of it as though it were in the past:

> As the service was subordinated to the sermon, so the church ceased to be a holy place and was turned into an auditorium. The altar was abandoned, and the pulpit, now become a desk set on a high platform, took its central place. The ministers' seats faced those of the congregation, so that the clergy could look over the crowd and in their turn be in full view of the people. The choir, regarded as a performing unit, was placed on a still higher level, immediately behind the pulpit, where it might be seen and duly admired. Then why not let the people have a lovely view of gilded organ pipes behind the choir; and what did it matter that the visible pipes were fakes?[3]

Some of us would qualify part of Dr. Hedley's comments. We may agree that Protestantism subordinated the service to the sermon, but it does not follow that the church thereby "ceased to be a holy place." "The altar was abandoned" because this place of priestly sacrifice gave way to the communion table of the commemorative feast. The pulpit was elevated as the place for the Holy Scriptures, the central basis for our faith. That the minister was also thrown into prominence is partly the result of Puritan emphasis.

Can we also explain away Dr. Hedley's remarks on the location of choir and organ? It is doubtful, since there is nothing in Christian symbolism or church history to justify this central position of the church musicians. However important the organ may seem, there is nothing to warrant the dominance of its gleaming pipes over the sanctuary. Music is not the highest act of worship, nor is the organ the most sacred symbol of the Church.

"What did it matter that the visible pipes were fakes?" asks Dr. Hedley with scorn. It mattered and continues to matter much, of course. The organ is in a sanctuary which is devoted exclusively to the worship of God. Every detail of construction and furnishings should lead the mind toward God. Is it not clear that rows of gilded pipes anywhere in the sanctuary would be a dissipating influence to the spirit of worship? The organ does need a covering; let it be a beautiful but unobtrusive screen or grill, not glittering artificiality.

Something should be said at this point on the fairly new trend of placing classic-type organs, with exposed pipes, in the sanctuary. Undoubtedly these modern versions of eighteenth-century European organs have brought into the church a tonal purity and clarity that are irresistible. Because of the beauty of the classic tone, and because these rows of pipes are no longer fakes, many churches have felt justified in placing them in plain view toward the front of their sanctuaries. In these churches the worshipers are virtually compelled to look at the interesting pipe arrangements and to watch the opening and closing of the swell shutters during the worship service. Although this point will be discussed later, two comments should be made at this time. There can be no valid objection to placing an exposed organ where it was commonly placed in the older European churches, in the west gallery, behind the congregation. But if a church wishes to place a classic-type organ near the front of the sanctuary, classic tone may still come from behind a light grille or screen, of enough substance to obscure the view of the pipes and swell shutters, but not heavy enough to impede the clarity of the tone. There is really no more reason to expose the organ to view than there is to make visible the wiring and plumbing that have to do with the lighting and heating of the church.

"The choir, regarded as a performing unit, was placed on a still higher level, immediately behind the pulpit, where it might be seen and duly admired." Thus Dr. Hedley describes the most disturbing feature of this standard arrangement. To the would-be worshiper the choir is a disconcerting element from the time it enters the sanctuary until the end of the service. Every time he raises his eyes, he is confronted by lines of faces staring back at him. During the sermon, when he would be intent on what is being said, his concentration is snapped by every movement behind the minister. It is worse in summer when lines of fans flutter before his eyes!

The effect of this arrangement on the choir itself is even worse. This confrontation makes it difficult for the singers to worship because the congregation, numerous and variously dressed, is interesting to watch. The worst product, however, is what has been called the "concert psychology" of the choir. Sunday after Sunday it stands and sings to and at the congregation. Perhaps minister and choirmaster remind the choir that its song is an offering to the Lord, and not to the congregation. Yet it is hard to feel that the music is not *for* the congregation. The members of the congregation may not applaud, but they do compliment the individual members. I have even heard a minister thank the choir for a job well done; this thanks was delivered in the presence of the congregation immediately following the singing of an anthem.

It is hard for choir members not to enjoy this congregational approbation. The next and natural step is to seek more approval. Soloists pursue more frequent and more spectacular opportunities to appear before the congregation, and resent it if they must share too much with other singers. Are they not giving their talent to the Lord and His work unselfishly?

This is the way a quarrel may start in the choir. This is the reason the church choir has the fabulous reputation for being the seat of church discord. Let us grant at once that the real fault is sinful human nature. Yet it must be pointed out that these humans who sing in choirs are led into temptation week by week as they sit confronting the congregation.

Is it impossible to worship in the environment just described? Certainly not! Man has learned to worship throughout the ages in varied circumstances. We as Christians can practice communion with God wherever we are. Yet through the centuries man has lavished great wealth and infinite care in building beautiful temples to God, not just to honor Him but also to make a place in which He can be most fitly worshiped. Man has so built, and continues to build, because he has found great blessing in worshiping with other men in a place of beauty. It is common experience, I believe, that our worship becomes more satisfying as our environment becomes more beautiful and appropriate. Should we then offer ourselves to God in an unworthy place?

Today in America we are building great numbers of churches, as downtown churches move to the suburbs and others are added in areas surrounding our cities. Also, many established churches, dissatisfied with the shabbiness, impropriety, or inadequacy of their sanctuaries, are rebuilding them as they think best. How should they build? This is the problem we would undertake.

How Shall We Build?

We began this chapter with Dr. Coffin's statement about the sanctuary: "Everything about it should suggest its devotion to one end." The end is worship. How do we achieve it? In our building, our method is twofold. On the one hand the sanctuary should bring into prominence that idea or symbol closest to the spirit and practice of worship. On the other hand, all other ideas and symbols should be placed in a secondary position. The problem is largely one of placing the pulpit, the communion table, the organ, and the choir. Since we may freely admit that the organ and choir should have a less prominent place, we may at once narrow our first problem to the placing of the pulpit and the communion table.

The free church, particularly in America, still tends to regard the open Bible on a central pulpit as its dominant motif. The "centrality of the Word" has been much emphasized. But the earlier Protestant tradition in Europe was quite mixed. Calvin liked to conduct worship from his position behind the communion table. But early the pulpit became prominent. It was, however, variously placed: sometimes high in a corner, sometimes directly in the center of the church with the congregation on all sides of it, and sometimes in front center. Significantly, like the ancient basilica with its two desks, a common feature in these churches was a second desk or lectern, often occupied by a reader. In many churches this lectern was *below* the high pulpit. The Scriptures were read from this inferior position. The result of this was to bring into prominence not the Word but the preacher!

Is it not fair to say that in this country we have likewise elevated the preacher, even though we have placed the Bible on his prominent pulpit? Certainly this seems to be the opinion of S. Arthur Devan, who has this to say on the question:

> It may not be such a handicap to worship to have the minister's elaborate throne (flanked by two lesser thrones) as the most conspicuous object in the front of the church. Certainly many persons do not seem to think so. Yet the hypothetical visitor from Mars whose judgments are so often invoked, could hardly avoid the impression that the congregation had gathered for the purpose of doing reverence to the occupant of this ornate and exalted seat. Of course in theory it is not the minister in his chair, but the Holy Bible on the pulpit desk which is the predominant symbol and focus for the eye . . . Yet the Holy Bible itself is sometimes treated rather shabbily by the minister (who puts his notes and his hymn book and his watch and even his elbows upon it). . . . The Bible is quite overshadowed by the windows, the organ, the choir loft, and by the minister himself.[4]

As to the selection of another symbol as the center of attention within the sanctuary, Devan has this to offer:

Above all it [the church] should have . . . some very conspicuous symbol of God for the eye to rest upon. What should that symbol be? Most appropriately, the communion table. . . . Nothing should ever be placed on the communion table except the holy elements and their appurtenances . . . The only exception to this rule is a cross, which may properly be placed upon it, but only *provided the table is not underneath the pulpit.*[5]

Dr. Hedley supports throughout the position taken by Devan:

If we are thinking of worship as primary, it is evident that the pulpit never should provide the focus of attention. This means that some sort of chancel must take the place of the pulpit platform, with all the lines of vision drawn compellingly to an altar which is dedicated to the glory of God, and whose cross is the perduring reminder of the sacrifice of the Christ.[6]

To this should be added the statement of Von Ogden Vogt, who makes it clear that he is not talking about an altar below the pulpit:

First, the one chief symbol of both artistic and religious unification in religion has always been the altar. . . . Artistically, no other device has been invented, and one might dare to say nor can be, so effective as the altar as the dominating centrality which gives unity to the entire work of structural art.[7]

It will be noted that, while Devan was speaking of the communion table, both Hedley and Vogt used the word "altar" which to many Protestants suggests objectionable formalism in worship. It is therefore desirable at this point to quote Dr. Brenner on the use of these terms:

The Altar of the Christian Church is frequently termed the Table of the Lord, or the Lord's Table, or the Holy Table. It is a wholesome practice to use all these terms synonymously, for they were thus used in the Early Church and to the Christian they mean one and the same thing. At any rate, the Altar is always the Lord's Table when the Lord's Supper is celebrated, and in like manner the Lord's Table is always an Altar, the Altar of the cross, offering "the broken body" and "the shed blood."[8]

Dr. Coffin wants made clear, however, what the Protestant means by the word "altar":

> An altar set against the wall or a reredos is incongruous with the Reformed tradition. The holy table of primitive Christianity was turned into a cubical or oblong altar when it was erected over or built to contain the relics of a martyr. . . . The table should be unmistakably a table . . . It should not be set against the wall.[9]

Finally, what is the optimum arrangement for the front of the sanctuary? Hedley is joined by Devan in favoring some form of chancel:

> This brings us to the question, now discussed in many places: pulpit platform or chancel? The latter has been winning its way in much modern church building . . . The chancel arrangement, even if not ancient, has much to commend it both on practical and symbolic grounds. Perhaps most important is the fact that in the chancel arrangement, *everything seems to have been cleared away to make room for God.* Minister, singers, preaching station, organ—all are as it were pushed one side or the other to make a clear path to the cross.[10]

The time has come to draw what conclusions we can from the writers on worship who have been quoted. The place of worship, which we may call the sanctuary, should be devoted to one purpose, and should contain a central symbol or focus of attention which embodies that purpose. Whatever else it should be, that symbol should not be the central pulpit, the minister, or his "throne." By the very prominence of other objects in the sanctuary, the Bible has already lost its traditionally prominent position. Wherever else they should be, the choir and the organ with its false pipes should not be in the center. There is a growing feeling that the focal point may well be the Lord's Table, on which may be placed the cross. Increasingly, writers favor the divided chancel, with the Lord's Table near, but not against, the east wall.[11]

Trust Your Architect, But Keep an Eye on Him

The congregation has decided to build a new church, or to rebuild the old one. The architect is hired (few churches now have the temerity to do without one) and prepares plans in accordance with his instructions. The building or rebuilding is completed. Then, sometimes at once, sometimes gradually during a long period, the congregation realizes that something has gone wrong. The church home does not give all the spiritual satisfaction that had been desired. Since so often music has entered into this situation, directly or indirectly, some reasons for these disappointments should form a part of this study.

The first such cause to be mentioned is the failure in knowledge and vision on the part of the congregation itself. Many books, architectural and church periodicals, and national church headquarters are ready with advice, general and specific, for any church. But the building committee gazes with nostalgia at the old church, and thinks of nothing but reproducing it, even bigger and better. What can the architect do about this? He has his orders!

A difficulty of a different sort comes from the architect who "gets carried away." His training, personal preferences, religious convictions (or lack of them), may cause him to violate the wishes of his employers. Thus an architect, serving a free church, may design a high, ornate pulpit, an elaborate rood screen between chancel and congregation, or an altar with reredos where a table is desired. What might inspire one congregation would offend another. No building committee should conclude that the architect knows best in matters of religious propriety and symbolism, but should keep a watchful eye over his shoulder.

A fertile field for difficulty is the little-understood one of acoustics. Part of our trouble comes from the spread of a strange theory: the best acoustics for speaking is the worst for music, and vice versa. We know that a little reverberation tends to give music vitality. We also know that much reverberation makes it difficult to understand speaking; it is hard, for instance, to understand a speech in a gymnasium. Yet we tend to forget two other demonstrable facts. First, music is as confused by much reverberation as is speech. On the other hand the suppression of all reverberation smothers the speaking voice as completely as it does music. A church with too much acoustic "treatment" may have at the same time both unsatisfactory speech and "dead" music; this church may have to amplify the minister's voice to make it heard. Experience teaches, however, that some reverberation is good, and that good acoustics for music is likewise good acoustics for speech.

Several common errors in dealing with acoustics within churches should be noted here. The first is making a judgment of operating conditions while the church is empty. A sanctuary with a resounding echo when it is empty may be virtually devoid of reverberation when the congregation is present. Bodies and clothing absorb a large amount of echo. Again, good acoustics may be destroyed by adding, for reasons of beauty or comfort, materials that happen to be sound-absorbing. The addition of wall-to-wall carpeting, or foam-rubber cushions for the pews, or draperies for doors or windows, may materially deaden the live acoustics of a room.

The acoustics "expert" is often not an unmixed blessing in church. His profession was born of the desirability of reducing sound within business offices and other places where large numbers of people noisily congregate, and in such places as music conservatories where "soundproofing" is needed. But he should seldom appear professionally in church. Whether or not he sells and installs the materials with which he is concerned, he undoubtedly enjoys prescribing acoustic tile or plaster for surfaces within the sanctuary which would be better left alone. Unfortunately, such tile or plaster, once applied, tends to remain. Mr. Ernest M. Skinner, the famous organ builder of a generation ago, once gave this sound advice: No acoustic treatment of a sanctuary should be applied, or even planned, until as late as possible in the room's construction. If, just before the final painting, the room is found to have excessive echo under full conditions, then, and only then, should some sound treatment be added. A small amount achieves much.

Were we to build churches today with the same deliberate care that was used by the builders of the great Gothic cathedrals of Europe, it would be interesting to speculate on the result, but it would not be profitable. This day of haste and pressure cannot think in fourteenth-century terms. It is true that in many of our towns and cities our most beautiful structures are churches, yet their beauty tends to be superficial. An imposing façade may be more important than a well-conceived interior. But sometimes more care is lavished on the educational building than on the sanctuary. Always speed of completion is important. A builder may be chosen, not for his skill, experience, and integrity, but for his willingness to complete his contract in six months. Also this organ may be chosen rather than that one because this builder agrees to install at an earlier date than that one would promise. To the degree that haste has determined the building of God's house, that house may not be worthy of Him, nor will our worship within it be wholly satisfying.

II

THE CHOIR

The location of the choir within the church is a complex subject, about which a whole book could easily be written. While the placing of pulpit or altar has followed logic or pressure of religious controversy, no such simple causality has dictated the disposition of the church singers. Sometimes reason, sometimes caprice, has put the choir in every conceivable place in the church proper.

Before there was a separate group of singers in the Christian Church, the word "choir" applied to the whole body of clergy that took part in the worship service. When the singing choir became a separate entity, it is probable that two locations near the altar were used for it. The first, an extension of the monks' chapel, placed the singers before the altar, facing each other across the nave or chancel to facilitate antiphonal singing. The second, still to be found in monastery churches, put the choir in the deep recesses of the chancel, behind the high altar, largely concealed from the congregation. It is possible in this type of church for monks to observe the canonical hours in this space behind the altar without disturbing, or being disturbed by, visitors in the church proper.

As the medieval church gained in prestige and power, so did the pomp of its Masses increase. The high altar became larger and more magnificent, and the number of celebrants at Mass grew. So crowded did the chancel become that the choir was moved out to one of the two locations where it is still commonly found in Roman Catholic churches: in one of the transepts, or in the rear gallery.

With the coming of the Protestant Reformation, the status of the choir changed—in two different directions. Martin Luther, wanting to give the Mass back to the people, felt that music would be his powerful ally for this purpose. His efforts to get a singing church by providing sacred words to tunes familiar to the people are well known. This movement gave the choir importance in the church.

From the beginning, the choir in the Roman Catholic Church had sung *in behalf of* the congregation. Sharing the words of the Mass with the priest, the choir also shared the priest's function, separate from the congregation. With the Protestant insistence on "the priesthood of all believers," the choir has a dual function: it still shares with the minister the leadership of worship, but now it speaks *for* the congregation, to which it also belongs, and in much of the worship it participates *with* the congregation.

This identity of choir with congregation reaches its highest point, in theory at least, in the Anglican Church. Nothing is sung by the choir in Anglican worship, whether canticle or Te Deum, which may not be joined in freely by the congregation. The fact that most communicants do *not* so join does not change the essential relationship. Why the Anglican communion, particularly since the Oxford Movement, has chosen to express itself architecturally by placing the choir in the divided chancel is a little hard to understand. Although the choir should work closely with the congregation, the two are separated by the pulpit and lectern at least, and frequently by an elaborate rood screen in addition. Yet the choir in the divided chancel has become the usual arrangement for Episcopal churches in America, and in recent years for many churches of other denominations.

While the so-called liturgical churches of Protestantism were giving music an important place in worship, the churches of the Reformed tradition were taking a different road. Because Calvin was so critical of Roman worship, he wanted no part of choir singing and organ playing in church. Yet, like Luther, he saw the value of congregational singing. This singing, however, he limited strictly to metrical psalms. Of course, someone must teach psalm singing to the congregations. Yet there was no choir, and no place for a choir was provided in the Reformed Church, and there was no organ. The Puritan movement in the British Isles further made straight the path of severely plain worship in free churches.

Seventeenth-century America became the home of settlers of all these faiths. As the country and the people reacted upon each other, so their religious practices changed. Since music was so important in Anglican worship, it would be natural to look for leadership in church music among the Anglicans of Virginia rather than among the Puritans of Massachusetts Colony. However, it was mainly from the toughened, self-disciplined settlers of the northern colonies that the vigorous religious leadership came. As Methodists, Baptists, Presbyterians, and Congregationalists led the great drives westward, so did these same denominations take eventual leadership in shaping musical patterns in American churches.

There was little progress until the nineteenth century. The American Puritans out-Puritaned their British forbears. In church music, the lowest point must have been American psalm singing, with the precentor "lining out" the music before the congregation sang it. The early Methodists could not have been much better than the Puritans: they wanted no part in the Anglican worship features given to them by their founder, John Wesley. Along with these groups, the various kinds of American Baptists could be depended upon to oppose all influences, musical and other, that came from the Old World, particularly any that could smack of popery.

However, the hot flames of religious intolerance slowly died. The hymns of Watts, Wesley, and others began to win their place in our church services as people learned to read music. Then the precentor was no longer needed. Music and art, pure extravagances in a pioneer society, began to make their impact in the settled communities. It was inevitable that people should seek more beauty in worship, and that music should play an important part in this movement. The singing society of the community begat the church choir.

But in many of our American churches there was no place for
a choir, and of course no musical instrument. In the front of
the church was the pulpit platform, which allowed room for
the central pulpit, the pulpit chairs, and the minister only. In
these churches, the choir had to be placed in the front pews, just
below the minister. This was its common position in the non-
liturgical church during the first half of the nineteenth century.

The struggle to bring musical instruments into the Church is
a fascinating phase of our not-so-early American history. Here
is a part of that story, as told by William Arms Fisher:

> Everywhere the singing in church was without any instru-
> mental support, and the introduction of the pitchpipe in order
> to "set the tune" properly was long bitterly opposed. The in-
> creased interest in group-singing led next to the use of the bass-
> viol (violoncello) which met with like opposition from the
> elders.
>
> After the bass-viol had found entrance into the church serv-
> ices, the inexpensive flute was introduced, for in the eighteenth
> century this instrument was extremely popular with men musi-
> cally inclined. Later the hautboy (oboe) found admittance, but
> its squeaking and squalling in unskillful hands caused it to be
> looked on with suspicion. The clarinet came next, followed by
> the bassoon, which for many years had general favor. When
> these instruments were played together, the necessity of tuning
> several times during the services, in the then poorly heated
> churches, was of no assistance to devotional feeling. When last
> of all the fiddle was introduced, with associations quite the re-
> mote of churchly, many felt and soon openly said "that Satan
> came also among them." The churches that used stringed instru-
> ments were known as "catgut" churches.
>
> It should be remembered that the same Puritan prejudice
> that impelled Cromwell's soldiers to destroy most of the church
> organs of England, prevented the use of this instrument in all
> Colonial churches until the Brattle organ was set up in King's
> Chapel, Boston in 1714. . . . The second organ in New England,
> the gift of Bishop Berkeley, was set up in Trinity Church, New-
> port in 1733. Even in 1800 there were less than twenty organs
> in all New England. As late as 1814 the singing in Park Street
> Church, Boston was supported by nothing but a flute, bassoon
> and bass-viol, and in Father Streeter's church in Hanover Street
> the sole instruments in 1845 were a clarinet, ophicleide, and a
> double-bass.[1]

The nineteenth-century struggle over the organ, the echoes of which may still be heard, was a continuation of the earlier controversy concerning musical instruments in church. Bitter as it was, perhaps it did not last as long because the forcible entry of string and wind instruments had prepared the way for the organ. Whether it was a cabinet reed organ, or a pipe organ powered by those fabulous gentlemen who, tradition says, had to be wakened in their hole behind the organ at the end of every sermon, more and more churches bought as good organs as they could afford But where should the new instrument be placed? The victorious committee decided—and who can blame it?—that the organ must be right in the center where everyone can look at it, shiny pipes and all. A space for the organ had to be provided behind the minister, so this space was made large enough to hold the choir also, in neat rows, facing the congregation.

Thus was born what has been called the worst possible arrange ment of organ and choir. It was an arrangement of convenience made without reference either to church tradition or to worship values. Once started, the plan became astonishingly reproductive Even though we now recognize all the evils that come with this undue prominence of church music and musicians, we still worship in hundreds of churches which have this essential arrangement

The Akron Plan, born in 1867, was an ugly duckling that never matured. However unacceptable its general arrangement, its plac ing of organ and choir along one side wall was definitely superior to the standard arrangement we have discussed. In churches of this type it is possible for the congregation to look at the minister without also having to look at the choir; the choir members by merely turning their heads, may also see the face of the minis ter. But further discussion of this plan is unprofitable, since churches of this type are rapidly disappearing.

Yet other attempts have been made to find a suitable place for the choir. There is, for instance, the old church in Boston that has two small choir lofts, one on each side of the central pulpit; pre sumably the real quartet sits in one, and a dummy quartet in the other. Also, there is the large church in Ohio that has the divided chancel in combination with a front-facing choir behind it. Since these are strange mutations, not apt to reproduce their kind, they require no further examination. Of the other locations that have been mentioned, three are of no further interest to us: the choir in the front pews below the minister, the "standard" arrangement of front-facing choir and organ directly behind and above the minister, and that of the Akron Plan. Four choir locations remain, all of them acceptable, and all deserving further study:

1. The choir in the deep recesses of the chancel, behind the altar, as in some modern monastery churches. We shall call this the Deep Chancel Choir.
2. The Divided Chancel Choir as found commonly in Episcopal churches, and increasingly in those of other denominations.
3. The Transept Choir, placed in one wing or the other of the cruciform church.
4. The Gallery Choir in the west end of the church, that opposite the pulpit.

Deep Chancel Choir

"The ideal situation for the organ choir is behind the chancel, veiled by some sort of screening device from the view of the congregation," says Dr. Archibald Davison,[2] that eminent authority on church music. If one has ever gone to a monastery church and has heard the unforgettable sound of plainsong coming from the deep recesses behind the altar, he will understand Dr. Davison's statement. It is indescribably beautiful, mysterious, awful. Were I a Roman Catholic, such music in such an environment would continue to bring deep satisfaction to me.

But as Protestants we need to examine this in the light of our own faith, our own architectural heritage and habits, and our musical capabilities. Let us put into this same monastery church not a choir of monks, who spend much of their lives perfecting these chants we have heard, but one of our "mixed" choirs, which cannot take time to practice adequately. Let our choir sing in English instead of Latin, as part of a service conducted in English. Will the musical and spiritual effect be as mysteriously moving?

I have projected our Protestant service into this monastic setting because Protestant churches built in this manner are so rare. I have seen only one, a large metropolitan church. Its visible chancel is only deep enough to accommodate pulpit, lectern, benches for the clergy, and a true altar. Directly behind the altar is a magnificently painted screen covering the whole chancel, except for an opening on each side of the altar. These openings admit the choir, which is concealed behind the screen, except for two or three singers who can be seen directly behind each opening. But when this fine choir stands to sing its anthems, as many singers as possible crowd into the space directly behind the openings! This is certainly not what Dr. Davison meant when he suggested that the choir be veiled from the view of the congregation. Yet, were the choir truly concealed, the music coming from behind the altar could be effective and moving.

Why are so few Protestant churches built in this style? Part of the answer should be that placing the choir behind the chancel is not in accordance with Protestant practice. A choir completely separated from the congregation is no longer identified with the congregation, nor can it in any real sense lead the congregation in worship. This is possibly why, in the church I have described, there is this awkward attempt to maintain some contact between the two. It should also not be forgotten that the choir itself would find it hard to worship under these circumstances. It is safe to say that, during a twenty-minute sermon, complete concealment from the audience would invite inattention. This is, however, not a problem in the Roman Catholic Church, in which the choir is busy throughout the Mass, and the sermon lasts only about five minutes! It is doubtful, therefore, that many Protestant churches will find it desirable to conceal their choirs behind the chancel.

Divided Chancel Choir

The plan of placing the choir in the divided chancel has the advantage of being the current vogue in church architecture. It recommends itself to those who feel that the pulpit should no longer command the central position in Protestant worship, as well as to those who feel that some other symbol should be the focus of attention. The cross is, of course, the usual symbol, but an open Bible or the baptistry could be in this general position.

At this point it would be well to note the various criticisms that have been made of the divided chancel. There are people who object to it because they feel that it makes easy those formal liturgical practices which they find distasteful in Protestant worship. I would say here only that the implied formality of the divided chancel discourages the casual irreverence that has so often characterized Protestant behavior in the house of God. I am more concerned with the musical criticisms that have been registered: The divided chancel splits the choir in the middle, making it difficult for the singers to operate as a unified whole. The conductor, at or near the organ console, cannot maintain perfect contact with the choir, part of which must watch him through the use of mirrors. Since the voices are projected toward each other and not out into the nave, the choir music is imperfectly heard by the congregation.

It should first be remembered that in many churches with divided chancel the choir normally need not be divided. If the capacity of the chancel is great enough to accommodate the choir for festival occasions, one half of it may be sufficient for the "normal" choir. Since this choir will be seated on the side opposite the organ console, it will not be divided at all. The choir is directly under control from the console; no mirrors are needed. It should be clear that this formation takes care of two of the criticisms cited against the use of the choir in a divided chancel.

There is little doubt, however, that the placing of inexperienced singers on both sides of a divided chancel presents some problems, at least for a time. These difficulties are, I believe, exaggerated. In fact, certain musical advantages may come from this division. Singers facing each other, although not looking directly at those opposite them, will tend to sing their words together; a certain mutual feeling, like that within a string quartet, may be developed. Also, a choir frequently hears better in this position than in any other. One of the difficulties of the forward-facing choir is that the back row may hear nothing but itself, while the front row singers hear only those sounds coming from directly behind them. Across the chancel, the sopranos and basses should always hear the altos and tenors distinctly. This is an advantage, particularly in unaccompanied singing. Perhaps the musical assets of this arrangement outweigh the debits indicated earlier.

Let it also be admitted that the conductor, guiding a divided choir from his position at or near the console, has some difficulties to overcome, because part of the choir must observe him through mirrors only. These difficulties can best be met by more practice "on location." Most, if not all, the rehearsals of a chancel choir should take place in the chancel, and not in a rehearsal room, in order that the choir may have the benefit of service conditions for as much of the time as possible. I say this in full recognition of the advantages that are supposed to come from the use of a separate rehearsal room: the piano is a more efficient teaching instrument than the organ; perhaps more work can be done in a room set aside and equipped for the purpose. Yet I believe that a choir that practices in a situation resembling as nearly as possible that of the service will have a patent advantage over the choir which gets little opportunity to "feel" service conditions outside the services themselves. There is another important entry on the credit side: the choir members, looking at the choral conductor or at his mirrored reflection, cannot be facing or looking toward the congregation. Likewise the conductor behind the console will be largely, if not completely, concealed from the eyes of the congregation; here the mechanics of conducting need not be a distraction to worship.

There is, unfortunately, no law to punish the conductor who, with his stand and baton, takes his position in the center of the chancel, in direct view of the whole choir but in even better view of the congregation. I know of one large Gothic church where this has been (perhaps still is) the practice. I can think of no condemnation too severe for this sort of thing. A symphonic conductor may be seen; a church music conductor should never be seen, unless he cannot possibly be concealed.

Is the choir that sings from a divided chancel at a disadvantage acoustically? That depends upon the construction of the chancel. If its air space is boxlike, the walls smothering and reducing the choral tone, the musical effect will be bad. If, however, it is so shaped that its walls may act as a sounding board for the choir, its tone may be distinct and full. Acoustical problems are no more to be found, perhaps, in the divided chancel than in any other church plan.

Without expanding them, here are several other reasons which make the divided chancel perhaps the best arrangement for the church choir: The closeness of choir to minister makes communication and response between them most direct and immediate. More significantly, the choir members, no longer facing the congregation, do not feel themselves the center of attraction, and may more readily lose themselves in the selfless task to which they have given themselves. Above all, perhaps, the congregation is no longer confronted by rows of faces as it looks toward minister, pulpit, altar, but may devote itself to the worship of God without this hindrance. Incidentally, the church processional and recessional may be done to and from the chancel most naturally and effectively.

Transept Choir

It is Dr. George Hedley who favors putting the choir into one or both transepts of the cruciform church. He says, reasonably enough, that there are few other sensible reasons for building transepts on any but a very large church. There is much else to be said in favor of this arrangement. The seating is compact, providing for optimum singing conditions. The choir will be heard from any position in the church, but need not be looked at. Choir members will also appreciate having something other than the rear view of the minister during worship. In fact, there are no serious objections to the transept choir, except the very cost of providing for it. It is, however, questionable that many churches of small or medium size could afford the luxury of a double wing of limited usefulness on a new church.

Gallery Choir

The choir in the rear or west gallery, long a chosen place for the Roman Catholic choir, has received widespread, if not frequent, acceptance in various Protestant churches. Its virtues are obvious. Like the choir in the divided chancel, the gallery choir members do not feel the attention of the congregation on them, and may work more easily, without personal striving, for the good of the whole group. Unlike choirs at the front of the church, these choir members face the minister, and will find active participation in worship an inviting experience. Unlike the choir in the divided chancel, the voices may here be arranged in the most advantageous manner, and the choirmaster may control them more completely. The *musical* result of the choir's efforts should be more satisfactory than that from any other location, except possibly in the transept.

This is not, however, the whole story. There are congregations who are unhappy about the gallery choir because they cannot *see* what is going on behind them unless they look over their shoulders! Also the processional and recessional cannot logically be led to and from the rear gallery, particularly with the minister going in the opposite direction. For no good reason I could give, the congregational participation in hymn singing seems to be somewhat reduced when the leadership of the choir is behind it. There also seems to be a loss in liaison between minister and choir when they are separated by the whole body of the congregation.

This somewhat brief discussion of the comparative merits of the various locations of the choir within the sanctuary has only the purpose of stirring up divine discontent within the minds of those who may read this. Are you building a new church? Are you restoring and improving an old one? Before you begin to plan, read all the books on church architecture you can get, and look at pictures. Travel, and worship with congregations in various types of sanctuaries. Then, and only then, begin to plan your own church, placing your choir with great care.

Shall We Remodel?

Many churches in this country have found themselves in recent years discontented with their sanctuaries. The beauty of the exterior may still satisfy them. The sanctuary is adequate for the church's membership. The pews are comfortable, and the organ is pleasing and in good repair. But they are weary of looking at shiny organ pipes behind their choir. They have been to other churches where they do not have to look at lines of faces whenever they look toward the pulpit. They have felt that worship in their own sanctuary lacked those values of dignity and reverence which they found in other churches.

For many of these churches a new satisfaction in worship has come after they have remodeled the sanctuary, replacing the old central pulpit and choir with a divided chancel. Not all churches, of course, can be adapted to this treatment, but where it is possible, it is usually rewarding.

First the front of the church is cleared to floor level; out comes the organ, the choir elevation, the pulpit platform. Then the organ is replaced, perhaps on one side, perhaps on both sides of what will become the chancel; its false metal pipes are replaced by an unobtrusive grille. Next comes the low chancel platform, not over two or three steps above the level of the nave. At the central point, but not against the front wall, is the communion table, on which will be placed cross or Bible. Then, on either side, the choir benches and rail face each other, allowing only the space for the organ console close behind the pulpit. The lectern will come on one side, and a slightly elevated pulpit on the other, with a bench behind each faced in the same direction as the choir benches behind them.

With a comparatively small fraction of the cost of a new church building, this congregation will have won for itself something more precious than a new church: here will still be the memories of the old sanctuary but also worship resources that have never been known here before.

Or Shall We Make the Best of What We Have?

Here is another church with central pulpit, choir, and organ, with the choir seated on benches, facing the congregation. The need for change exists here, but not the conditions. Perhaps the architecture of the interior will not permit the change to a divided chancel. Perhaps the church needs a new educational building, and does not feel it has the money for a major change. Perhaps the organ is a memorial gift and cannot be touched. Whatever the reason, no great change within the sanctuary is possible.

Can anything be done for the worship of this church, so far as the music is concerned? Yes, there are at least two forward steps most churches can make. The first is to remove the benches from the choir, replacing them with individual chairs. All the chairs should be placed so that they face the organ console, not the congregation. (It must be assumed that the church has a console disconnected from the organ case, in the center of the choir loft.) Although a few of the chairs will still face the congregation, most of them will be at an angle of 45 to 90 degrees away from the congregation. With few singers directly facing the congregation, none of the remainder should be permitted to change their direction under any circumstances!

If the choir rail is so low, or the organ console so high, that the organist is in view at all, a screen sufficiently high to conceal him should be placed on the rail behind him. Whether the organist is also conductor, or the church has a separate organist and conductor, the mechanics of conducting should not be permitted to show.

These physical changes will not prove satisfactory unless the choirmaster and choir by attitude and resultant behavior make the best use of their environment. These topics will be considered in a later chapter.

III

THE ORGAN

The organ is the proper instrument for the sanctuary. This we may agree upon. But beyond this point it would be hard to get organists to agree on anything. A variety of answers would come at once from each of these questions: How much should be spent for the organ? If sufficient money is not presently available, should we use a temporary expedient, or should we "hold out" for a completely adequate instrument? Should the organ be electronic or pipe? How may we know the correct size and specifications of the instrument? From whom should it be purchased?

Variable factors make all answers to these questions "iffy." The first of these is cost. A set of pipes that cost $500 in 1936 will cost about $1,650 now. There is no reason to believe that organ prices have stabilized. The second is the highly individual nature of the pipe organ. Every instrument that is worthy of the name is "custom-built" for the room in which it is to be installed. In this day of assembly-line production, the pipe organ still remains largely the complicated product of hand manufacture and assembly. The end product represents the combined efforts of the church architect, organ designer, factory hands, engineer, voicer, installation crew, etc. The result is not predictable; the best-known organ builder will occasionally go wrong, and the obscure builder now and then will produce a masterpiece. The third factor is the rapid technical changes taking place in the electronic organ industry. In this vigorous new field, most of the companies are now engaged in sharp competition with each other for the low-budget home and church business. Few are seriously challenging directly the pipe organ builder. But improvements in design and resulting tone are already known to the better electronic organ firms, improvements that now make it possible for the electronic organ to compete with the pipe organ on almost even terms. Unfortunately, most of the trained organists of the country have not heard the electronic organ at its best. Therefore, for some time to come the pipe organ will remain the preference of the church that can afford it.

Where shall we start in making a choice of organ? With the church, as with the individual, the starting point will probably be the financial one. Since the organ is the last item to go into the new sanctuary, it is usually the last to be planned. Before the organ committee can do its work, some costs that increased after the original estimates were made have to be met, and other purchases that were forgotten or neglected in the original plan must be made. When these bills have been paid, frequently the organ committee finds itself with far less to spend than was originally planned. Even when this is not the case, the committee is left with many difficult choices. Let us begin with this general yardstick:

1. For between $2,700 and $7,500 an electronic organ may be purchased. Cheaper ones than $2,700 are available, but these would not meet exacting needs. Likewise more expensive electronic organs can be found, but these lie outside the usual range of this type of instrument.

2. In general, $5,000 to $12,000 is the range of "unit" pipe organs. Made partially to compete with electronic organs, they sound like pipe organs because they *are* pipe organs, but they do not require permanent installation.

3. Ten thousand dollars, approximately, is the minimum price for a standard pipe organ. But not much may be bought for less than $15,000. From $15,000 to $20,000 will buy an adequate organ for a fairly small church, or a minimum organ for a larger church, with future additions planned and "prepared for" in console and organ space. An adequate organ for a larger church will call for a greater investment, depending on the size of the sanctuary, its acoustical quality, the builder chosen, and the type of service expected from the organ.

Although a church may, by careful planning and sacrifice, install an organ completely adequate to its present and foreseeable needs, it often faces the temptation or necessity of the temporary expedient of a cheaper electronic or smaller pipe organ than seems desirable for more than present use. Such a choice is frequently regretted. Although the church has every intention of replacing or enlarging the instrument with which it started, the time to make this change never seems to arrive. At any given moment in the life of the church, other demands appear to be more urgent than those of music, and the day of change is postponed again and again, with a consequent impoverishment of worship. It is certainly desirable that such a church make and follow a long-range plan for improvement which will keep its whole program moving, without neglect of any phase of its life.

If the Organ Fund Is Ample

If a church has raised or received all the money it needs for an adequate organ, what will it buy? Let us take, for instance, a church that plans to spend $300,000 for a new sanctuary, and has set aside $30,000 for its organ. How will this money be spent? Should the organ committee consider the rather new possibility of a custom-built electronic organ? Most organists would not consider this a question worthy of discussion; the answer would be an emphatic, "No." This statement by the eminent Leo Sowerby is typical:

> It is depressing to be obliged to record that far too many churches have installed electronic inventions, which short-sighted people, whose eyes are fixed on the money bags rather than toward the Fount of all art, have caused to be used as substitutes for the king of instruments; these electronic devices are definitely more suitable for the theatre or the beer-hall. The use of such an instrument does not represent progress in the Church, for it is too obviously an inferior substitute.[1]

Probably the greatest reason why most organists have had little praise for electronic organs is that most builders of electronic organs have made little effort to produce instruments that could challenge the pipe organ. These builders have been content to satisfy the larger low-budget market offered by residences, funeral homes, night clubs, and small churches. One has only to examine the advertising of these firms to realize that their primary effort is not toward the creation of a wondrously new instrument of artistic superiority, but rather to earn a fast dollar. Here is a chord organ that a person may learn to play in a few minutes, whether he knows how to read music or not. Here is an inexpensive electronic organ with a short pedal board and two abbreviated offset manuals; this instrument promises to be the center of the social life of the family that possesses it. For a little more money an attachment is furnished which will supply a full repertoire of percussion sounds. (None of these organs can play an appreciable amount of organ literature, but that seems to matter little.)

These same firms do have models which they recommend for chapel or church. Each has several standard designs; the higher the cost, the more adequate the specification. Each model is carefully priced to meet the competition. Some, but not all, of these firms have as their best model or two a "complete" organ, with standard console measurements approved by the American Guild of Organists; but most of the designs have shortened pedal boards and other "economy" characteristics. Only about two of the electronic organ manufacturers in this country really try to plan and custom-build an instrument to satisfy the specific musical needs of a particular situation or building.

The reaction of most of the trained organists to the electronic organ has been predictable and justifiable. They have not liked it. They loathe the "economy" spinet models, with truncated manuals and pedal board, which builders continue to push on unwary nonmusicians. They despise the tone, sometimes thin and superficial, sometimes harsh and shrill. Used to dealing with organ designers who plan an instrument for a room with loving care, they cannot become enthusiastic about an instrument that comes in just five sizes and three colors!

But this is the day of the radio tube and, more recently, the transistor. The electronic marvels we are witnessing must in-

evitably have their effect on music. Mr. William Leslie Sumner
makes this rather grudging prophecy in his 1952 book:

> What of the future of the organ?
> There are no indications as yet that electrical devices have
> been able to imitate the major effects of the genuine pipe
> organ, in particular its major choruses. No doubt the prevalence
> of the loudspeaker in our daily lives has blunted the ears of
> many to the subtle beauties of really first-rate organ tone, and in
> view of the complexities and expense of the real organ there
> will be a temptation to the uncritical to purchase electrical
> substitutes. It is better to regard these latter as separate instru-
> ments than as imitations of the organ. It cannot be doubted
> that the future will bring great improvements in the electronic
> organ and that it may displace the more expensive pipe organ
> where the retention of the latter necessitates large expenditure
> to keep it in repair or to effect its rebuilding.[2]

Mr. Sumner's prophecy has largely come true, even during the
decade in which he wrote it. Great improvements have already
come in the electronic organ, and it has already displaced more
expensive pipe organs that have worn out in service. Moreover,
an increasing number of larger churches are making the deliberate
choice of the electronic organ, custom-built, as against the pipe
organ, where the saving of money is not the most important consideration.

The well-known American organ designer, Dr. William H.
Barnes, reports on one of these:

> The recently installed Allen electronic organ in the new First
> Presbyterian Church of Stamford, Conn., is a milestone in the
> development and perfecting of electronic organs. It is not only
> the largest and most costly electronic organ ever built anywhere
> by any builder, but it seems to me to have the sound and attack
> of a first-class, four-manual pipe organ. . . . After hearing this
> organ, one feels that the sound of a large, fine pipe organ has
> been successfully reproduced electronically. . . . I will leave the
> conclusions to be drawn to others who are not such dyed-in-the-
> wool pipe organ enthusiasts as I. I am honest enough, how-
> ever, to report what I have seen and heard with my own eyes
> and ears. By this time I should know what the sound of a
> good organ is like, whether it be pipe or electronic.[3]

Many organists have visited this remarkable church and organ of which Dr. Barnes was writing. Almost without exception those of us who have heard this great instrument played by its capable organist, Mr. W. Raymond Randall, must agree with Dr. Barnes' estimate of it. Here is a large chancel organ of seventy-five speaking stops, completely duplicated in the west gallery, except for a giant harmonic trumpet that speaks from the gallery only. Either organ may be played independently, or the two may be combined, completely enveloping the sanctuary in thrilling sound. An eminent organist of one of our greatest churches, describing this church and its organ, said, "What they have done there is unbelievable." Many organists would agree with him.

Mr. Randall, who had to be "sold" on the idea of a large electronic organ for the church he serves, is happy to point out the advantages of the instrument he plays. It occupies only a fraction of the space required for a comparable pipe organ, which would cost over twice what this organ cost. He is easily able to make desired adjustments of the electronic organ, which operates without the expensive tuning and repair contract that goes with every large pipe organ.

Yet it should not be stated or implied that the days of the pipe organ industry are numbered. At the present time only two electronic organ firms are making any serious effort to challenge the pipe organ; these are the Allen Organ Company of Macungie, Pennsylvania, and the Haygren Organ Company of Chicago. The rest of the electronic organ builders are still content to compete with each other for low budget business. It is also true that for some time to come the pipe organ will continue to be favored by most organists. Even Dr. Barnes, whose 1958 report in *The Diapason* helped to bring national attention to the Stamford electronic organ, has recently said that if he were to spend as much money for an organ as the Stamford church did (about $60,000) he would buy a pipe organ. Perhaps it should be pointed out that not all organists would agree with him even now. We may not know what will be true several years hence. It is probable that certain electronic organ firms will continue to make improvements which should narrow, then erase, any apparent advantages the pipe organ now has over the electronic organ.

Whether the organ committee has $15,000 to spend for a new instrument, or several times that amount, let its members take time to hear and ask questions about numerous types of organs. If any custom-built electronic organs are to be found near at hand, let the committee hear them. Only after they have listened well, let them decide whether the organ of their choice will be electronic or pipe.

If the Organ Fund Is Modest

If a church proposes to spend less than $5,000 for an organ, it must choose one from among the electronic organs. The selection of manufacturers is not broad. There are only about ten firms, large and small, in this field in this country. Only four or five of these maintain retail and service outlets that are really national in scope; the remainder are only regionally active. In even a fairly large city perhaps only three or four electronic organ agencies can be found. Each one offers several models, with specifications and prices close to those of their competitors.

How do we choose among the companies and models? Before we seek an answer, perhaps we should define our terms. Properly speaking, an electronic organ's tone is produced by the activation of vacuum tubes. However, the word "electronic" now is applied to any organ the tone of which comes from speakers rather than from pipes, although the tone may be produced by other methods, such as the revolving notched disc, the vibrating reed, or the electric eye and scanning disc. All electronic organs have three basic components: the console in which the tone is formed, the amplifier in which it is increased, and one or more speakers which put it into the air. In smaller models, all three components are placed within the console. But the better models place the amplifier and speaker or speakers at some distance from the console.

From different means of tone production have come different results, which at the beginning were uniformly unsatisfactory.

There was a percussive thump that came with each tonal attack, particularly when the swell shoe was open. When the organ was loud, there was a harshness that came from the speaker, as when a radio is turned up beyond the point of tolerance. Then, like the pre-stereophonic phonograph, most electronic organs blended their qualities within the instrument instead of in the air, where we are accustomed to hearing various qualities blended.

These early tonal defects of electronic organs are mentioned here because they continue to be characteristic defects, particularly in organs priced below $5,000. Most, but not all, electronic organs are now free from the percussive thump. Most of the smaller electronic organs still have a harsh, shrill quality when they are played loudly, particularly when their speaker or speakers are not carefully installed in recessed and elevated chambers. The third defect, of qualities artificially mixed within the instrument, remains in most smaller electronics. Its correction lies in the use of several speakers, well separated, each voicing a different set of stops; not many organs in this price class have made this change, which is found in larger electronic organs.

This is not to say that smaller churches cannot find an effective electronic organ for an investment of less than $5,000. At the present time there are about six firms which build instruments capable of giving beautiful music and reliable service. Two more firms have let it be known that they expect to produce improved church models in the near future. At the same time it is easy for a church, by not choosing with sufficient care, and by not making a large enough financial investment, to select an organ which will serve it poorly. In the face of rapid change, it is hard to make definite statements on the choice of electronic organs. But there are some basic principles by which buyers may be guided:

1. Do not buy on the basis of national advertising. The company with the largest advertising budget, or the one making the most attractive claims for its product, may not build the best organs.

2. Do not buy on the basis of a showroom demonstration only. Artfully placed speakers and tricks of demonstration may give an entirely different impression of an instrument than the same one would give in the sanctuary. Organs—perhaps two or more in

direct comparison—should be heard in the room in which they are to be used.

3. Do not buy cheap "economy" models. The "spinet" models —with shortened manual keyboards, and pedal boards of one octave only—should not be considered under any circumstances. It is also well to avoid all instruments with shortened pedal boards. The usual competitive models have a twenty-five note (two-octave) pedal board, while the standard organ pedal board has thirty-two notes, or over two and a half octaves. The shortened pedal boards not only have all the pedals out of position, but most of them lack the radiating-concave characteristics laid down by the American Guild of Organists. The result is that any organist who has learned to play the substandard organ will be handicapped if he ever tries to adapt himself to a standard one. It should also be pointed out that the shortened pedal board is a competitive device with various companies; these models, made to sell at a low price, tend to lack other qualities desirable in an instrument adequate for church use.

4. Ascertain the dealer's ability to service the organ he sells. Contrary to common opinion, electronic organs do require occasional repairs of a sort that cannot be met by the local radio or television repair man. If nearby service is not readily available, the church may find itself without the use of its organ while it sends expensively for a distant repair service.

5. Do not install an electronic organ without properly recessing and elevating the speaker or speakers. Some of the best installations are those with the speakers placed in old organ chambers. Speakers placed near choir or congregation almost guarantee dissatisfaction.

6. Pay especial attention to the quality and general effect of the full organ with the expression pedal open. This is what you will hear, at least during the singing of hymns. Choose the organ with the most pleasant as well as the least percussive quality.

7. If the gift horse is an electronic organ, look it carefully in the mouth. Because a church does not want to offend a well-meaning donor, it accepts an inadequate or unsuitable electronic organ, and then suffers from the results of the bad gift for years.

Having accepted it, the church dares not replace it. Since this is unfair to the church, every church board should insist quietly that it have a share in the choice of every gift, no matter how generous.

A church should not attempt to buy an electronic organ for any less than about $3,000. It is true that cheaper instruments can be found. It is a temptation for a small church which has been slowly accumulating an organ fund to lose patience with waiting and saving, and to buy an instrument that is "almost as good" as they had originally planned to get. Let that church select an instrument fully adequate for its needs. (Appendix A lists a number of these.) Then let that church accept no lesser goal for itself than that which will serve it best.

Electronic or "Unit" Organ?

If a church plans to spend between $5,000 and $10,000 for a church organ, it may choose between an electronic organ and a "unit" pipe organ.

What is a unified pipe organ? It is a small pipe organ, with as few as two sets of pipes, and with a top limit of seven or eight sets. The true unit organ is so called because all its pipes are a single unit, placed together in one chamber. Ingenious electric circuits have made it possible for these few pipes to play at different pitch levels from two manuals and a pedal board. Thus a typical three-set unit organ, with a total of only 233 pipes, will use each set six or seven times on between four and six pitch levels on the two manuals and pedal, and the three ranks of pipes will appear as an organ of twenty stops! For many years this type of organ has been a favorite for use in practice rooms of music schools. More recently it has served as the pipe organ industry's answer to the challenge of the electronic organ for the smaller church.

How do organists regard the unit organ? Here is the opinion of Mr. Allan Bacon, a California organist:

> Few people know . . . that a small, compact unified pipe organ, which requires very little more space, for console and pipes combined, than two upright pianos, and which can be moved easily, as you would move a piano, can be purchased for a very little more than some of the electronics are charging.[4]

Since Mr. Bacon earlier in his book had expressed his general distaste for electronic organs, his preference for the unit pipe organ should not be questioned. However, many organists would not agree with him. It should be remembered that if an organ has only three ranks of pipes, only three qualities of tone are available individually and in combination. Even an expert chef can do only so much with three ingredients! Attempts to add to its variety by making use of lower and upper octaves and other "partials" may result in a "tubby" tone on the one end, and a shrill one on the other. This remains the great weakness of the unit organ.

Should a church with $5,000 to $10,000 to spend buy an electronic or a unit pipe organ? Perhaps the best answer is made by Dr. William H. Barnes in the seventh edition of his standard book on the organ:

> Considering the matter of the relative merits of electronics and organs in the year of grace, 1959, the author is now of the opinion that unless a church has $10,000 to spend for an organ, they should certainly buy one of the electronics of the largest size made by Baldwin, Connsonata, Wurlitzer, Lowry, or one of the other oscillating-tube electronics, as second choice.
>
> My first choice is the Allen Model C4. This model of the Allen, a development of the past year, employs three tone generators, with suitable amplifiers and gyrophonic projectors for each generator, and costs between $7,000 and $8,000. It has the elements of a true organ ensemble. Outside of the big and very costly Allens, this electronic really comes closer to sounding like an organ costing at least $15,000 than any that I have ever heard. . . . With organs costing between $1,500 and $2,000 per unified rank, one cannot go far with $7,500 today in buying an organ. One can go a lot farther with this Model C4 Allen, and get an instrument that will create the impression that the congregation is listening to reasonable organ tone.[5]

If You Decide on a Pipe Organ

Once a church has decided to buy a pipe organ, a set of complex, interrelated questions is raised. It is not the province of this book to supply definite answers to them, but rather, guiding principles which may be applied to any local situation. Ultimately each church must seek its own solution.

First, we should define *pipe organ* in the sense we mean it here. We do not include the unit organ, which is built to a standard specification and assembled in the factory. We refer rather to the custom-built organ, designed only for the room in which it is placed, and in relation to the specific purpose for which it is used. It need not be a large organ. It does need to be carefully designed.

How Much Shall Be Spent?

Several methods have been devised for determining the size and cost of an organ for a given sanctuary. Mr. Leslie Norman Leet[6] offers a table which suggests first a minimum, then a fair number of manual stops for a sanctuary of a certain seating capacity. The table is not very helpful, since the range between "fair" and "minimum" is so broad that the answer is largely meaningless. Dr. Barnes' suggestion, that a church should have a minimum of one pipe for each seat in the sanctuary, but that two or three pipes per seat would be better, is subject to the same objection.[7]

Any scheme which seeks to link organ size with seating capacity will not be adequate because it fails to take into account at least three variable elements. The first is the acoustical quality of the room. A large organ may be smothered and lost in a room in which the walls and ceilings have been treated with acoustical tile, the floors carpeted, the pews cushioned. On the other hand, a smaller organ might be more than adequate in a room of the same size with live acoustics.

The second variable element is the character of the instrument. A large organ may be put entirely "under expression," buried deep in a chamber, and shut off from the sanctuary by too small organ openings. On the other hand, a smaller organ, partially unenclosed, and closer to the congregation, may speak brilliantly beyond its size.

The third variable element is the use to which the organ will be put. A church that does vigorous hymn singing will need one type of instrument. A church in which the organ mostly plays services behind a small choir will have more modest needs. Again, the church which wants good organ recitals will have another type of need.

Faced with standards so broad that they are almost meaningless, and variable conditions that are difficult to assess, what is an organ committee to do? If its members lack knowledge, there is no better source than Dr. Barnes' book, to which repeated reference has been made in these pages; unfortunately, its overpowering amount of knowledge may confuse the non-organist more than it helps him. It is clear that the committee should also seek expert advice. The person consulted need not be an organ architect, but should be a discriminating organist who, as the agent of the committee, would work with the various organ firms considering the contract and would help the church obtain an organ appropriate to its needs.

How may a church know what it should spend for an organ? With certain businessmen in the church pressing for economy, while pastor, music committee, and organist seek a fully adequate instrument, some definite yardstick would be helpful. Dr. Barnes offers one: let the church put one-tenth of the value of its church building into its organ.[8] This formula has the advantage of being precise, and merits further consideration.

It should be clear that the Barnes formula should be applied to the cost of the church proper, not including the other parts containing educational and recreational facilities. In this day of increasing emphasis on Christian education, the educational parts of our churches are receiving an increasing portion of all building funds. Obviously, a large investment in a church school wing should not influence the cost of the church organ.

Some organ designers feel that the Barnes formula, about right for organ and general building costs in 1935, should not be applied now. The great inflation of recent years has multiplied costs, both in organs and in general building, but at somewhat different rates. However rapidly organ costs have risen, general building costs have advanced more rapidly. Some organ builders feel that at the present time ten per cent of building costs applied to the organ would be generous; perhaps eight per cent would be sufficient.

However, custom-built organ costs have recently advanced ten per cent; at the moment, Dr. Barnes' formula is not far wrong. Considering that the variable conditions mentioned earlier may change the figure in either direction, let us agree that the cost of the church organ should be between eight and ten per cent of the cost of the church sanctuary in which it is placed.

"Romantic" or "Classic"?

The past few years have brought a remarkable "classic" revival into the whole field of the organ. The movement has made itself felt in several ways. First and most obviously, we now have in this country many instruments designed to sound like their European prototypes of two centuries ago. Sitting out in the main room of the sanctuary, a large proportion of its pipes are in the open where they can be seen. Because it is no longer in a separate room, the most convenient place for it within the sanctuary is in the west gallery, where the choir is also placed with increasing frequency. Because these organs make early organ compositions sound more like they must have sounded when they were written, organ recitals as well as service music tend to be more heavily weighted with the works of Bach, his contemporaries and predecessors. The next and predictable result of the different sound of this organ has been a definite change in the style of organ playing itself. An extreme result of this movement has been an attempt to restore the cumbersome mechanical tracker action of these early organs. It may certainly be said that the "classic" or "baroque" movement has become a cult.

Before we discuss this modern classic instrument further, a word should be said about the "romantic" organ that preceded it. Until almost the present century, the development of the organ had been retarded by unwieldy mechanics and a lack of adequate wind pressure. The coming of electricity solved both problems by making available the electromagnet and the high-pressure blower. Rapidly, and particularly in America, the organ developed great power, tonal variety, and flexibility. The tendency was to think of it as an orchestra put into one instrument, with all the instruments present. But above all towered the great diapasons, which furnish the characteristic windy quality the organ alone possesses. Most of the instrument, if not all of it, was put behind swell shutters (under "expression") and the whole was concealed behind a "front," which was an elaborately carved grille, or a broad expanse of gilded false pipes.

The causes of the revival of the classic or baroque organ are interesting, but not within the scope of this work. We shall just say that suddenly, during this century's second quarter, organists became absorbed in a study of eighteenth-century organs still in use in Europe, particularly in Germany. These organs tended to have certain common characteristics. Because all action was mechanical, and the larger the organ the more energy required to play it, these organs were limited in size. Because bellows power was limited manpower, the pipe sets tended to be small in size, requiring less wind at lower pressure; big diapasons and large pedal stops tended to be avoided. Since the balanced swell was not known, most of the organ was unenclosed, only one section being put inside a "swell" box. The tone quality of these instruments tended to be bright, clear, pure, not too powerful or heavy.

The classic organs built in this country, first in concert halls and then in churches, followed their ancestors in both design and nomenclature. The lower manual of a three-manual organ, once known as the Choir Organ, now became the Positiv, and the stop knobs took on long German names. Then this renewal of an old instrument began to win its place in this country, at first against massive opposition. Its clarity, brilliance, and general responsiveness became almost irresistible to American organists and organ lovers. A large proportion of our new organs today are of the classic variety; some enthusiasts have named them "contemporary" organs.

There has already been time for some second thoughts on some of the features of the baroque organ. These beautiful graduated ranks of pipes, unlike the gilded false ones of our organs a few years ago, although completely honest, still may distract the attention of the worshiper if the organ is near the front of the sanctuary; the opening and closing of the swell shutters during the organ music are more disconcerting. It must also be admitted that the classic organ in its pure form is not entirely adaptable for accompanying the solo voice or the choir.

The fact remains that the coming of the baroque organ to America has been good for music and good for the Church. Musically it is already being altered to make it more acceptable for worship purposes. Although the Great Organ continues unenclosed, some designers have either replaced the unenclosed Positiv with an enclosed Choir, or else have put both a Positiv and a Choir Organ in the same instrument. These and other changes in choice of stops have made this type of organ not only more effective for service playing, but also more versatile in the music it can play adequately.

As to the placing of the ranks of pipes in the open for all eyes to see, there should be little or no objection if the organ is in the west gallery, behind the congregation. It must also be admitted that few voices have been raised against the exposure of the same organ at or near the front of the sanctuary. In fact, there are those zealots who insist that such exposure is appropriate and right. Others have apparently accepted it as a necessary provision of the classic design. Without arguing the matter at this point, let it be said that neither statement has to be true. "Classic" sound can come from behind a grille or screen with no appreciable loss of effectiveness. One of the expensive processes of classic organ manufacture is the finishing, polishing, and racking of pipes for public view. Money saved on this process could be spent on the grille or screen; if this outer covering is not too costly, conceivably a church could save some money on what would otherwise go for appearance only. This would also provide satisfaction for those who feel that during divine worship the seeker's eye should be confronted primarily with Christian symbols.

How Do We Proceed?

One does not have to visit many churches before he finds organs that fail in one way or another to serve their churches well. Church A bought too small an organ, but has no space in the sanctuary for its expansion; the only way the organ may grow is to rebuild a portion of the church. Church B has purchased an adequate organ, and then buried it so deeply in a chamber behind small openings that its tone is smothered and ineffective. Church C has spent so much money for a harp, chimes, and a Vox Humana that not sufficient funds were left to get an organ sufficiently large to support the hymn singing. Church D obtained at a bargain a secondhand organ from a church that was being torn down, but found that the organ has never sounded well in its new home, and never seemed to be in good repair.

All of these churches are victims of insufficient planning. Perhaps their organ committees have been unaware of the complexities of their task. Perhaps they have taken the easy solution because they wanted to avoid the difficulties they might otherwise have to face. Since the life of a church organ tends to be forty years or longer, any church pays a high price for a job thus poorly done. First, then, the church and its organ committee should bring themselves to the realization that the task of selecting an organ is both important and difficult.

Beyond an idea of how much money it has to spend, the organ committee should begin its work with no preconceptions. It should travel extensively, listen to all kinds of organs and organists in all kinds of churches, and ask questions. Rare is the organist who will not gladly demonstrate his instrument, discussing fully its good and bad points. If the committee probes for information, in a short time its members will have a fund of knowledge on builders and specifications, and will use with confidence the technical language having to do with blowers, wind trunks, relays, contacts, chests, pipe work.

The committee, thus equipped, is now ready to take one of two forward steps suggested by Dr. Barnes.[9] If the church has no more than $30,000 to put into an organ, it should write to a modest list of builders, say three or four in number. Dr. Barnes discourages the practice of indicating to the companies the approximate cost of the organ desired, and permitting them to offer their own specifications; in this way three or four quite different specifications might be suggested, and the committee might have a difficult time comparing them. Rather, a discriminating organist should be asked to furnish a sample specification which would be submitted to the several firms. They may be expected to alter the specification to conform to their own standards. The resulting specifications and bids, while not identical, will offer the committee a better basis for comparison.

A further word should be added here concerning the choice of firms from which bids should be requested. If the committee examines some issues of the Chicago publication, *The Diapason,* "a monthly publication devoted to the organ and the interests of organists," in it will be found several "big name" firms which build most of the large organs found in big churches, colleges, and auditoriums. Next there are the smaller firms which usually build neither as large nor as many organs as the first group, but still build well. In the third place, there are the organ technicians whose first task is to provide tuning and repair service to organs, but who also rebuild old instruments, and provide new ones.

Different types of organ builders should receive different types of treatment from the organ committee. Certain of them, particularly the "big name" ones, require little guidance. The designer will probably come from the company. After ascertaining the general price range of the proposed organ, and the uses to which it will be put, he will draw what data he needs from the actual building or its blueprints. The resulting specification may or may not be close to the one submitted by the committee, but it should be treated like a work of art; it may be rejected, but it may be altered very little. In fact, some organ firms would rather lose a contract than materially to alter that which the designer has proposed. The committee should accept this as evidence of the integrity of the company, which is considering not only its own reputation, but also the long-term satisfaction of its customers.

Certain other builders, perhaps smaller ones, sometimes lacking heavy backlogs in their order books, may be more flexible in their treatment of prospective customers. This willingness to meet the customer's desires, even to a limited degree, offers the organ committee both opportunity and danger. With guidance and wisdom the committee may make the organ dollars of the church go further. Yet with less wisdom the errors we have seen in the choice of organs all about us may be made again and again. In this field the customer is not always right. The committee should hesitate before it insists on its own way, against the advice of the organ builder.

There are many firms of organ tuners and repair men in this country which are technically able to build good organs. They are able to operate more economically than the standard organ builders. Since they get new materials from organ supply houses as they require them, they need neither a factory nor a large inventory of organ parts. Since they may arrange to build organs during their "off" season, when they are less busy with their regular service contracts, they may keep their labor costs at a minimum. It is therefore possible for a church to buy a beautiful organ from a firm of organ technicians for less money than the same organ would cost from a regular builder. Yet a church runs two risks if it does business with a service firm. The first is in the quality of materials used. The greater part of any organ—a complex of wood, metal, leather, electromagnets, wiring, contacts, motors—is hidden from view. It is possible for a service firm, less responsible for its acts than an established organ company, to use inferior materials that will offer continual trouble. The second is in the matter of design and engineering. Rare will be the firm of technicians that will include both an artistic designer who can conceive a beautiful instrument, and an engineer who can build it well. There are many good firms of organ technicians in this country which can qualify as able organ builders. The church, if it employs a firm of organ technicians to build its organ, should be certain that the firm is both competent and responsible.

If a church has more than $30,000 to invest in its organ, Dr. Barnes counsels it to proceed somewhat differently. Let the church select one of the established builders, whose organs are familiar to the committee. Then let this builder, with the full knowledge of how much the church has to invest, proceed with a free hand to plan the instrument for the church. Any of the better builders, given this opportunity, will take pride in creating for the church an organ on which it will not be ashamed to place its own name, and by means of which the church will enjoy beautiful worship for many years.

It should not be forgotten that no organ committee should buy
and have installed a new organ without the continuing advice of a
competent organist, particularly if the organ funds are limited. For
instance, every church organ should contain one very soft stop, to
give pitches to the choir, and to furnish other very soft music;
since such a stop costs about as much as a louder one which would
carry more weight in the organ ensemble, builders easily persuade
themselves to use the louder rather than the softer. Every church
organ should have ample adjustable pistons to enable the organist
to make quick necessary shifts in registration in the course of a
service; again, when costs need to be pared, builders are apt to cut
out these "mechanicals" first, to the organist's discomfort. Unless
a competent organist is on guard throughout, the church may lose
much in service it might otherwise realize from a new organ.

The Place for the Organ

The first statement to be made on placing the organ within the
sanctuary would seem to be self-evident: this place should be
planned before the church is built. There are, however, too many
known examples of failure to do this to take this proposition for
granted. Of course, a building committee will make its wishes
known to the architect before he begins his work. But this is not
sufficient. The committee should also satisfy itself that the architect has consulted at least one organ builder, and that the plan
include within the church building the proper and full preparation to receive the organ. This should include provision for a
soundproofed motor room, remote enough from the sanctuary to
prevent even its vibration from being felt; available to it should
be a clean, warm air supply. It should also not be too near other
rooms in which meetings are held on Sunday mornings.

Of greater importance is the allotting of space to the organ itself. If the organ is to be in a separate room or rooms, not only
must width, depth, and height be adequate for their sounding
and tuning, but the openings into the sanctuary should be large
enough to avoid smothering its tone. If the organ is "contemporary," sitting out in the sanctuary proper, the same care

must be given to its air space. No general statements should be made here concerning how much room is needed, since it should be tailored to fit the instrument that is to occupy it, and should be planned from the beginning.

Where should the organ be placed? Again, the first and obvious answer is near the choir. But this answer seems not to be so obvious. In my limited experience I have visited at least two churches in which the organist and organ are at one end of the nave, and the choir at the other. In these churches, of course, the organist cannot direct the choir. It is difficult enough merely to keep the choir and the organ together! Both of the churches to which I have referred had skilled choirs which were able to work under these adverse circumstances. Less able singers would have found the task too difficult. It should be quite evident that this arrangement does not favor good church music.

The large church that can afford it may, of course, place its organ in more than one location. If the choir is in the gallery, a gallery organ may be provided, with another section of the instrument in the chancel, with sometimes two different consoles. Most churches, however, cannot afford all this. If the choir is in the gallery, that is where the organ should be.

Where the choir occupies a divided chancel, the organ may also be divided, with one half behind each side of the choir. If the two halves are in chambers, and the church is in a climate where there are cold winters, precautions need to be made by insulated walls or special heaters to give both sides balanced, even heat. Otherwise the two halves may not agree in pitch on a cold day when the wind blows heavily on one wall. Moreover, when such an organ is in two chambers above the choir in a divided chancel, the organ openings should be toward the chancel or choir, and not toward the nave. If there were other openings toward the nave, it would be difficult for the organist to balance the organ with the choir. The devotees of the classic or baroque organ (call it "contemporary" if you will) say with a certain complacency at this point that neither of these items would be any problem at all for the classic organ!

The Place for the Console

Two purposes should determine the placing of the console: i should be concealed from the congregation, and it should b within view of the choir.

Why should it be concealed from the congregation? If worshi is to be God-centered, and all details that cloud or vitiate ou contemplation of Him are to be suppressed, then the keepin of the console from a point where it can attract interest become highly desirable. To the nonmusician, the very process of playin the organ is a fascinating sight. If the organist further "puts o an act," either in his playing or in the directing of the choi his performance becomes a serious deterrent to worship. The cor sole, then, should never be permitted in the nave proper, near th congregation. If the console is in the middle of the choir lo behind the pulpit, it should be lowered enough to conceal th organist behind the choir rail; if this lowering is not sufficient t achieve its purpose, a concealing curtain above the choir ra should be used. Where the console is in the same center positio in transept or gallery the same should be true, although it is nc as important a matter when the organist does not sit directly be fore the congregation.

Should the console be exposed to view during organ recitals Not at all. The primary purpose of the sanctuary is worship; th recital should not suggest any change in this attitude. One ha only to sit during a twilight organ recital in a church which is l only by the rays of the setting sun to know the beautifully reverer experience that may come in this environment. The sight of th organist playing can add nothing good to this experience; indee the opposite may be true.

It should be quite obvious that the console should be near th choir, and in a location from which the organist may condu the choir. Even if a church now uses different persons as organi and choirmaster, this arrangement could change. I have in mind church in which the organist was responsible for placing the cor sole so that he faced the congregation, with his back to th choir. He made it clear that *he* had no intention of ever conduc ing the choir. He certainly gave no thought for those who would follow him. Surely in this general arrangement the organist should be in the center of the choir space, facing the choir, within view of all its members.

The divided chancel offers a different problem. With the communion table near the east wall in the center, the organ console normally is placed on one side or the other of the chancel. The organist should sit with his back to the chancel wall, facing the opposite side, as do the choir members who sit on the same side. If the console and music desk are not too high, the choir members on the opposite side should have a clear view of the organist. Those sitting on the same side must observe him through a mirror or mirrors extended above the heads of the choir on the opposite side. This arrangement works out well so far as choir control is concerned.

For reasons not wholly clear, some consoles have been placed on the east end of the chancel, near the communion table, as well as the farthest possible distance away from both minister and congregation. Two difficulties result from this position: First, the organist cannot as easily maintain close contact with the minister. Second, the choir will tend to turn faces away from the congregation in order to get a better view of the organist. To the degree that the choir does this, its tone and enunciation are reduced in clarity. Even if the choir is instructed to turn only the eyes toward the choirmaster or his mirrored reflection, the tendency will remain to turn the head also. For these reasons, this position for the console is not the best one.

Rather to be preferred is the placing of the console close behind the pulpit, nearer the congregation. It is effectively hidden by the pulpit. If the choirmaster and organist are different persons, this position is good both for choir control and for concealment. Communication between minister and choirmaster is easy. Also, choir members need make no adjustment in position of head or eyes to see clearly the choirmaster or his reflection.

However, for the church that is willing to use new ideas there is a still better place within the chancel for the console. Let us visit again that unique church in Stamford, Connecticut, the First

Presbyterian Church. Its sanctuary, shaped like a giant fish, contains the finest electronic organ in the world as of now, and a most effective arrangement for worship. Its communion table above which is suspended a tall cross, is just outside the chancel midway between the pulpit and the lectern. The entire chancel then, may serve the purposes of music. The space between the opposing choir stalls, for the full length of the chancel, contains a pit four or five feet below the level of the chancel floor. On the end nearest the congregation, the west end, is the console, facing east. From his position there, the organist is concealed from the congregation, yet may be seen perfectly by the choir members on both sides. The remaining space in the pit, to the east wall, may be occupied by a "pit" orchestra for festival occasions, or built up to provide for an augmented choir. I can think of no more perfect arrangement.

Finally—

It is now evident that this chapter has not given many answers. The subject is too complex to compress into precise formulae. Organs, like homes and automobiles, are in constant process of change. The great resurgence of baroque or classic design came during the second quarter of this century. What will emerge in the third quarter is not yet clear, but it appears that the day of the electronic organ is at hand. Also, the addition of electronic pedal units to the pipe organ now appears practicable, although other combinations of the two do not now seem to have great promise. Direct amplification of pipe organ tone has not yet been tried extensively, but offers assurance of making a small organ sound larger, and also may double a chancel organ in the gallery, and vice versa.

Whether it has a large or small amount to spend, today's organ selection committee has a variety of attractive possibilities opening before it. It is easy for its members to succumb to good salesmanship, or to choose at once what can be delivered most promptly. If the committee thus gives way quickly, it will be missing the exciting chance to explore tomorrow's organ, and may also miss giving the church the best organ available.

IV

MUSICAL ACCESSORIES

The Choir Room

Every church that uses a choir needs a choir room. It is the storage place for robes and music. But of more importance is its function as a place of withdrawal and final preparation for the choir on Sunday mornings.

It is needful that this room be reserved for the choir alone. In some busy, crowded churches the choir members must wait outside the room until some class vacates it. In others the choir has no place at all to call its own. It rehearses on Sunday mornings in some classroom, then dons robes in some corridor, where it must wait until time for its entrance into the sanctuary. That choir works under a severe handicap, since it has no opportunity to grasp that quiet moment of withdrawal which is so necessary in preparation for worship.

The choir room should be equipped with robe cabinets for all choirs, storage space for choir music, a piano or organ, and chairs sufficient for the largest choir in the church. The robe cabinets should be as dust-proof as possible. Choirmasters have varying ideas about music storage. Some methodical souls have all music filed in permanent cases, arranged alphabetically according to composer or first line, with a separate card index containing significant data, including when each item has been used. Other more casual and economical persons may be content with manila folders for the music, with the data written on the outside. I would not want to say which method is better. That depends upon how the choirmaster prefers to spend his time, as well as the money of the church.

The choir room should be arranged with one purpose foremost the saving of the singers' time and nervous energy on Sunday mornings. As nearly as possible the arrangement of chairs should correspond to that in the choir loft or chancel. Rehearsal conditions should be made to approximate performance conditions Since the rehearsal time is short, none of it should be wasted in arranging persons or things. Singers should at once find their proper chairs, on which the music has already been placed. I should be clear at this point that such preparation would not be possible if the choir had no choice but to move hastily into a room a class had just vacated. The requirements described here are modest. It would be easy to add other details toward the making of the ideal situation. But since the gap between the real and the ideal is wide in most of our churches, it is unprofitable to go further at this point.

As to location, this room should be remote enough from the sanctuary for its Sunday morning rehearsals not to disturb the early arrivals in the sanctuary. It would also be helpful if choir loft and choir room be not so far separated that needless time and effort are constantly used getting from one to the other.

Choir Robes

Choir robes have two functions in worship. They suggest the status of the choir as it differs from that of the congregation They also achieve a certain uniformity of appearance which seem desirable among a group of people who share the same task. Like other changes made in Protestant worship, the adoption of robes was accompanied by a certain amount of controversy. But this ha largely disappeared, and most large churches, whether free or liturgical in their approach to worship, now robe their choirs There is, however, some variety in the way it is done.

The trend today is toward "multiple" choirs within a church; the larger the church, the greater the number of choirs. There is a tendency for each choir to have its distinctive costume and color largely based on the academic robe. But some churches clothe all choirs in the more formal black cassock and white surplice (with the younger choirs perhaps omitting the cassock). Some churches use both methods of dress for the various age groups.

Both historical and practical considerations may well enter into the choice of choir robes. The cassock and surplice are associated with the Roman Catholic priesthood, for, as Macalister wrote, "When the priest was vested in professional attire . . . the lower end of the cassock appeared very prominently under the surplice, and its presence was consequently essential to complete the processional outfit."[1] This garb was adopted by the Anglican priesthood, and then extended to Anglican choristers. The place of cassock and surplice in this country has largely been in Episcopal and other liturgical churches.

Almost from the beginning academic costume became a symbol among Protestant clergy, as told by Wilhelm Pauck:

> A telling symbol of the new religious and social status of the Christian minister of the Age of the Reformation was his manner of dress. The gown of the secular scholar, commonly worn by the men of learning among the burghers and called *Schaube*, became the outward sign of ministerial vocation and social status. Zwingli was the first to introduce it in Zürich, during the autumn of 1523. In the afternoon of October 9, 1524, Luther too began to wear it. Clothed in the *Schaube*, he then preached from the pulpit which he had occupied in the morning for the last time wearing the monk's cowl. Henceforth, the scholar's gown was *the* garment of the Protestant minister. It symbolizes all the changes that were wrought by the Reformation in the nature and the work of the ministry.[2]

Whether or not the *Schaube* is identical to what we now know as the Geneva gown is not important. It is sufficient to recognize that within the Protestant Church the academic gown has a certain historical advantage over the cassock and surplice. The choir is garbed in the same general attire as that worn by the minister, and shares some of the worship functions with the minister.

For the adult choir which sings week after week, the academic gown is more practical than cassock and surplice. It is more easily donned and removed. It requires less cleaning than the white surplice, although the stiff white collars on the women's gowns require occasional laundering. The academic gown is available in numerous colors, and may be tailored in fabrics of light enough weight so that they may be worn in all but the hottest weather.

The cassock and surplice have one advantage over the gown, and that is one of cost. They may be made by the ladies of the local church from fairly inexpensive materials, while gowns need to be made to measure and factory-tailored. These ideas suggest the most practical solution, one used by many churches: the adult choir, which sings regularly, is vested in well-made academic costumes. The younger choirs, which sing less often, are vested in cassocks and surplices; the surplices may be all that are needed for the smaller children.

A word of warning should be raised against the spectacular in choir vesting. It is possible today to buy choir robes in shining materials and brilliant colors, sometimes with contrasting colors in sleeve facings. Such a mode of dress may be suitable for a concert choir; it is not proper for a church choir. Since choir gowns may not be changed as often as the flowers on the table, it is well that the gown have a modesty and dignity appropriate at any solemn occasion in the life of the church.

The stole has no proper place in the choir. For many centuries it has been a symbol of ordination, and should be worn by ordained ministers only. Its use by either a church or a school choir is an impropriety.

We must also deal with Paul's statement directed against the appearance in church of women with uncovered heads. For the choir, many creations have been advanced in various shapes, sizes and colors to obey what some have regarded as a Biblical injunction. But it is fairly safe to say that none of these has enhanced either the beauty of the wearers or the dignity of the ensemble. Whatever Paul's reason may have been for his initial statement, many feel that the need for it has departed with the centuries. No evil effects have been recorded, so far as I know, from the appearance of women in the church choir with uncovered heads. By all means let this symbol of women's traditional abasement be forgotten!

Were there not so many examples to the contrary at hand, this last word would appear to be unnecessary: Since one purpose for vesting the choir is to give its members a uniform appearance, no unnecessary deviation from this uniformity should be permitted. (I use the word "unnecessary" because no vestment has been devised which can make uniform various shapes and sizes.) I refer specifically to hair ornaments, earrings, necklaces, or bright-colored neckties which may be in evidence in spite of proper robing. I also know of a choir in which the women members, not being confident concerning the security of their handbags in the choir room during the service, carry them on their arms during processional and recessional. Then there are the women of another choir who were indignant at their choirmaster for refusing to permit them to wear their corsages on the outside of their choir robes on Easter morning!

The Hymnals

The hymns of the Church change, as indeed they should. This is partly because the hymns we sing reflect the current activities and concerns of the Church. A hymn like Frank Mason North's "Where cross the crowded ways of life" could not have won acceptance within the Christian family until Christians had developed a concern for the social conditions under which many are living. Our hymns change partly because the great souls of each age express some of their finest thoughts in hymns. The Church must, for instance, make room for such a challenging utterance as the 1930 hymn by Harry Emerson Fosdick, "God of grace and God of glory."

Any church should use the same care in keeping its hymnal up to date as in keeping its sanctuary in repair. Above all, it should avoid clinging to an old hymnal just because it contains the "good old songs" the congregation loves to sing. Perhaps each church should have a standing committee which from time to time reviews the various materials used by the church, including its hymnals.

First consideration should go, I believe, to the hymnals suggested by the denomination of which it is a part. The larger denominations have, in general, given thought and care to the preparation of a series of hymnals for different age groups, culminating in the hymnal for the worship service. These hymnals are occasionally revised, with outworn and unused materials discarded and desirable new materials added. The advantages of using a uniform series of hymnals throughout a church are too obvious to require expansion here.

Another fairly new type of hymnal should also be mentioned: it is that produced by interdenominational co-operation. Two examples come to mind (there may be others): In 1941 commissions from the Northern Baptist Convention and the Disciples of Christ worked together to bring out a hymnal, published by Judson Press and called *Christian Worship*. More recently the Presbyterian Church in the United States, the Presbyterian Church in the United States of America, the United Presbyterian Church of North America, and the Reformed Church in America issued a joint hymnal, known as *The Hymnbook*, copyrighted in 1955, and circulated by all these denominations. It should be admitted at once that when two or more denominations co-operate on something as important as a hymnal, the result will be a compromise, not altogether pleasing to any one group. Against whatever loss there may be should be placed at least two gains: First, a joint hymnal exposes a church to an unfamiliar hymn literature, one which should stimulate new musical and spiritual thought within the church. Also, the very practice of sustained co-operation among a number of denominations during a period sufficient to bring out a hymnal certainly must help the cause of Christian unity.

Other general hymnals, such as the series edited by H. Augustine Smith a few years ago, appear from time to time. Some have a particular emphasis which makes them unsuited for corporate worship. Some are good and merit examination. Space will not permit here a detailed discussion of this type. It remains only to repeat that each church should force itself periodically to re-examine its hymnals. Where a way to improve opens, it should be followed.

The Choir Library

To many a choirmaster the selection of anthems and responses is laborious and irksome. For this reason congregations suffer from hearing, again and again, a very small repertoire. Some choirmasters attempt to make a virtue of this iteration by calling certain solos, anthems, or cantatas, presented at fixed points in each Church year, "traditional" celebrations. But, no matter what they are called, too frequent musical repetitions are deadly to the spirit both of the congregation and of the choir.

For the choirmaster who has limited time and opportunity to examine unfamiliar choir music there are a number of aids. Of increasing helpfulness are those which come from certain denominational offices. This assistance takes three forms. Some denominational offices offer lists of service music. Some go a step further by occasionally publishing books of anthems and reponses for various voice groups. Some denominations find that they can serve their choirmasters best by issuing anthem periodicals; at least some of these have been successful.

Of a quite different sort are a number of commercial choir periodicals. For many years there have been these monthly magazines which purport to contain all the material a choir should need for its regular services. The materials are uniform in approach and easy. They are also mostly bad music and of deadly monotony. Let the choirmaster who follows this easy path beware; the road leads only downward. And let those hundreds of churches in this country which keep closets full of back issues of these periodicals beware; they are maintaining a fire hazard. These issues are worth more as waste paper than they are as music.

Another aid for the busy choirmaster, by no means as bad as the one just mentioned, is the use of volumes of collected anthems. There are many such collections, printed by various music publishers. They offer to the uncritical choirmaster tempting fare. The musical quality of many of these is fairly good. Here within one cover are a variety of topical sources, musical styles, and degrees of difficulty. It is also true that the cost per anthem within these volumes is much lower than that of the same anthems bought individually. The discriminating choirmaster will soon realize, however, that the bargain he thought he had in a collection is not as good as it first appeared. Anthem A is too difficult. Anthem B has a too difficult solo. Anthem C the choir does not like. Anthem D has an unsuitable text. Anthem E the choir uses from another collection.

When the choirmaster has eliminated all materials in the collection that will not be used, what remains is no bargain. If he buys the most venerated of all collections, *The Church Anthem Book* of Oxford University Press, with its hundred anthems, he will find that, unless he has a choir of oratorio proportions, much of the book will not be suitable. Remember also that any collection becomes a problem in handling. It is bulky in choir loft and storage space, and offers an added problem in indexing and keeping anthem records. But where the individual octavo anthem is to be preferred for the adult choir, the anthem collection is often more useful for the younger choirs of the church. While individual copies will get lost, soiled, or torn in a child's hands, the stapled or bound anthem collection should fare better.

The choirmaster should make a consistent effort to keep his operating repertoire ample. Although it may not be wise for him to buy anthem collections for the full membership of his adult choir, individual copies of the best of these collections should be in his own library. He will also seek help from his denominational central office. He will examine other church music libraries. He will make use of materials submitted by music stores and publishers. Also, one book is available to serve him.[3]

How much music should be bought for an adult choir? A choir that has grown out of the beginner class should have a working repertoire of at least a hundred anthems. Three hundred would be better. A new choir may need to buy thirty or more anthems in its first year. Thereafter, as some anthems are retired and more added, fewer sets will be needed each year thereafter. But a choir, in order to grow, should learn at least twenty new anthems a year. If thirty copies of each are bought, at an average cost of 20¢ to 25¢ a copy, the choir's anthem budget should be between $120 and $150 a year. This does not include "specials" for the holiday seasons. The budget for the younger choirs is harder to fix. It would depend upon the degree to which departmental hymnals are used, the frequency of public appearances, and various other factors.

One of the mistakes made by some churches is the buying initially of too few copies of an anthem. This is false economy.

Suppose a choir of twenty starts with twenty copies. Several copies are taken home, and some fail to return. Perhaps seventeen are filed away. A year later there are seventeen copies for a choir that has grown to twenty-four; copies have to be shared awkwardly between two people. If more are lost this time, shortly there are not enough copies to go around. The choirmaster does not take the trouble to order the few needed copies; the anthem just drops from use because too small an investment was made at the beginning. A better plan is to buy thirty copies for a choir of twenty. The extra copies do not cost much, but will provide for a growing choir, and for a certain amount of lost music as well.

No choir library should be without its repair department. The backs of octavo anthems, folded and refolded during use, wear out. Individual sheets become separated and lost, and the edges tattered. The least that should be done before this happens is the liberal use of adhesive tape. Particularly helpful is a Scotch Tape Edger, obtainable from some music or business supply houses, which, at the turn of a crank, quickly puts a neat binding on individual copies.

Were its services not unique, I would hesitate to mention the work of one company. Gamble Hinged Music Company (312 South Wabash Avenue, Chicago 4, Illinois) promises that "Gambleizing adds twenty years of life to your music." Gamble Leaf Hinge Tape, known by its users as Gamble Hinge, consists of two or more strips of gummed linen that are strongly sewed together, making a durable hinge. The company offers three ways of using its service. New music of all publishers may be ordered through its mail order service, and the hinge is added for a few cents a copy before it is mailed out. Copies new or partly worn may be sent to the company for the addition of the hinge. Also, for the do-it-yourself church this hinged tape is available in rolls of different length and number of hinged strips.

For choir efficiency as well as neat Sunday appearance, the chorus folio is helpful. Within durable covers a choir's current repertoire may be placed. Each choir member should have within his folio, which should bear his name, all the music that is to be used at a given time. No time is lost during rehearsal in distributing and returning music. There is no shuffling of music during the Sunday service. For the choir that operates in full view of the congregation, the folio offers Sunday after Sunday a neat, inconspicuous appearance.

PART TWO

We Belong to a Church

THE MINISTER

CHOIRMASTER AND ORGANIST

THE MULTIPLE CHOIR SYSTEM

THE ADULT CHOIR

THE MUSIC COMMITTEE

V

THE MINISTER

The Captain of the Team

Minister, director of music, choir, ushers, and congregation—these are the members of the team directly concerned with the worship of the church. Behind them work other members of the church staff, the church governing boards, the operating committees, the church school teachers. If all of these do their jobs well, and in relation to each other, beautiful and effective worship may result. That they may know their jobs and their relationships is the task of the minister, the captain of the team. Perhaps this is his most important task.

It may be said that the most significant furnishing of the church is not the pulpit, nor the Lord's Table, but rather the desk within the pastor's study. Its primary importance is not the study done beside it, nor the sermons and letters that may go out from it; its highest function is that of conference table. Over it should proceed the ideas which, hammered and shaped together, form the framework for the strengthening and growth of the church.

Exchange of ideas is important. They must not move all in the same direction. If a minister has become charmed by the sound of his own voice, talks much, and listens seldom, his church will tend to listen well and do little. Wise is the minister who listens much, and patiently. Yet it must not be forgotten that the minister is the captain of the team.

What may a minister do to control the music of his church? Should he select the hymns? Should he feel free to tell the organist when to begin and how long to play, even what to play? Should he make his wishes known if the hymns are not being sung to his liking? Should the minister choose anthems and choir responses? Should he risk the harmony within his church by suggesting, say, a change of organists?

The answer to all these questions varies, of course, with the amount of authority vested in the minister by the various denominations. It is probable that in most churches, even where the minister must seek the agreement of his supporting board, he may do all of these things if he so chooses. But it would be hard to imagine a situation in which a minister would be justified in doing all these things. He is the captain, but will be at his best only as he works with his team.

The minister is confronted by two very real limitations. The first is his lack of musical knowledge. Rare is that minister who has more than a rudimentary knowledge of music. He may have sung in his college choir or glee club, and may have taken the seminary course in hymnology. But these things together are just a beginning toward the knowledge he should have of music if he alone expects to deal with it.

The other limitation is that which any man faces who tries to do great tasks by himself. Ministers are very busy men. There seem always to be more demands on their time, labor, and sympathy than they can possibly meet. They must therefore be selective, choosing for themselves those tasks which are peculiarly their own, and then assigning every other possible task within the church. Unfortunately, assigned tasks in this situation may not be long forgotten, but must be checked to see that they are being done, and in the right way. Yet sermons have to be prepared and calls made. How is the minister to do all of this?

The minister would do well to make more use of his study as conference room. The minister should confer each week with his choirmaster, and at least once a month with his whole staff. Worship should have a large place in all these discussions. The staff members should be the minister's eyes and ears, giving him perspective in observing a problem which he stands too close to see. His staff is also, of course, an extension of his arm.

The wise minister will also not forget that the congregation is an important part of the team. His members need to share his great concerns for the church, including those of worship. Unless they know what the goals are, they cannot be expected to work toward them.

The Minister and the Choirmaster

The best operating relationship between the minister and his choirmaster will vary with the relative capabilities of each. It is fairly safe to say, however, that a perfect operating relationship exists between the two in few of our churches. The tendency is for each one to do his assigned task as he sees it, with not too much concern for how the result "ties in" with the work of the other.

Let us examine the various methods of choosing hymns, for instance. Some ministers like to make their own selections. There is the rare minister who knows his hymnal from front to back, his congregation's singing capabilities, and exactly what he wants his hymns to say. He selects with sureness and wisdom. Then there is the more common variety who knows his hymn lyrics well, but has very little notion concerning the music that goes with a set of words, and which hymns his congregation can sing. Frequently his hymns may express the idea he seeks, but musically his congregation cannot achieve the desired result. There is also that minister who feels he should select the hymns but neither knows nor greatly cares how he should go about it. His selections consist in making the rounds of about fifty of the best-known hymns, using them without any particular reference to their suitability in a given situation. There are far too many of his type in the world.

Then there are those ministers who prefer to let their choirmasters pick the hymns. At the bottom of the scale is the minister who either sees little value in planning the hymns as part of the worship, or just never gets around to that phase of service organizing. He asks his choirmaster to choose "any good devotional hymns," which rarely prove relevant to the occasion. There is also the well-meaning minister who, busy and troubled about many things, seldom manages to plan his full service with care.

84 MUSIC IN PROTESTANT WORSHIP

One minister, asked by his choirmaster on Saturday morning for his sermon topic for the following day, frequently said, "I have not quite made up my mind what I shall preach about tomorrow." It is not to be expected that such sermons turned out to be world-shaking. And what chance did his choirmaster have to help him?

There are, fortunately, those ministers who give their choirmasters topic, text, and key point of the sermon to be delivered a week away. Thus prepared, the choirmaster may do a fair job in planning the hymns, and sometimes other music, to lend significance to the preaching. However, this is frequently not enough. The choirmaster may have in mind just the anthem to go with next Sunday's sermon, but the available rehearsal time is not sufficient to prepare it, and this opportunity to enrich a particular sermon is lost for lack of sufficient notice. Then there is the choirmaster who has done his best to fit his music to the sermon of the day, only to find that the data given him was insufficient. Often the choirmaster may say with feeling, "If I had only known that this sermon would begin with that particular illustration, what I could have done to make it live!"

None of these ministers, then, can be said effectively to use the resources available in their choirmasters, although some have done better than others. Unless a minister not only grants, but insists on, frequent conferences with his choirmaster, he is hampering the effectiveness of his church music and also limiting the force of his own preaching. If the minister considers himself too busy for such conferences, he has no moral right to blame his choirmaster for shortcomings in musical support.

There should be several choice fruits of frequent conferences between minister and choirmaster. The first of these is the benefit to both parties resulting from long-range planning. There is little doubt that the minister who plans his reading and preparation for sermons some months in advance will meet the needs of his congregation better than the man who waits for last-minute inspiration for his next sermon. If this is true for the minister, it is doubly true for the choirmaster. If the choirmaster knows in March that there will be a series of sermons on the Beatitudes in May and June, he may plan, order, and prepare anthems that will give an impact to the sermons not possible by last-minute methods. What is true of preparation for series of sermons is equally true for individual sermons. The choirmaster who knows somewhat in advance the sequence of ideas which are to appear in a certain sermon may give emphasis to the thought by the studied addition of anthem or even solo directly before or after the sermon.

A close working relationship between minister and choirmaster brings other benefits. The two together can best plan an expansion of the congregational hymn repertoire. The choirmaster's counsel may serve the minister well in the occasional restudy of the order of worship. Likewise the minister may often be of real help to the choirmaster in the meeting of personal problems, which are not infrequent within the choir. In fact, the weekly conference between minister and choirmaster is an invaluable aid toward a rich worship service.

The Minister and the Choir

It is a truism to say that the church choir has an important influence on the quality of worship within the church. This is particularly true where the choir is in view of the congregation. Whispering, smiling, and exchanging greetings with members of the congregation are common devices by which choir members may annoy and distract those in the pews, and impede the efforts of the minister. Conversely, choir members who are invariably reverent and attentive during worship encourage the same attitudes in those who may see them. Less obvious is the feeling of support, or lack of it, a minister may sense within the spirit of his choir. The feeling of well-being a minister has as he faces his congregation, knowing that behind him is a group of worshipers seeking to advance his every effort, does much to make those efforts successful.

How may this rapport between minister and choir be achieved? This is partly the function of the choirmaster. Certainly the choir will not be deeply in earnest and dedicated to its task in worship if its choirmaster is indifferent and trifling in his attitude. However, his devotion may not be sufficient if the minister does not keep fresh his own interest in his choir. One way he may express this interest is by occasionally "dropping in" on a choir rehearsal. He need do no more. His very presence shows his interest.

However, the minister will find it rewarding occasionally to discuss with the choir its duty in relation to his in the life of the church. The choir needs to be reminded of the importance of its task in sharing with the minister the leading of worship, for its members cannot lead in worship unless they themselves worship; they sing not to the congregation, but rather to God Himself. The minister would do well to recognize privately, never publicly, a job well done by the choir.

In one area where the minister has been traditionally active, it appears that he would sometimes do well to withdraw. That is in the area of the choir's devotions. For many years many ministers have routinely led the choir in prayer just before the morning service has begun. It is altogether appropriate that this be done, but I have been witness to a better way. May I illustrate with this story, which is true:

In a certain church, where a volunteer choir had replaced a solo quartet of some years' standing, the minister inaugurated the usual practice of praying with his choir just before the morning service. After this had gone on for some little time, on one Sunday morning one choir member said to the minister, "Preacher, if it is all the same to you, we would like to do our own praying." The minister, a man of tact, after he had overcome his surprise readily agreed. Then began a remarkable practice which went on for years, and may continue to this day. At the end of each Sunday morning rehearsal, one choir member, asked in advance by the president of the choir, offered his own free prayer for God's blessing on the choir, the pastor, the service, the church; with this prayer the choir weekly rededicated itself to its task in a way scarcely possible when the minister was "praying for" the choir. Although the minister was frequently present, and the choirmaster always there, they were rarely asked to lead. All the choir members, young and old, took their turn in leading the weekly fellowship of devotion.

It would be hard to explain what has happened to that particular choir, and to others which follow the same practice. Perhaps these shared devotions become the symbol and model for the unity of spirit which should characterize all its work and worship together. A choir which experiences such unity of feeling will resist all those selfish and divisive influences which could make dissension within the group, or could separate the choir from the main stream of the thought and worship of the church.

There are, however, other areas in choir affairs where the minister's co-operation is not only appropriate but needed. The first of these is in choir enlistment. The minister has access early to the list of new arrivals in the community. Increasingly, ministers have on file questionnaires submitted to old and new church members concerning their abilities and interests in the line of church work. Therefore, the minister has a fund of information on potential choir members which no one else possesses. He should be prompt in putting this information to use. He should *never* invite a person to join the choir until that person's acceptability has been assured by the choirmaster or by the committee within the church responsible for choir membership. The risk of a personal or musical misfit within the choir is too great. He should, however, make available to the choirmaster what information he gains, and should be willing to aid in the enlistment to the choir of any person desired by the choirmaster.

In many churches, the minister should also act to protect the choir from talent "raids." It is common knowledge that the truly active members of most churches are a small percentage of that church's full membership. It is also true that a fair proportion of the workers within the church are also in the choir. It is natural for the director of Christian education, the church school superintendent, or (too often) the minister to turn to those who are already active and acceptable workers in the church when a new task is to be performed. Often a choir member is asked to accept just one more job than the two or three he is already doing. If this person feels he is already doing all his time and energy will permit, it is easy for a church official to press the need of the new task against those the member is already performing. So it is not unusual for a good tenor to leave the choir to become a poor scoutmaster; in that case both services lose. The minister would do well to discourage such a transfer.

The minister's interest should, however, carry further than the avoidance of errors in leadership management. It is certainly obvious that he should seek to add to the "active" members. Mrs. A. sings in the choir, and has also in times past been a successful church school teacher. The regular teacher of a high school class has just moved away, and a new teacher must be found for the class. Mrs. A. is available, but would probably drop her choir membership to fill her teaching responsibility. On the other hand, Mrs. B. has just joined the church, and has not yet taken up any church activity. She might make a good teacher for this class, but can we be sure? Too often the church will choose the safe way, place Mrs. A. in charge of the class, and hope that the choirmaster may find a replacement for her. In the meantime Mrs. B's talents may go unused. In the end the church has gained nothing, and may have lost the use of a fine worker. The minister needs to remind himself as well as his church leadership that choir members are not easily replaceable, and that every effort should be made to find others to do a needed task in the church before weakening the choir, whose place in the worship life of the church is so important.

The Minister and the Ushers

Although the ushers have no direct relationship to church music, their chief activities take place during the performance of music, and their ways of working will have a bearing on the effectiveness of the music as well as the smoothness of the whole service.

It is generally agreed that the worshiper should enter the sanctuary on Sunday morning in silence. The sound of the organ is the bridge by which the seeker is brought from the outside world into the presence of God. His first personal contact is with the usher who meets him at the door. If the greeting is a kindly glance and friendly smile without a spoken word as the bulletin is proffered, the worshiper may enter the sanctuary fully prepared for the quiet meditation with which the service should begin. If, however, the greeting is hearty and a little noisy, and if, after he takes his seat, the worshiper is aware of conversation behind him between the ushers, he will see no necessity of silence if a friend sits down near him. The period of silent meditation is lost, and the worshipers are not spiritually prepared for the beginning of the service. Unless the ushers' work is well done, the organ prelude is wasted, and the beginning of worship will not be what it should be.

Ushers' carelessness concerning the periods for seating late comers frequently destroys the feeling of worship. Perhaps it is the hurried clearing of the aisles just before the processional. Perhaps it is failure to close the doors promptly, permitting entrance during a reverent choral introit. Perhaps an usher feels called upon to seat a deacon toward the front during the singing of the early anthem. In every such case the usher has been permitted to mar the air of sacred solemnity the church musicians have worked hard to create.

Another point at which ushers may be said to create a diversion comes from the American propensity for keeping step. One of my earliest recollections of church is the performance of four good men and true who, after carefully sighting across the church at each other, struck out down the side aisles in perfect military cadence, and thundered on toward the pulpit to get the plates for the offering. That is what usually happened. But now and then one got off on the wrong foot, and had to do a little dance step to get himself into the correct relationship with the others. This practice continues in many of our churches. It is a pointless injection of the military into a situation in which the military should have no place. The offertory should be a high point in the service. It is the time for quiet meditation. In most of our churches there is music during this period. Such measured heel-thumping certainly destroys its solemnity.

There is also a tendency in many of our churches to hurry the taking of the offering. Sometimes the ushers, and sometimes the minister, want to "get on" with the service, with no time wasted. The ushers need frequently to recall the importance of their act at this point in the service, and to give it the solemn pace it merits.

The ushers are an important part of the church team. They are responsible to the minister, who should constantly observe their labors. Here again a regularly scheduled conference between minister and ushers is profitable. At such a conference he needs to remind them of the aims and methods of their task, and they need to study together ways by which their contribution to worship may be improved.

The Minister and the Congregation

Some congregations seem to worship fully and with understanding. A visitor will feel that each person around him is seeking one experience, the glorification of God. Every act is directed toward Him. His presence fills every silence. There is a warmth in the singing, an earnestness in the prayers. During the sermon God remains at the center of all thinking.

Other congregations seem not to worship, but merely to react. An air of casualness seems to pervade the service. Friends chat in vestibule and pew during the prelude. After minister and choir have entered, more or less attention is given to carrying out the instructions given by bulletin, by minister, or by both. The emphasis is not on seeking, but on responding. The attention is given to the minister, the choir, the organist, to that which at a given moment occupies the center of the ecclesiastical stage. God is somehow on their minds—choir and congregation sing about Him, and the minister preaches about Him—but He is not at the center of the service.

It must not be supposed that one type of congregation is more religious than the other. One congregation has been taught how to worship. The other has not. It is easy for a minister to infer that his congregation has and uses knowledge it really does not possess. He may have explained the duties of church membership, and the significance of the ordinances of Baptism and the Lord's Supper, but has he explained *why* we worship as we do? The wise minister will preach at least one sermon a year on worship. As he has made clear to choir members and ushers the *why* and *how* of their place in worship, so must he do the same thing for the congregation. Each worshiper should know why there is an organ prelude, and what he should do with his mind and spirit during

that time. He should be told why an anthem and choral responses
are used, why we begin with praise and end with personal dedication, and what the significance of the offertory is. The minister
should patiently teach the principles of worship until his members
have formed the habit, and the whole church the tradition, of
reverent worship.

The Minister Behind the Pulpit

> Many of the best denominational preachers do not know how
> to conduct a formal service of worship because they cannot keep
> themselves out of it. They are like the golf players who cannot
> be rid of the fault of pressing the ball. The good golfer knows
> that the right form will itself do the work. The proper club
> swung properly will lift the ball. No extra intrusive pressing is
> required. It is precisely so with a liturgy.[1]

There are now few churches of any size without their bulletins
containing an order of worship. Yet many ministers feel that
their congregations must be helped to follow the order. It has been
said that some worshipers will not go to the trouble of looking
for the numbers of hymns and responsive readings in the bulletin;
the minister must therefore furnish this information. It might be
observed that a person who will not exert himself sufficiently to
look up the numbers in the bulletin will not go to the trouble of
opening the hymnal after they are given to him! (There are, of
course, those people who look with disapproving eye on the
printed bulletin just as they have opposed robing clergy and
choir; their grandparents probably fought against bringing an
organ into the church.) The congregation may easily be trained
to rise for the hymns when the choir does, yet countless ministers
seem to prefer to order it by their own gestures. Then there is
the minister who, at the close of each hymn, tells his congregation
to "please be seated." In one of his services I found myself wondering what would happen if he should forget to order his congregation down at the end of the "sermon" hymn. Would his flock
continue to stand throughout the sermon? Or would his ushers
fail to come forward if he did not remind them and the others that
"the morning offering will now be received"?

What the minister of this sort has forgotten is that in general his congregation is there for the purpose of worship, and *will* worship up to the limit of its ability without his help; those who did not come to worship will not worship with the type of help he has given. His words and gestures, where words and gestures are not necessary, may obscure the contemplation of God for many who do not find it easy to look beyond the minister who continually presents himself before them.

Rather to be preferred is the humility of another minister who would not permit himself to take the central chair behind his pulpit. During the early part of each service he would stand at one side of the pulpit, standing directly behind it only when he read from the Bible and preached. It is doubtful that his congregation understood fully what he was doing, but it was quite clear that he did not want himself to be considered the center of the service of worship.

The events that brought the pulpit into the center of the church have conspired to make the minister's position behind it difficult. The side pulpit of the divided chancel does much to correct the situation. From his side bench, the minister may be, during the early part of each service, a worshiper among worshipers. When his voice is heard—in prayer, in the reading of the Word, and in his sermon—it will come with more power when it has not been used for such trivial things as calling out hymn numbers. If a minister still must do his work from a central pulpit, let him treat it, and himself, in the same fashion.

The Minister's Wife

Some ministers are fortunate enough to marry wives who have had musical training. A musical wife is a great asset. She may add to her husband's musical knowledge and skill, teach him new hymns, help him toward musical discrimination. She may extend her usefulness into the life of the church by serving as pianist for the church school, the young people's group, or the women's organization when the need is there with no one else to fill it. She may become a regular member of the church choir and, by her voice as well as her spirit, act as an important lengthening of her husband's arm in the life of the church.

The point of this section is, however, that there are things she should *not* do. While she may safely be a regular member of the choir, she should not ordinarily accept assignment to any regular musical post in the church. It may well be that she plays the organ better than anyone else in the community. If she becomes organist in her husband's church, the development of others who might later play the organ tends to stop, and the field is left to her. Whether or not others in the church resent her position—and such resentment is not unusual—she should not permit herself to accept this or a like position for more than a short time. Otherwise she might be doing the church, and her husband, a real disservice.

VI

CHOIRMASTER AND ORGANIST

Minister of Music?

In recent years in this country there has appeared a movement to name the person who heads the music of a church the minister of music. In fact, at least one of our larger denominations has made this an official title. It has been felt that the competent musician who has taken specialized work to prepare for service within the church merits such a designation. By the same reasoning the status of all who serve under him would also be somehow dignified, not only in their own eyes but also in the regard of the congregation. The effort, then, has been to give to those in the choir loft a sense of mission they have too often lacked in the past.

It is true that the training of church musicians has advanced rapidly in recent years. So, to a degree, has the quality of church music. This does not, in the opinion of some of our church leaders, justify the use of the word "minister" in this connection. The minister of the church has been set aside and specially trained and ordained to conduct worship, to administer the sacraments, and to perform other priestly functions. The minister of music is not so equipped.

Certain of our music schools, however, are now providing a type of training which should meet the objection we have just stated. Not only are these musicians trained in the technique and art of producing beautiful church music, but they also are prepared to enter fully and satisfactorily into the life of the church; they are no strangers to the study of theology, church polity, and worship. The man or woman so trained may perhaps be properly set apart for his task in a service of dedication. The church should hesitate, however, to give the title of minister to a church musician unless he, by his training and personal commitment, shows himself worthy of it.

Organist-Choirmaster, or Organist and Choirmaster

Electro-pneumatic organ action made possible the detached console. The detached console is placed, or may be placed, where the organist is in position to conduct the choir. There are still some churches in which the organist cannot do so. There are also many churches, particularly in smaller communities, in which the organist is either unwilling or unable to conduct. But in the large proportion of our medium- to large-sized churches, the music committee has the privilege of deciding whether the organist and choirmaster be one or two persons.

From the ideal standpoint, there is no real argument on this question. If one person can perform two tasks better and more efficiently than can two, why should two people ever be hired? There are several reasons why the organist should take complete control of the choir. The first is efficiency. In rehearsal, loss of time cannot be avoided when a separate conductor must give instructions and signs separately to accompanist and to choir. One step in this double process is eliminated when the organist is both conductor and accompanist. The second reason is that the result of unified choir production will be more harmonious and musically adequate than would be possible with a separate conductor and organist. When the two are personally and musically congenial, there still remains the technical problem of blending, in amount and quality, the singing with the organ accompaniment. This is the responsibility of the conductor, who may not have sufficient knowledge of the organ to make his wishes known. There are, however, many cases where conductor and organist are not congenial. The organist tends to feel that he is musically more competent than this singer-conductor. The conductor, on the other hand, is within his rights in insisting on his own way of doing things. In the resulting clash, both choir and church suffer.

A third and obvious objection to the separate conductor may

be registered whenever he performs his task in view of the congregation. The waving arms, with or without baton, may be appropriate for the concert hall or the park bandstand but are disturbing and out of place in the sanctuary. It is usually possible to hide the organist by lowering or otherwise screening the console, and this should always be done. If a conductor is as well screened, there would be no objection to his appearance in church.

It is not sufficient that we agree on the ideal. The practical consideration of supply and demand enters the picture. The organist who can conduct the choir and accompany at the same time is not always easy to find. He must have sufficient command of his instrument to be able to give most of his attention to the choir while it is singing, and still furnish an adequate and musical accompaniment. If he lacks this command, either the choir's singing will suffer as he attends to his playing, or his playing will suffer as he devotes himself to the choir. For this reason many organists, capable of playing an artistic service, will quail at the suggestion that they also take charge of the choir. This partially explains why so many churches still have separate organist and conductor.

Our colleges and conservatories have not been sending out enough well-trained organists to meet the demand. At the same time, our schools are preparing a quantity of singer-conductors. Often a church which would like the one must settle for the other. The result, somewhat less than the best, may be as good as can be obtained from an inadequate supply of trained church musicians.

Member of the Church He Serves?

Increasingly churches are requiring that the choirmaster be a member of the church he serves. At first glance this seems to be a right decision. The church does well to protect itself from the secular-minded musician whose interest in the church may not go further than its ability to pay his salary. But those churches which have not already made this an official policy would do well to question its wisdom. Is not this stride too long? Would not a shorter step have reached a more desirable end?

There is no doubt that the chief musician of a church should be a Christian. He should be more than a nominal one. He should be a dedicated one, committed fully to the life and program of the church. The minister and music committee should give as much attention to a prospective choirmaster's spiritual and moral qualifications as they do to his musical ability.

The choirmaster should be a member of a church, but there is some doubt that he should be required to join the church he serves. His position is comparable to that of the minister. Whether the minister actually joins the church he serves, as is common in churches with a congregational form of government, or his membership is held in a conference or presbytery, he is not completely part of his church. He may be in it, and yet not completely of it. He must stand somewhat aside in judgment of his church, as indeed his church also judges him. In the same way a choirmaster should maintain a certain objectivity in relation to his task, an objectivity he would lose if he were too deeply immersed in that church's life.

Like the minister, the choirmaster should have the courage to separate himself from the church he serves whenever he feels that such action will benefit the church. This may be a simple, fairly painless operation if he is not a member. The separation should be equally easy to achieve if the church desires it. On the other hand, disengagement becomes more difficult if the choirmaster must leave his own church. Many examples can be found of a choirmaster or organist entrenched in his position because he is entrenched within the life of the church, to the degree that he cannot be dislodged without a major operation endangering the unity of the church; yet this person may have ceased to serve his church well for some time.

As Musician and Person

Much has been written concerning the musical qualifications of the church organist and choirmaster. This book will add little to that literature. Often this type of advice serves no purpose, as most churches can make little use of it. They have to accept their church musicians as they find them, so far as musical quali-

fications are concerned. Whether a church uses a different o
ganist than choirmaster, or the organist serves both purpose
from now on in this book they will be considered as one, and wi
be known as *choirmaster*. Although freely admitting that muc
more might well be said about his training, let us move on t
the other characteristics he should have as a person, or shoul
acquire, to make him valuable to his church.

An important tool for the choirmaster is *musical taste*. Mar
sensitive musicians avoid attending church because they canno
endure hearing so much bad music poorly performed. We mu
admit that their judgment is largely fair. Lack of musical sk
within our choir lofts is only half the explanation. More to l
deplored is the great quantity of unworthy music which is co
tinuously circulated and performed in our churches. Referen
has already been made to choir periodicals largely filled with tri
commonplace material, which is often the complete choral di
for those churches that lack resourceful choirmasters. Yet tl
"standard" publishers cannot be trusted. Most of them contin
to put out stacks of anthems in utterly bad taste. Too many u
wary choirmasters, attracted by "nice" words, and chorus pa
within easy reach of the choir concerned, continue to commit the
sins.

How may a musician of limited training acquire good music
taste? How may he learn to select good materials? The first
quirement is that he have ample basis for comparison. Unless
has at hand plenty of material, and spends time examining it,
cannot even start in the right direction. He should get new issu
from a number of publishers. He should examine the music
braries of churches that have well-developed musical progran
He should seek the help of the headquarters of his denominatic
(See "The Choir Library" in Chapter IV.) Although he shou
examine with respect the choices of leading choirmasters,
should look with suspicion on lists of "favorite anthems" or "b
sellers" submitted by publishers. Many of these will contain t
worst characteristics of so-called church music. If he makes
occasional visit to a church music conference, clinic, or scho

a project which his church should be willing to subsidize, he should be on his way toward musical growth.

To musical taste needs to be added a high degree of *idealism*. No one can visit many churches without finding in a number of them choirs and organists who seem to feel that what they are offering is good enough for the time and place. If the minister and congregation seem satisfied with the music they are getting, why should the church musicians try to improve their part of the worship, when what they do may not be appreciated anyhow? After all, the music in this church is as good now as it has been for years, and is even better than that in some other churches we could mention. Such an attitude as this is understandable in the church musician whose object is to please his music committee and his congregation. But if he remembers that he really serves not these, nor even the minister, but the Lord Himself, and if he repeatedly reminds his choir of this, then no effort is too great, no result too perfect for which to strive. Let that choirmaster be happy if he is called a perfectionist.

If the choirmaster truly serves the Lord, he needs also *integrity* to resist those who would lower his standards. No minister worthy of his calling will let his congregation or any part of it dictate his preaching. Likewise the choirmaster will think of the musical needs of his church before he considers its likes. He will be wise, of course, not to lead either choir or congregation so far beyond their understanding and appreciation that he loses contact with them. On the other hand, he must never permit the tastes of congregation and choir to stand still. The choir must frequently be challenged with materials just beyond present grasp. If he quietly ignores congregational objection to new hymns, which he will add and repeat with discretion, the new will become the old, and the congregation will finally forget to object.

Last in this list of needed qualities is *humility*. Why is it that church musicians are so often short in this quality? Do we forget that our talents are a gift from God, who expects us to develop them for His glory and not for our own? Any choirmaster may see the evidences of pride among his choir members. But is he aware of his own self-importance? If he is not, no matter how completely he may possess the other attributes of success, he may fail. But if he works in humility for the glory of God and the good of the church he is serving, his choir will work in the same spirit. Such a spirit will go far toward producing genuine worship within that church.

In Rehearsal

Since this is not a book primarily for the training of choirmasters, time will not be taken here to discuss rehearsal techniques, on which excellent books have already been written. We shall state only some general principles of rehearsal management, with particular attention to the personal relationships between the choirmaster and the members of his team.

Few volunteer choirs are able to achieve more than one rehearsal between Sundays. During this one period, long or short, much work must be done, and an important task for the choir master is to divide rightly the available time among the materials to be prepared. Shall we take time every week to practice all the hymns and responses to be used, or shall we briefly "spot" the places of need and then get on quickly to weightier matters? Shall we insist on a long, deliberate rehearsal, or shall we attempt to save everyone's time by a shorter, "snappier" period?

Many excellent choirmasters insist on a rehearsal period of at least two hours. Since it is impossible either to command full attention, or to work amateur voices strenuously, for so long a period, the pace of such a rehearsal must be a bit leisurely, and provision be made for a short break midway. The slow pace makes an opportunity for social exchanges, which in turn should improve the choir's *esprit de corps*. Other good choirmasters feel that a hour and a half should be the rehearsal maximum, and that occasionally the choir should be surprised by being permitted to leave even earlier than this. The emphasis of the shorter rehearsal is on unremitting activity and concentrated work. The choir's social life must flower at some other place and time.

The vote of this writer goes to the shorter rehearsal. The busy adult who gives to his church choir the effort he could have used otherwise will appreciate the choirmaster who does not propose to waste anyone's time. The teen-ager, who should be well represented in every adult choir, will always prefer the shorter sitting period. Nearly everyone will be glad that he does not have to "kill" a whole evening for choir practice. Of course, every rehearsal which closes promptly must also begin promptly.

A shorter rehearsal should not mean a less thorough one. The temptation to neglect the hymns and previously rehearsed responses should be resisted. There is a tendency for choir members to become careless with familiar routines. The choirmaster should secure as careful performance of hymns as of any other part of the service. If processional and recessional are done, they should be frequently checked to see that there has been no deterioration in either sight or sound. When the need to rehearse a response has ceased, the response should be changed. It would have worn out its usefulness. Of course, anthems must be adequately rehearsed, but without leaving other materials unrehearsed.

That every item of the rehearsal be planned in advance is essential. There must be no wasted time. In this connection should be mentioned one of the most flagrant time-wasters: the talkative choirmaster. This sequence happens too often: A musical passage is called for; the pitch is given; the conductor raises his arms, preparatory to the attack. At that precise moment he recalls a delightful anecdote concerning the composer of the work sung, the period from which it comes, or some other place this work has been performed. He drops his arms, the choir members exhale the preparatory breath, and "let down" for two minutes or more of wasted time. It makes little difference whether or not the anecdote is significant or interesting. The point is that the people before him are there to sing, not to listen, and are annoyed that they cannot realize their purpose.

Somewhat less culpable is the conductor who feels that the best road to musical interpretation is a thorough discussion by him of the passage to be sung, with attention called to each expression mark. Again, the choir, ready and eager to sing, is not prepared for a dissertation, and will not hear anything that is said beyond the second sentence. The wise conductor will keep a tight rein

on his own tongue. He may ask that expression marks be followed, and even call attention to one that is being neglected.
Always he will keep his instructions to minimum length, and
depend upon his gestures and facial expression to do the rest.
At the end of the rehearsal, the choir that has worked at top
speed may be tired, but it will have a warm sense of achievement.
It will not be the exhaustion of sheer boredom.

Another wasteful process within the choir is that of moving
toward a result after general discussion. A choir cannot operate
successfully by the democratic process. The members should not
decide what they are to do and when they are to do it. The
choirmaster must be the unchallenged dictator. If his musicianship
is superior to that of any of his members he has the advantage.
If he is not musically more adept than anyone else present, his
right to command must be accepted as a necessary rule of procedure. It is not hard to explain this if it is remembered that
many small decisions must be made during any rehearsal and these
cannot possibly be debated one by one if any work is to be
accomplished.

Since the choirmaster is the "boss," he has an obligation to
make his control fair, and as pleasant as possible. The application
of one rule will go a long way toward bringing this about: the
choirmaster should keep all criticisms of the choir general, and
not personal. If one bass is singing below pitch, *the basses* are told
that they are singing flat. The men who are not offenders will
know to whom the criticism is addressed, yet the person who is
in error has not been singled out. The repetition of the passage
will give the stronger the opportunity of helping the weaker, and
no one's feelings will have been hurt. This does not mean that
the choirmaster will always be pleasant. There is a rare time for
sharp rebuke, but without rancor and sarcasm. And any such
corrective period should be followed speedily by the restoration of
normal friendliness.

As in any other human relationship, injured feelings and
jealousies will occasionally appear within the choir. These become
the ultimate tests of the choirmaster's influence upon the individuals in the group. The frank person-to-person conference is

ere the best tool—usually the only effective tool. When there is doubt in the choirmaster's mind that he can resolve the difficulty, he should not hesitate to seek the minister's help. However, the choirmaster's friendship with his members should be so strong that seldom should there be any cause for taking difficulties outside the choir family.

The Organist of the Future, or, Is the Organ Locked?

With the idea of looking inside the organ console, let a person approach it in almost any church when there is no one around. The probabilities are high that he will find it locked—perhaps doubly locked. (I know of one organ that is almost as hard to get into as a bank vault after closing hours.)

If this person should then go to the minister and ask permission to play on the organ, there is a good chance that the minister's answer will be in this wise: "Personally, I would be happy to let you play, but the official Board (or Session, or Deacons, or Trustees) has passed a rule that nobody but our organist may play on it. You know we have a great deal of money invested in this instrument. And it is delicate, easily damaged, and expensive to repair. So we have to protect it if we want it to last. I hope you understand." If the person does not understand, and pursues the matter further, he will probably find that sometime earlier the church organist prevailed upon the board of control to pass this regulation.

Unfortunately, part of what the minister said is clearly not true, and the regulation is all wrong! The organ may be expensive; if it is of any size, it is expensive. But it is not delicate. It would be more accurate to say that it is sturdy and not easily damaged. Of course, if the motor bearings are not adequately oiled, it would not be a good idea to forget to turn the power off at the end of practice. Otherwise the organ *needs* to be practiced on. If it is not played sufficiently, its electric contacts tend to corrode, and its "mechanicals" to "freeze" from inactivity. An organ thrives on practice!

Then why have this senseless regulation against practice? Only because some organists, like other human beings, tend to be selfish, jealous, fearful, suspicious. They like their jobs at the console on Sundays. They may complain about what they have to do, but they would not give up their positions under any circumstances. (I once knew an old lady who had played the same organ for many years. Her fondest wish was that, when she should finally die, she might die on the organ bench!) But if no one except the organist practices on the organ, no one else can learn to play it, and he need have little fear for his position.

Unfortunately there are not enough good organists to begin to meet our needs in this country. Any church that locks its organ against its own young people is not only mortgaging its own musical future, it is hurting the whole Church. For organists, to be really useful, must start to learn while they are young. This organist himself will always be grateful to that organist he knew many years ago who, with no other motive than her own kindness and generosity, took him beside her on the organ bench when he was still quite young, and told him some of the things she had learned about organ playing, some things he has never forgotten.

Therefore, if your church has on its records a regulation restricting the use of the organ, let it be brought out and rescinded. In its place let a policy be put in motion to encourage the young people of musical ability within the church to learn to play the organ. If the regular organist is unable or unwilling to help train these, let them, with the blessing of the church, seek their help outside. If this young girl or boy who has been playing faithfully for a department in the church school is unable to pay for further study, the church would do well to subsidize such study. A church can meet the future best if it plans for it.

VII

THE MULTIPLE CHOIR SYSTEM

During recent years the Church in America has developed an increasing interest in the use of younger choirs. Historically this probably has been little influenced by the use of boy choirs in the Episcopal Church. It has come rather from our increased emphasis on the educational process within the Church. We recognize music as one of the tools by which spiritual growth may be fostered in our youth. With this recognition has come the training of more people who are qualified to take charge of the complete music program within the local church.

This use of more than one choir in the activities of the church may be known loosely as the multiple choir system. It is important to note at once that the system requires careful tailoring to fit each church. The program for a "stable" church with a large proportion of older members and comparatively few children in attendance will be quite different from that of a young congregation with many children in an expanding suburban situation. The downtown church with widely scattered membership would find it difficult to maintain a program that could be well managed by a closely knit community church.

Here is a general yardstick suggested by Dr. Whittlesey to measure the possible program: "The size of the church and church school must be considered. Eight to ten per cent of the combined membership are potential participants in the choir system."[1] There will be, then, smaller congregations that cannot easily grow beyond one choir. Others slightly larger may maintain two: an adult and a junior choir. Large churches may have five or more.

The optimum number will depend not only on the resources available, but also on the results expected in a given church.

What are the fruits of multiple choirs? So far as youth is concerned, "through choirs we can help children and young people to find their places in the life and work of the church," says Dr. Whittlesey. "Churches are in the long run built from the children up. The church school is chiefly for them, but the worship service, which is the central act of the life of the church, often makes little provision for children. One excellent way to help youngsters feel that the worship service is for them as well as for adults is to have children's choirs take a regular and active part in the worship. . . . *Frequent appearance of the children's choir fosters a church-attending habit.*"[2]

Dr. Whittlesey follows his argument to its logical conclusion: "One test of a children's and youth choir program is how many join the church as a result of it—not children alone, but parents too. The children will be reached largely through the church school; the parents, largely through the children. . . . (A note to the finance committee: many churches feel that a well-organized graded choir system pays its way by the contributing members it brings into the church.)"[3]

We would not be entirely fair to Dr. Whittlesey if we did not at least list other fruits of the multiple choir system mentioned by him: the teaching of reverence and worship, the teaching of fundamentals of music, correct singing habits, and the great hymn literature of the church, the development of singers for future adult choirs, and the provision of a large body of singers for festival occasions. These points are sufficiently obvious not to need expansion here. There are, however, dangers inherent in the use of multiple choirs *primarily* for the increasing of attendance, church membership, and financial returns, which should be discussed more fully.

What, for instance, may be the effect of the use of younger choirs on worship itself? Let us quote Dr. Whittlesey again:

> The accusation is sometimes made that children's choirs detract from the worship service because of poor singing and unbecoming deportment. This need not be true. A choir of children

can be taught to sing beautifully, to conduct itself with decorum, and to add worship values to the service. Whether this is done or not seems to be wholly up to the director. However, if the children receive something of definite spiritual value from participation, that is of more importance than that the adults be pleased.[4]

Dr. Whittlesey would probably be the first to say that this quoted statement oversimplifies a problem. Certainly not every church may have beautiful singing from its younger choirs. In parts of the country where the public school music program is lagging, children may be so backward in their approach to music that good results may not come in the time available for training. Particularly is this true where the juniors in a small church are so few that their singing is timid and self-conscious. Moreover, we must not forget that host of smaller churches that do not have, nor can they find, competent leaders for their younger choirs; from poor leadership come poor results, and it can scarcely be otherwise. But may we justify these efforts by saying simply that the spiritual value of participation is of more importance than "that the adults be pleased"? We cannot be sure. The answer depends upon the weighing of those spiritual values of participation that may be gained against other values that may be lost.

What spiritual value may be gained by members of a junior choir who are pressed to sing partially prepared numbers too often, and who realize how badly they sing them? The repeated experience may be harrowing alike to the children, to their parents, and to the remainder of the congregation. Could we not agree that such a choir, which had been expected to sing one Sunday each month, might not better sing once every two months or every quarter, when it might be better prepared? Let us agree that no matter how badly a junior choir may sing, it should be given an occasional opportunity to sing for the worship service. But how often this choir should sing should be determined not by how well it pleases the adults, nor on how it influences church attendance, but on the total result of its singing on the life of the church, not forgetting the lives of its own members.

The very success of the multiple choir system may bring problems to a church. Here, for instance, is a church with five choirs, each with its distinctive robe, and a sense of its own importance. Each is heard regularly and often in the morning service. The magnitude of the musical program of the church, and the number of people involved in it, tend to exaggerate its importance. Even when the singing is not of high order, the congregation may admire the discipline of a choir, its beautiful robes, enjoy the "fresh young faces" of the juniors, the "cuteness" of the smaller children. Perhaps the musical emphasis will attract larger congregations, particularly the parents of the performing children. (The use of the word "performing" is intentional.) But it should not be forgotten that to the degree that the *children themselves* are the attraction, to that degree true worship is not served.

However, this is not the whole story, for the greatest harm that may come from the high development of multiple choirs is that done to the young singers themselves. If a church has a full program of Christian education, and that program is interrupted, as it must be, every Sunday a group of children sing in the worship service, that program and the children in it will suffer. For on this day there must be the special rehearsal, the robing, the special instructions, the "lining up." The brief time, if any, allowed for the educational program will serve little purpose, since the children clearly will have something else on their minds besides the lesson.

Less tangibly, it is quite possible for a type of musical exhibitionism to develop among children of the church that has overemphasized its choral program. In this situation, music, which should be a means, might become more important in the thinking of the church, and particularly of the children themselves, than the end, which is worship.

In spite of all that has just been said, we may be sure that the multiple choir system is one of the significant movements of the day in the advancement of the church. It has already contributed much to effective worship, and its promise for the future is boundless. Yet safeguards are needed, in order that the program may best serve the purpose for which it was designed.

The first of these safeguards is organizational. All of the choirs except the adult choir should be made firmly a part of the church educational program. The way—the only way—into any of these choirs should be through the church school. The purpose of such a restriction should not be to exclude members; rather, the activities of all of these choirs should be so closely tied to those of the church school that they would have little significance aside from it. A child who is interested in joining the junior choir would be encouraged to do so, but he would be asked to join the junior department of the church school at the same time, since the junior choir will be drawn from this department. The choirmaster will look first and always to the church school staff for help in organizing a new choir, or in enlarging an old one.

The goals and activities of these choirs should also be determined by the needs of the church school. The choirmaster and his helpers need constantly to inform themselves in regard to what musical materials are called for within the various departments. These will, of course, vary greatly. But first of all, the musical leadership will work within these departments, not outside them. This means, in the final analysis, that educational needs will take precedence over those of the worship service for the attention of the younger choir. For instance, the choirmaster in his planning would give priority to the church school Christmas celebration over that of the church worship service.

Another safeguard needed is a well-defined philosophy of the relationship of music to the whole program of the church. This is largely the minister's responsibility. Music is the servant of the church, and its service should be well understood. We recognize the hymn as one of the great forces in Christian education. We also believe that church music is one of the few ways all men together may express their acknowledgment of God's Kingship. Each church, then, should direct its musical activities toward these ends. Music should never be permitted to glorify man rather than God within the church. Particularly as applied to our younger choirs, music must never be allowed to become an end in itself, but rather a means of praising and glorifying God.

The Junior Choir

The beginning of a multiple choir program is the formation of a junior choir. The proper ages included in this group should be eight through eleven, and its size as nearly unlimited as possible. The capacity of the choir loft needs to be considered when appearance at worship services is involved. But that capacity should not limit the number of children who receive the training. In the rather small church, it may seem wise to extend the age limit in both directions, depending upon the type of community and the degree to which children of various ages are mingled in the public schools. On the other hand, the choirmaster may wish to keep children out of the junior choir until the ninth birthday, in the interests of faster learning; this is a procedure that should be admitted only with reluctance. But no general statements here may be applied universally.

Whittlesey's plan for the junior choir merits careful study, although it need not be accepted fully. He stresses, for instance, the need for individual tryouts before admission. These tryouts acquaint him with individual vocal problems and also single out the "monotones." He points out that some children need only a little coaching and encouragement to start them singing. But if a little training does not teach the boy to modulate his voice (a girl monotone is rare indeed) he may never learn to sing successfully. It is clear that if the choir's singing is to become really beautiful, the non-singers must not participate. But to refuse admission to children may do them serious and lasting injury. This presents a dilemma not easy to face.

In a small church, where perhaps only one or two "monotones" are involved, the choirmaster should be very hesitant about refusing admission to so few. But where a larger number of children are involved, a speech choir may be formed. Such a choir, not requiring singing skill, may serve well both the educational and worship programs of the church. The effective reading of passages of Scripture or religious poetry by a group of children, trained to speak in pefect unity, may be a moving experience to readers and listeners alike. A teacher with patience and imagination may cultivate from a group of children beautiful results that would give satisfaction to the children themselves, to their parents, and to the church. The children would be entirely free of the feeling that they had been rejected because they are unable to do what most children do. Besides the benefit of learning great Scripture passages and poetry, the development of speech skill is itself important. These two things together may bring lasting improvement to the personalities of these children.

Whittlesey also speaks of the desirability of having a waiting list. There is little doubt that the waiting list stimulates regularity in attendance. It is to be regretted that the waiting list also keeps children from the choir—children who should have its training. But the size of the choir loft or the rehearsal room may impose a definite limitation. Here again the speech choir may meet a need. Let the church school divide its junior department between the singing and speech choirs, keeping the two on an equal footing and moving the children from the one to the other as need arises to strengthen the one or the other.

This is not the place to discuss the complex problems of organization, rehearsal techniques, length and frequency, keeping of records, and repertoire, which go with running a junior choir. Let the reader who seeks more information consult the experts mentioned. It only remains here to discuss the actual use of the junior choir in the worship service.

It is usually agreed that juniors should not sing often in church. Perhaps the "fifth" Sundays in addition to Christmas and Easter would be sufficient. More frequent use would shorten the choir's preparation period, as well as interfere with the educational program of the church.

There is a tendency today to suggest that the junior choir, when it appears in church, should sing early in the service and then leave to attend junior church. But what are you going to do with the great number of small churches that have neither the facilities nor the personnel for a junior church? Obviously, the junior choir in this situation has no place to go, and it is not perfectly clear that they should go even if a junior church service were provided.

If the junior choir is merely an "added feature" that brings an extra musical number into morning worship several times a year, it is not worth the effort that goes into it, even if it brings some extra parents to church! It can be justified only in terms of what it does, in Christian training and experience, to the children themselves. It should be for each junior choir member a source of valuable training and experience in the practice of worship. This can only happen if the junior choir is the choir of the day. Let the adult choir be given the day off, and let the juniors assume responsibility for *all* that the adult choir has been accustomed to do. This is the way the juniors like it, and this is the only way the experience may mean the most to them.

"What," says the hypothetical critic, "are you going to do with the people in the congregation who just do not like the junior choir?" Let us agree that they should be considered. First, the junior choir should appear rarely, perhaps not over two or three times a year. It should prepare with the greatest of care the anthem and responses it will offer. Its members will be made to feel the responsibility of their task. Then on a certain Sunday the junior choir will appear—I say this without shame—without previous announcement made to the general membership. If the church is not willing to go this far with its junior choir, then the choir should be banished permanently to the junior church.

The repertoire of the junior choir should be primarily good hymns, to which should be added a few simple anthems and responses, mostly in unison. Although some two-part singing could be tried, it would not be rewarding in every case. Good unison singing is to be preferred to indifferent part singing from this group.

The Beginners' Choir

Where there are a sufficient number of children six through eight years of age in the church school, a beginners' choir may be formed. Such a choir presents serious transportation difficulties in a downtown church, and probably should not be attempted there. It is best tried in a parish where most of the children live close to the church.

That children of this age should be placed in an organization sufficiently formal to be called a choir may well be questioned. Its purposes are primarily educational; training in group discipline, rudimentary use of the singing voice, and a small start on hymn literature are all that should be expected of it. Its membership should be, therefore, as all-inclusive as possible. No attempt should be made to separate the singer from the non-singer, since it is too early to make firm choices. Children who begin apparently as "monotones" may suddenly acquire what they seemed to lack. Certainly no child at this age should be labelled a non-singer.

Since the purpose of this choir is primarily to provide beginning training, little thought should be given to public performance. If it disrupts its own departmental activities very little, an occasional appearance before another church school department may be arranged. No appearance in the worship service of the church needs to be intended or planned.

The Junior High Choir

The Junior High choir, while it is probably the most difficult of all to manage, may be the most important in the lives of its members. Its ages should be twelve through fourteen years. Since it is a period of difficult relations between the sexes, it is rather a good idea for boys and girls to practice separately, even though they may sing together in performance.

The Junior High choir poses the biggest challenge the choirmaster may have to face. If, through the choir, he can hold the loyalty of its boys and girls to the church, there is a good chance that they will always remain there. On the other hand, those who are lost to his choir may also be lost to the church. The boys are the more difficult half of the problem. They feel that they are growing up, and want to feel that their voices are becoming deeper. They convince themselves quite easily that they can no longer sing with the girls. The choirmaster should not be too severely censured if, after he has tried his best to use them, he lets the boys go and works on the more submissive girls. However, if he is able to keep the boys around during this period, he should win the deep gratitude of his church.

This choir should do two-part, rarely three-part, singing. The older children, or those with more musical background, should take the lower part or parts. The choirmaster is obligated to hear the individual voices rather often, to see that they are being properly used. Boys' voices will usually begin, and some of them will complete, their change of register before they would normally leave this age group. They may be used as alto-tenors for a period, but may have to be moved on to the next choir. The choirmaster should be constantly aware of the condition of each boy's voice, to know whether or not he should be advanced.

No general statement may be safely made in regard to the nature and frequency of this choir's public appearances. It probably should occasionally replace the adult choir for the morning service. The choirmaster should also give consideration to the increasing literature of anthems which combine adult and youth choirs, particularly at festival times.

The Senior High Choir

The Senior High choir is the last which should be added to the multiple choir system. Practically speaking, it is an adult choir. If it is at all possible, Senior High singers should belong to the adult choir.

There still seems to be the feeling in some churches that the adult choir should be the exclusive domain of the adult, with the accent on middle age and older. One does not choose to join this type of choir; he gains election to it as to a secret society. If the choirmaster should have the audacity to invite several high school students into this group, they probably would not remain long, since they would not feel themselves welcome. It should be fairly evident that such a choir shows a lack of truly Christian attitude, and cannot make very beautiful music either.

We are not concerned here with this attitude, but rather with the musical results of it. Here is a church which has, in effect, excluded its high school students from the adult choir by organizing a separate choir for them. Its members are not eligible for the adult choir until they have finished high school. But at the precise time when they are permitted to enter the adult choir, many of these high school graduates leave the church and the city to attend college or to seek employment. When they return to their own church, there will be no choir home to which they belong, since they have outgrown the choir in which they last sang. They have not, on the other hand, established membership in, or loyalty to, any other choir. It may not be easy for these potential members to take the step which will place them where they belong in the adult choir of this or any other church.

Let us look next at the church which takes its Senior High young people into the adult choir, and makes them welcome there. Obviously many of these will make little musical contribution, at least for a time. The boys' voices may be changing. Some of them can sing only the higher notes of the tenor part. Timidity will keep the girls' voices from counting at first. But neither boys nor girls will harm the choir in any way. They are far less a hindrance to the choir than the flat-singing older soprano, or the ancient bass whose voice "sticks out." In the meantime they are learning musically and spiritually, and acquiring those habits of service which may stay with them for life. Their skill improves. They do not now experience the gradual deterioration that comes with later years. When they do leave for college, they have a place in the choir to which they are welcome on Sundays home and particularly during vacation. When they later come back to the home church or go to a new home, it will be natural for them to continue membership where they have belonged for years—in the adult choir.

There are large churches with adult choirs of maximum size which cannot admit high school students because there is no room for them. The Senior High choir is needed here. Although some of these may have to start with three-part music (SAB) with all the boys singing on one part, the Senior High choir should be able to sing the same music as the adult choir. In some city churches, the skill of the younger singers may rival that of the adults, and the church may give the Senior High choir some important assignments, even in other churches. Such a choir merits the support of its church, since it holds the loyalty of its members as effectively as can any other organization within the church.

There is no good reason why a church that has both adult and

Senior High choirs should keep the two mutually exclusive. The wise choirmaster will permit members of the Senior High group to sing in the adult choir also during the final year or half-year they are in the younger group. In this way these singers will help maintain the strength of the younger choir while they also develop a loyalty to the older.

Names?

Kettring suggests the use of imagination in selecting names for the various younger choirs.[5] Certainly the use of departmental names is not particularly stimulating. The calling of one group of children "cherubs" and another one "angels" is not to be recommended if for no other reason than that such names are highly unrealistic, at least as applied to growing children! But our several denominations have words around which precious associations have been formed: Luther, Augsburg, Wesley, Epworth, Calvin, Knox, Westminster, Pilgrim. To give a choir one of these names, hallowed in the life of the Church, is to give it a dignity it would not have attained with a departmental name.

VIII

THE ADULT CHOIR

This is the day of the "mixed" choir. Increasingly this main choir of the church tends to be "volunteer," although in the cities any number from a core of soloists to the entire choir may be paid. Single soloists and quartets may still be found alone in choir lofts, but they are becoming rarer. Is the movement toward the mixed choir just a vogue, or does this choir offer resources for worship which cannot be matched by other and smaller groups? Is the volunteer choir more trouble than it is worth? These and related questions should be asked periodically by every church that maintains a program of music. Whatever that program is, it should be able to justify itself in the clear light of repeated examination.

Just what is the advantage of the mixed choir over other types of organization? What advantages, if any, does the volunteer choir have over one that is partially or entirely paid for its services? The answers to these questions furnish the criteria by which any church may judge its own program. They can best be arrived at by a brief examination of the different types of personnel in the choir loft.

The Single Soloist

The single soloist has been the easy, trouble-free device of the church that has not seen the need to do anything better. It has been pleasant for the indolent organist, who has little rehearsing to do. It has simplified the task of the music committee, which has only to enter into contract relationships with two people perhaps once a year. Since most of the music budget has gone into one basket, the best soloist available may be chosen. But the church cannot escape the poverty of this program. Solo literature appropriate for worship is limited. A broad choice of music will be partly unworthy, while the narrower choice will be oft repeated. That the soloist should project his songs by full use of his personality is taken for granted. This is wholly inappropriate to the worship situation. There is little to justify the use of the single soloist in the choir loft.

The Boy Choir

The boy choir, adopted from liturgical churches, has had little success when transplanted. It is musically inefficient, since boys are the hardest to teach and results come slowly. It is spiritually inadequate, since immature boys cannot transmit what they do not feel. It is ineffective musically, since the proper tone for the boy voice is light in texture and size, and does not lend itself well to contrast in quality and amount of tone.

The Male Quartet or Choir

The male quartet or choir has had little better success in church. The male quartet is at its best in "barber shop" music with which it is associated, and is at the same time too sentimental for worship as we conceive of it. The male choir is quite different. From it may come reverently beautiful music. Yet it is music limited in variety and breadth. If a church can assemble a fine male choir, how much more beautiful a mixed choir could the same church develop! Another limitation of the male choir is its literature. So little good music has been written for it, the choirmaster frequently must use ill-adapted arrangements, or write his own music for his own choir.

The Mixed Quartet

The mixed quartet, once described by Dr. Peter Lutkin as a baneful medium for the glorification of four people, was for many years acceptable in many churches, and still clings stubbornly to its place in the choir lofts of some of them. A choir in miniature, its literature is choir literature, or that portion of it that does not require the singing of more than four parts at a time. It was a creation of convenience. Organists liked it because little rehearsal was required to get the job done. Churches liked it because it made little trouble. Its members could be hired, and fired if need be, with little personal involvement. Since they were hired to do no more than to sing, little thought or interest was given to the personal lives of its members.

In some city churches, particularly those that were able to hire big names with big voices, normal limitations on four voices were largely ignored. If an oratorio chorus was written in four parts, it could be sung by the quartet. It has not been unusual, for instance, for a church quartet to sing the entire Christmas portion of the *Messiah*, and many people thought it was wonderful.

But since it is just a miniature choir, it is no more effective doing full choruses than a string quartet is in doing symphonies, or a monologuist performing a Shakespeare tragedy. Its further weakness is that when four voices are put together they tend to remain four voices, with their individual characteristics remaining.

The Mixed Choir with "Solo" Quartet

The mixed choir with "solo" quartet has been an important step forward in church music. In many cases this has been just an expansion of the mixed quartet. When other voices were added to the quartet for Christmas music, perhaps the church liked the result so much that its continuation was sought. But the church acted without much faith, since the old quartet was kept around, just in case!

There are three clear advantages of building a full choir around a solo quartet. First, the church will always have on hand competent soloists, which it doubts it could find otherwise within its own congregation. Second, the four mercenaries are good insurance against that bad time that can happen to any choir. If, on a too unpleasant or too pleasant a day all the other tenors fail to show up, the hired tenor will be there to save the choirmaster, who might otherwise be forced to abandon the anthem on this particular Sunday. It is also obvious that the four trained singers are able to carry the more timid voices during rehearsals, leading each section and shortening the learning time for new materials.

Yet the three advantages just named are also the fatal weaknesses of this type of organization. First, a church that goes outside its membership to get soloists will not develop its own talent. In fact, it may not know what fine voices it already has. Second, in the presence of a quartet which is expected to be on duty, choir members may find it easy to be absent. There is always the temptation to leave the job to the person who is being paid to do it. Finally, there is an almost irresistible tendency among inexperienced singers to rest on the leadership of the soloist. The vocal "leaner" will learn little and contribute little in this situation. And such a choir in performance is likely to exhibit its practice weakness: the quartet leads and the rest follow.

It would not be fair, however, to leave our discussion of the quartet-choir without indicating that the weaknesses referred to can be, and often are, completely overcome. The hiring of a quartet is not in itself an error. Errors will result if the choirmaster does not carefully control the conditions under which choir and quartet work together. A prejudice has grown up in some quarters against the paid singer. Such a prejudice is justified if the paid singer is that and no more. That singer must not only enjoy singing; he should enjoy singing to the glory of God. If he is not a religious person, he should not be singing in church, no matter how beautiful his voice. But if the quartet members are humble, devoted, generous, and co-operative people, the choirmaster's problem should be small.

There are other conditions desirable to ensure the success of the choir with a solo quartet: First, the choirmaster should seek and develop all the singing talent he can find in his church. Whatever solos there may be in anthems, they should not automatically be given to members of the quartet, but should be spread as far as they can be done effectively among other members of the choir. Next, the choirmaster and minister should do everything possible to stress the attendance and activity of volunteer members in the choir. Each singer should be made to feel that the choir's success comes little from the four quartet members, and mostly from the combined efforts of all the members. Finally, the choir master should not permit his soloists to carry the burden of the rehearsals. They should privately be invited to sing very lightly on all sight-singing and note-learning projects, in order that all members be led toward musical self-reliance.

The Fully Paid Choir

The fully paid choir is a device that has brought many churches beautiful music they could not have achieved any other way. Reference has already been made to the prejudice against paid singers. Some of this prejudice has been merited. One has only to listen to the perfunctory performance of sacred music in some great metropolitan churches with tremendous music budgets to realize that genuinely religious music is not a commodity that can be bought. It has to be won by devotion and effort. Yet more than one writer has pointed out that there is no less reason to pay the choir than to pay the clergy. There are some who feel that all choir members should be paid something.

It is obvious that this suggestion could not be applied universally. However, there are certain situations in which the fully paid choir seems quite appropriate. There is, for instance, the city church whose membership is so scattered that a choir of members could be brought together only with great difficulty. There is the church in a college town that needs to make use of non-resident student singers. In both these situations a reasonable music budget may obtain an effective choir.

Here is a typical plan for such a choir. Let the base pay for each member be modest, from $3 to $5 a week. (This may not be sufficient for some parts of the country, or with an inflationary state of economy.) Since the pay is for work done on Sunday, none is offered for a given week unless the singer has attended both the stated rehearsal and the Sunday service. There should be a modest bonus added for each month of perfect activity, a bonus that increases with cumulative perfect records. Balancing this should be a system of fines for tardiness or other failure to fulfill all reasonable requirements. The system should be so devised that fines and bonuses are approximately equal, in order that budgeting may not be too difficult. It takes not too much figuring to realize that a church may maintain a choir for as little as $3,000 to $4,000 a year.

Mention should be made of the plan frequently used of giving each member of the choir voice lessons in return for service. The choirmaster provides the lessons, to which some pay for the singer may be added. In general, it may be said that this plan is somewhat limited in its application. Not all choir members are interested in voice lessons, nor would they necessarily benefit from them. It must also be admitted that there are plenty of choirmasters who are not competent voice teachers.

It is sometimes difficult to make a fully paid choir a body deeply concerned with leading worship. Its members, some of whom do not belong to the church, will tend to think of their jobs in terms of so much music to be performed. This aloofness from the spiritual life of the church is the weakness so often found in the paid choir. This does not have to be the case, but it takes the best efforts of the choirmaster to keep it from being so. Somehow each singer must be led to involve more than his voice in the church. Nothing less than the sincere devotion of the choirmaster to the spiritual aspects of the whole task will achieve this.

The "Volunteer" Choir

"Volunteer" choir is the recognized name given to that group of singers serving the church week after week with no more recompense than the personal satisfaction received by its members. The word "volunteer" as applied to "choir" has an unpleasant connotation, because so much bad music has come from volunteer choirs. Yet much that is beautiful has also come from them, and through them many of our Protestant leaders hope to raise the quality of worship in the church. Until a better word is found, "volunteer" is the word we must use to describe this type of organization.

It is easy to find fault with the volunteer choir. It is plagued by absenteeism; the best efforts of the choirmaster and singers may go for little on any Sunday when a number of chairs remain vacant. Vanity has often exposed its ugly side, while jealousies and quarrels have never been too far removed from the saints in some choir lofts. An unwillingness to recognize that vocal skill has departed has often characterized aging singers, whose continuance in the choir often does more harm than good; with this comes unfriendliness toward younger singers who would add their efforts to the organization. Above all, there is a great hesitancy on the part of choirmaster, minister, and music committee to come to grips with these problems where they exist, lest the evils thereby unleashed prove to be greater than the good which should be accomplished.

Yet the volunteer choir remains one of the great forces for good in the life of the church. For smaller churches, it may be the only type of organization possible. For an increasing number of larger churches, it is bringing values in Christian training and worship not achieved by other types.

What are these values? First, the choir provides an avenue of service for a substantial part of every congregation. Let us take the history of one rather small church. For years it had been served by a paid quartet, with which it considered itself reasonably well satisfied. Then one Sunday, stimulated by the visit of a college *a cappella* choir, many members came to feel what a few of them had known: their church had been missing something musically. After some self-examination, the church decided to make a change, and employed a new organist-choirmaster for the purpose. A survey of the membership revealed vocal resources that had been only dimly suspected. These were ample to start a volunteer choir. It would not be accurate to say that at once the church was supremely happy with its change. It took perhaps two years before the collection of voices began to sound like a choir. Then the dividends began to appear. Singers, some of them newcomers to the city, were attracted, first to the choir, then to church membership. A new organ was purchased. Young people growing up in the church found the choir a stimulating activity. Above all, the church began to know a depth of worship experience it had not known before.

What has happened to this church has happened to many others. The volunteer choir helps meet the need so often experienced within a congregation of finding constructive, absorbing tasks for its members. How often have members come into a church, only to become totally inactive in its life because they have never found a place in which they could serve! The choir may often provide this vital link that holds the loyalty of some who would otherwise drift from the congregation.

The choir also brings spiritual growth to its members. Unless they themselves worship, they cannot effectively lead in worship. As they give themselves fully to their task week by week, they are blessed in the giving. A minister backed by such a choir will feel its strength supporting his, and will lead and preach more effectively with that support.

What can be said of the music of the volunteer choir? One may fairly say only that it is improving. The quality of our public school music is advancing. There is more choral activity within our colleges and universities. More choirmasters and organists are being trained. More churches are setting up choral programs for the children. All of these things bring promise for the future. The change will not be spectacular, but slow and steady. In the meantime, the hope for the present is in making the best use of the choirs we have, in meeting wisely and firmly their problems, and in expecting great things from them.

Who Should Sing?

The first requisite of a healthy choir is a broad age span. If your choir is aged thirty years and up, it needs treatment. The best voices are the younger voices, and the organization's future can be assured only by constantly adding to them. Unless the choirmaster is overcome by a surplus of talent (there are few in that class), he should even add voices that are only potentially useful. If he keeps them out until they develop, he may lose them. This is particularly true of high school young people. The boy with the changing voice, for instance, who may be able to sing only the upper notes of the tenor part when he begins, may grow into a valued tenor or bass later if he stays in the choir during the settling period. If he is not invited into the choir until later, he may never come.

Should church membership be required? Certainly not! It would be hard to conceive of a volunteer choir in which a majority of its members were not concerned with the program of the church, and therefore members of it. But there is no good reason why such membership should be asked, although it may follow as the singers' interest draws closer to the church, as it should.

It should not be necessary to suggest that choir membership should be in no way dependent upon social acceptability. There is the story of the membership committee of a certain choir, which decided against inviting a certain interested woman into the choir because she was known to dye her hair! (It is needless to say that this happened some years ago.) The choir has no more right to be exclusive than does the church of which it is a part.

Tryouts?

Some years ago I listened to a distinguished choral conductor as he addressed an assemblage of choirmasters on the subject of tryouts for the choir. The proposition he confidently made was that each candidate should be tried out by the choirmaster before he should be admitted to the choir. If a voice not up to standard should be found, it should be rejected, and the choirmaster should find some tactful way to make the fact known to the possessor of that voice. It was quite evident, first, that this conductor had never dealt with a small volunteer choir in his life, and second, that he was accustomed to dealing with voices rather than with people.

Voices do not try out for a choir, but people do. When a person is told that his voice is not acceptable, the voice is not hurt but the person is. The extent of the hurt is not easy to determine, but it may be very great. It is highly doubtful that the choirmaster as a Christian should under any ordinary circumstances use this privilege.

What is the alternative? Is the choirmaster bound to accept whatever voice comes to him, no matter how bad it may be? The answer is not easy, because the choirmaster has a dual status. He is responsible to the church, and also to its members. His first task is to give the church the best music possible. His second, by which the first is achieved, is to train its members musically in any way he can. Is it his clear privilege to decide which of its members he chooses to work with?

If he decides that it is his privilege so to choose, can he be sure of his choices? He will not ordinarily have to deal with a real monotone, since this person will have discovered his condition earlier, and usually avoids the embarrassment of singing with others. Rather he will have to deal with borderline cases, with people who match tones imperfectly, or have difficulty staying on a part. He is wise indeed if he knows surely which of these will improve and which will not. There are too many cases like the budding tenor who cannot sing anything except the soprano an octave lower, but who by dint of sheer determination labors at the job until he becomes a good part singer. Then there is the soprano who definitely flats, but later becomes a good choir alto.

Suppose, then, that the choirmaster ordinarily accepts whoever is interested in coming into the choir, up to the capacity of the choir loft. He will try them out privately only if they so desire, in order to find their proper section. Otherwise he will let them start where they feel they belong. That he will admit some vocal problems is a certainty. Some of these will improve; some will not. As a rule, the latter will eliminate themselves in time. Rarely, an alto will come to him and say, "Mr. S., I just cannot seem to stay on my part. I believe I really do not belong in this choir." The choirmaster should not argue with her. More often, the singer will become too busy to continue with the choir, will develop a regular conflict on choir practice night, or will just drop out without notice. Again, the choirmaster will accept any offered excuse, or none at all, and will not pursue the person who has just disappeared from the choir. It is fair to assume that most people who find themselves in a situation in which they do not fit will in time remove themselves.

Yet choirmasters will find now and then a singer whose love for singing and whose loyalty to the choir will obscure his awareness of his own shortcomings. Although, in spite of all the help the choirmaster can give him, he does some musical damage to the choir, frequently his spirit makes an equivalent contribution. It would be my opinion—and we are now at the level where personal opinion must operate—that these rare persons should be retained in the choir for the pleasure and satisfaction they derive from it. In this I believe the choirmaster will also be serving his church well.

The New Singer

The choirmaster has worked hard to bring a certain new singer into the choir. The singer comes to one rehearsal, and does not return. The choirmaster wonders why. If he seeks out the person, he should not be surprised if the person delivers some plausible-sounding reason for not returning. It may be that he has discovered a meeting he had forgotten about that will keep him away from choir on that night. It may be that he has just decided that he is too busy to go on with choir at this time. Rarely the real reason comes out: the singer is bewildered by the amount of new music thrown at him; the others seem to get it but he doesn't; this choir is just too good for him, and there is no use in his trying further.

It is easy enough for the choirmaster to forget the difficulty the new singer faces. Unless the person is an accomplished musician (few choir singers are), he will feel himself beyond his depth at once. The chances are that the rehearsal will begin with responses and anthems the choir has partially or completely prepared earlier. What is old to everybody else is new to him. By the time the rehearsal reaches new material which he might try on an even footing with the rest, he is convinced that he just can't get this stuff and there isn't any use trying.

The choirmaster needs to prepare his new singer before he lets him sing a note with the choir. He should be told that most of the material will be more or less familiar to the old members, and that he should not be surprised if he does not get as much as the others seem to. He should just hit what he can, and not worry about what he misses. Better luck next week. The rest had to start

some time, and they did not get much right to start with, and n
one would expect any more of him. Such reassurance is importan
to the new singer, and may be what will keep him coming.

Retirement?

All singers grow old, and there comes a time when the
voices will not respond to their wishes as they used to do. Pe
haps, like their slowly declining physical vigor, the vocal deteriora
tion is so gradual they do not realize it. Yet some *do* realize it bu
choose to ignore the evidence, and do not even ask themselve
whether or not they should stop singing. With this flat refusa
to give up comes resentment against the young people in th
choir; their very presence seems a threat.

Although in many fields of employment there is automatic retir
ment at a fixed age, I have never heard of a choir with a simila
regulation, nor can one easily be applied where service is voluntary
Yet choirmasters would agree that there should be some painles
way to remove the singer who has reached the point at whic
his voice does more harm than good.

I recall reading some years ago of a plan devised by a hopefu
choirmaster of making a real occasion of choir retirement by givin
a party with speeches and gifts for the person about to be pu
on the choral shelf. But—to mix the metaphor—there is no wa
to make the bitter pill palatable to the taker. He is being di
missed from this organization to which he has devoted so muc
time and effort, while he is still willing and able, so he think
to continue to serve. The act is still too cruel to perform withi
the Christian Church.

Yet in the interests of musical and spiritual harmony a wa
needs to be found to make it easy for the over-age singer to see
retirement. The choirmaster's unspecific criticisms may occasional
help. If the section to which the singer belongs is having pe
sistent pitch trouble, for instance, and is having to do extr
practice to overcome it, the choirmaster may well suggest tha
each member listen carefully to himself to see if he is the offendi
member. After the rehearsal the older person may well go to th
choirmaster and ask, "Is it I?" The choirmaster has the oppo

tunity to suggest that his singer leave out some of the higher, more difficult notes. If the singer is a tenor, the choirmaster may ask if he would not like to try singing bass, where there would be less strain on the upper notes. Our singer will realize that these are not the type of suggestions that would normally be made to younger singers, and may see the light.

A continued flow of fresh young voices into the choir is always a tacit suggestion. The old singer cannot always escape the thought that he is less needed than heretofore. Finally the day may come when he feels called upon to say to the choirmaster, "Mr. S., you have a fine bunch of new singers in the choir now, and really don't need me as much as you used to. I think I have about served my term, and should take a rest from the choir." The choirmaster will make every effort not to look relieved, will compliment his singer on his long period of service, and will thank him for his generous attitude; he will *not*, however, argue with the singer over the decision he has reached.

Unfortunately, a little more must be said on this topic. Our choirmaster may have done everything he can to quiet and minimize the bad quality of this man's aging voice, and to overlook his crotchety behavior. He has made it as easy as possible for the singer to retire, but nothing has happened. The singer's voice continues to ruin the choir's best efforts, and his attitude makes choir harmony difficult. A change must be made, but how? Perhaps this is the sort of situation Christ contemplated when He suggested cutting off the offensive right hand. If cutting must be done, who is to do it? In my opinion, this is the responsibility of the choirmaster alone. He should discuss what he proposes to do with the minister, but he himself must do it.

Why should the choirmaster take this burden on himself? Precisely because his action can most readily confine the area of possible conflict. The fact that many jokes have been made about quarrels that explode out of church choirs does not obscure the fact that the danger of such quarrels within the church is no joke. There is no wrath like that of an aggrieved choir member. If his wrath, reinforced by that of his relatives and friends, is directed against the choirmaster alone, there is a good chance that the struggle may be localized. The only head that might roll would be that of the choirmaster. But should minister, music committee, or other part of the church judiciary become involved, the result could be far-reaching. It would be better to sacrifice one person than to endanger the life of the church.

Organization

This is the day of organization. It is not uncommon to find a social creation in which the organization is more important than the work it is designed to do. Beyond a certain fine point, organization does more harm than good. This is certainly true in regard to choirs. It is possible for a choir to have, in addition to its choirmaster, a president, vice-president, secretary, treasurer, librarian, choir mother, social committee, membership committee, service committee, and chaplain. Unless the object is to give each member of the choir a title of which he should be proud, most of this organization is not worth the time taken to put it together.

All most choirs need in the way of organization is a president and four section heads. The vice-president is clearly not needed. Any secretarial work should be done by the choirmaster and section heads. Little money changes hands, so no treasurer is needed. The choirmaster should be his own librarian. The choir mother's task should lie between the choirmaster and the music committee, whose members should also work with him on membership. Social affairs should be dealt with by the president and the music committee. All members of the choir may be chaplain in turn. What little service is required may be done by the president.

The four section heads should be busy and responsible persons. They may be elected by the several sections, or appointed by the choirmaster. They need not be the best musicians in their sections. Their chief qualifications should be their concern for the well-being of the choir, and their willingness to work for it. The principal task of each head should be to obtain the full and regular attendance of the choir. They should, first of all, keep attendance records for their own use. If, say, a soprano is unaccountably absent on a certain Sunday, the soprano section head should reach this person immediately by phone or letter, letting her know that her absence is of concern to the choir. A singer should never be permitted to feel that his regular attendance is of little importance. The section head should, whenever it will help, enlist the aid of other choir members in the pursuit of an errant singer.

The section head should also keep an eye on the future. When a singer or a number of singers know that they will be absent on a certain week end, this information should be in the hands of the section heads as early as possible. The choirmaster, knowing that three weeks hence certain singers will be absent, should plan his music for that Sunday accordingly. That a large-scale anthem should not be done by a half-scale choir is rudimentary. Likewise, an eight-part anthem would not be chosen for a day when one or more of the divided parts is greatly weakened or missing. It is also possible for the section head, knowing that his section may need insurance for a certain period when absences are promised, to take extra care that all others in the section are present to take up the slack.

Summertime

Summertime offers a special problem to the choir of the church that stays in business. It is taken for granted that the minister will be gone for a month, and that congregational attendance will decrease. It is a temptation for the choir to follow the same easy pattern, and cease all activity for one to three months. This is to be deplored. It is trite to point out that God does not take a vacation, and that the same care should be given His worship in summer as in winter. But many of His followers have decided that He can take care of Himself during the summer. However, thought needs to be given to those of the regular congregation and visitors who choose to worship in His house during the hot months. It is important that they be assured that the church's homage to Him is not halfhearted or negligent.

It should also be pointed out that the choir that ceases activity for a season of each year loses during that time a momentum that it is not easy to regain. Advances that are made during the spring are lost during the summer, to be recovered not without real effort in the fall. There is a slow return to full strength and effectiveness. On the other hand, the choir that has not ceased entirely to function goes into the fall season without losing a step

It is important that the choirmaster's vacation *not* coincide with that of the minister. The low ebb of the summer is usually that time in which visiting ministers serve. During that period the choirmaster should remain on duty, in order that the effectiveness of worship in the church may be equalized.

The summer plans should begin with a week-by-week check of the vocal resources available. About the last week in May a chart should go up in the choir room or other appropriate place listing each singer's name with blanks covering each Sunday of the summer season. Each member should be asked to check after his name those Sundays on which he confidently expects to be present. Those with stated vacations should indicate the Sundays when they know they will be absent. Those with less definite plans may use the convenient question mark until more definite plans are known. The section heads should now take this data and seek to ensure a certain minimum choir for each Sunday of the summer. On some Sundays the effort will need to be made to increase the number present. On others, some members may be offered an additional vacation.

During the summer the section heads should make a weekly advance check on probable attendance. Earlier plans may change that will remove singers who had planned to be present; replacements for these need to be sought. Fortunately, there are usually some singers who are willing to change their plans to meet a particular need.

The choirmaster should arrange the program for the summer so that the least possible effort produces the most effective service possible. A repertoire of "summer" anthems, requiring a minimum of vocal resources and rehearsal, should be laid out and practiced in advance; response music should be likewise simplified. If the proper advance preparation has been made, there should be few or no evening rehearsals during the summer period. A short Sunday morning rehearsal each week should suffice.

The Choir in Action

When the choir confronts the congregation during the worship service, certain rules of behavior should be carefully observed. The word "confronts" is used, because these rules are partially unnecessary for a choir in a divided chancel. But where the choir faces the congregation, each member is exposed to the gaze of the assembled worshipers, and what he does under that gaze may influence the effectiveness of that worship.

The choir rail should be treated as though it were a curtain, beyond which nothing may be seen further than the minister. In far too many churches, large and small, it has been a common practice for choir members to nod and smile to their friends in the congregation. While all movement within the choir is distracting, these greetings are particularly so, since they cause people in the area toward which the greetings are directed to look about them to locate the recipient. More serious damage is done to the spirit of worship, which is above all directed toward God. To the degree that personalities interpose themselves between the individual worshiper and God, to that degree has worship been lost. All exchange of glances, smiles, or whispers between choir members should be plainly disapproved. Even the show of undue interest on the part of choir members in anything that happens in the congregation should be discouraged.

The use of hand fans in hot weather should not be permitted in the choir loft. Not only is this ceaseless movement behind the minister annoying to those in the pews; in some people it can produce vertigo. If the church is not air-conditioned, several electric fans can keep the choir comfortable.

In some churches in which choirs are forced to sit in a widely spread position, some choirmasters have sought to improve the singing of the group by having the singers move closer together whenever they stand to sing. Although the singing may thus be improved, this musical improvement comes at the expense of worship. The choirmaster can justify such a procedure only if his choir cannot sing acceptably otherwise. For in this period of God-centered devotion, every detail that calls attention to man un-

necessarily weakens the intensity of that worship. If this movemen
must be done, let it be done for the anthem only. To have such a
parade before hymns or other service music would be imprope
and unthinkable. A worse example still of what to avoid ha
already been mentioned: the movement of choir members, largely
hidden behind an altar screen, so that as many as possible may be
seen through the openings, during the anthem singing. A prope
justification for this would be hard to find.

One other rare choir movement calls for attention. Some choirs
seated behind a central pulpit, make a practice of leaving the choir
loft and of sitting in the congregation during the sermon. Variou
reasons are given for doing this. The minister may not like people
behind him while he preaches. Perhaps the congregation's atten
tion to the sermon is dissipated by the presence of the choir behind
the minister. It may also be hard for the choir members to follow
the sermon closely when they can see little of the minister's face
Let us admit that each of these reasons has some validity. There
is no question that the position of the choir behind the minister
facing the congregation, is disadvantageous. However, all of these
reasons together cannot justify that amount of movement at the
very time the worshipers should be quiet and expectant just before
the sermon. The choir can learn to attend well while sitting be
hind the minister. In fact, if its presence in the choir loft may no
be forgotten by the people in the pews, the very concentration o
the choir on the words of the minister may be an unconsciou
stimulus toward attention on the part of the congregation. Finally
if a person seeks any symbolism from movements at the front o
the sanctuary, the implication of the coming down of the choir
is all wrong!

If we can agree that worship should be God-centered, th
members of the choir should frequently be reminded that their
singing is directed to God, and not to the congregation. As ha
been indicated earlier, this is particularly difficult for the singer
to remember while they remain in front of the congregation and
seem to be singing to and at the people in the pews. The choir
master should seek in any way he can to counteract this semblance
Every evidence of staginess in behavior or attitude among th

singers should be quietly suppressed. If the choir sits facing the console as it should in the front-center choir loft, it should keep the same position while standing, in no way facing toward the congregation during either anthem or hymns. Any soloist, whether doing an anthem "bit" or a whole number by himself, will keep the position of belonging to the choir, in no way projecting himself outside the group. A soloist in a divided chancel will, of course, not face toward the congregation while singing. While there are people in the congregation who wish to see the faces of the singers, as well as singers who are quite eager to be seen, the avoidance of all such "concert" situations may help to bring the meaning of worship to both choir members and congregation. If choir and soloists are occasionally reminded of the nature of their tasks, there should be little difficulty in obtaining full compliance with proper suggestions toward the realization of devout worship.

IX

THE MUSIC COMMITTEE

The music committee exists, in one form or another, in most churches. It is usually rather inactive. In those churches that take an inventory once a year, its annual sitting measures the fitness of the chief musicians to continue in office, and replaces those who have been weighed and found wanting. In the churches that mark the passing of a year mainly by filing reports and raising a budget, the committee has even less to do. But this should not be, if the musical life of the church is to remain vigorous.

It should not be necessary to suggest that the members of the music committee should be people with some knowledge of music. Yet the choice seems frequently to have fallen on people with committee know-how plus business sense. This may not do much harm unless a committee member happens to be one of those people who says, "I know very little about music, but I do know what I like," and then tries to get what he likes. But even with musical knowledge, most, if not all, of the committee members should *not* belong to the adult choir.

The first task of this committee, of selecting and employing the musical leaders, calls for little comment beyond what was given in an earlier chapter. The longer pull which follows requires from the committee a nice use of restraint. Once the choirmaster has assumed his post, there should be no supervision from the committee. In this regard its work is like that of the pulpit committee that selects a new minister; once he is chosen, the committee should no longer seek to exert any control over him.

On the other hand, the music committee should be a valued

source of information and advice to the new choirmaster. Care needs to be exerted, of course, on how this information is given. It should never be in terms of "This is the way we have always done this," with the implication that this is the way it should always be done. There may be some blind alleys of personal relationships the choirmaster should be warned about. But in the main, suggestions and information should be on the constructive side, and usually not offered unless they have been sought.

It has been suggested that the organization within the adult choir be simple, in order that valuable rehearsal time not be lost in wasteful procedures. Sixty to ninety minutes of choir rehearsal should be filled with sixty to ninety minutes of singing. Let every auxiliary task within that choir be performed by those outside it who do not sing. These tasks should be the responsibility of the music committee.

One of these should be the searching out of new choir members. Neither those already in the choir nor the choirmaster are in position to discover singing talent in the congregation, either among the members or among the occasional visitors; such information will frequently not reach the minister. The music committee should be alert to find talent that may be used by the choirmaster. Whatever is found should be transmitted to him. Under no circumstances should an invitation be issued to a prospective singer unless or until the choirmaster has suggested such an invitation. Not everyone who sings lustily and not too inaccurately on the hymns will make a good member of the choir. If misfits find their way into it, the responsibility for their being there should rest on the choirmaster, and on no one else.

The resources of the music committee should also be available to the choirmaster for any projects requiring financing. If new hymnals, robes, or music files are needed, the committee should see that the money is provided. The day is past when the church choir should dissipate its energies from its main task by entering into time-wasting projects for money raising.

Finally, the music committee may properly assume interest in the social life of the adult choir. Since all the younger choirs should be organized under the auspices of the church school, no responsibility need be taken for these. But, in behalf of the whole church, it is appropriate for the music committee to provide one or two social events a year for the adult choir. It may be a supper-rehearsal in some home at the beginning of the season, or a picnic at its end. There also may be sometime a Family Night Supper given in honor of the choir.

Now and then the music committee may be faced with the unpleasant task of terminating the services of organist or choir-master. When this proves wise, the committee should act decisively. It will, however, act in clearer conscience if it has consistently supported the program of the musician in question during the time he served this church.

PART THREE

We Go to Church

X

THE HYMN

It has been said that, next to his Bible, the Christian minister should know his hymnal best. Whether or not this is true when he must know so many things well, we may say confidently that the minister needs to be able to command the resources of his hymnal, and to use it with the greatest effect. He not only needs to distinguish the good from the bad in hymns, but he needs also to be able to lead his congregation away from the bad toward the good. He needs to know the purpose and place for using hymns, and what he expects to achieve through them.

Why Sing Hymns?

In many of our churches hymn singing is in a sorry state. The only churches in which we may be sure to hear vigorous, enthusiastic congregational singing are in those of the fringe "sects." There are country churches in which it seems agreed that hymn singing is for women and children; the men remain aloof from it. In many sanctuaries a considerable portion of the congregation hold the hymnbook in silence during singing, perhaps scrutinizing the words, or else gazing stonily into space. The few people who sing are careful not to raise their voices, lest they be suspected of trying to attract attention. Many of us have been to services where, were we to sing with any enthusiasm or conviction, we would attract furtive and somewhat shocked glances from those around us, as though we had done something not quite genteel. The final act to put hymn singing into a lowly place and keep it there is the custom in some of our churches of the congregation's remaining seated during at least one hymn each Sunday. The attitude of a large part of such a congregation seems to be this: "Let those people who insist on singing the hymns do so if they must, but why do *we* have to stand while they do it?"

Yet, if the Protestant Reformation was a movement of preaching, it was also one of singing. Much of Luther's effort was given to finding and developing chorales for congregational singing during worship. This was one of the chief methods by which he hoped to give the Mass back to the people. The more austere Calvin favored the singing of metrical psalms during worship. But Wesley went further: he laid down a set of rules concerning congregational singing, urging that everyone "sing lustily and with good courage"; all should sing; "If it is a cross to you, take it up and you will find a blessing."

Why should we, as Wesley says, find hymn singing a blessing? First of all, as we sing hymns we are joining in a religious practice that reaches back toward the beginnings of worship. Except for a mere thousand years when the lips of the faithful were silent as they observed the drama of the Roman Catholic Mass, hymn singing has been perhaps the most characteristic act of adoration through the ages. It is a means by which we participate in the "communion of saints." Then, hymn singing is perhaps the chief means by which we experience Christian fellowship. Let us sing together one stanza of that great Chadwick hymn, "Eternal Ruler of the ceaseless round":

> "We are of Thee, the children of Thy love,
> The brothers of Thy well-beloved Son;
> Descend, O Holy Spirit, like a dove
> Into our hearts, that we may be as one;
> As one with Thee, to whom we ever tend;
> As one with Him, our Brother and our Friend."

As our voices move together, our hearts are lifted together toward our God, and at the same time reach out to join others in a way and to a degree it would be hard to achieve by any other method.

Music tends to give vitality to religious ideas with which it is linked. Religious poetry speaks primarily to the intellect and mildly to the emotions, while music speaks at once largely to the emotions. When poetry and music are brought together, their effects are also brought together. When thought and emotion are combined, it is easy for action to follow. This action may be the immediate one known and used by the mass evangelist. Properly used, it may also be the means for sustained, consistent living.

Hymns Good and Less Good

If worship is the practice of communion with God within the Christian fellowship, then those hymns are best which lead us most completely toward that communion. It is scarcely possible within the limits of this book to add anything to the excellent discussion of hymns made by Henry Sloane Coffin[1] and Andrew W. Blackwood[2] in their books on worship, or in the broader discussion of what is proper in church music as covered so ably by Archibald T. Davison.[3] Let us rather briefly illustrate several of the basic principles which may suggest only the general direction of our thoughts on this subject.

1. Hymns should be "praise to God with song"—St. Augustine's definition. To achieve communion with God most directly, hymns should be addressed to Him. Yet it is necessary at once to add that there are many great hymns that are not so addressed, such as "A mighty Fortress is our God," "All hail the power of Jesus' name," and "Faith of our fathers, living still."

The hymns that sing about God are no less great for that reason, but hymns addressed to God achieve immediate contact with Him scarcely possible otherwise. Not considering the music, a comparison of hymns of both types should help. Compare

> "O worship the Lord in the beauty of holiness!
> Bow down before Him, His glory proclaim;
> With gold of obedience, and incense of lowliness,
> Kneel and adore Him: the Lord is His name!"

with

> "We worship Thee, almighty Lord,
> Our hearts revere Thy gracious word
> When it goes forth from heaven o'er all the earth.
> Holy, holy, holy art Thou, O God!"

Although perhaps the lyric of the first is better poetry than that of the second, the second establishes immediate contact with God, while the first is merely an exhortation to do so. Let us make another contrast. Compare

> "Give to the winds thy fears;
> Hope and be undismayed;
> God hears thy sighs and counts thy tears,
> God shall lift up thy head."

with

> "There is no sorrow, Lord, too light
> To bring in prayer to Thee;
> There is no anxious care too slight
> To wake Thy sympathy."

The first of these last two stanzas discusses a proposition, but the second opens the heart to God at once.

2. There should be an attempt in our corporate worship to move toward the objective hymns without, however, losing sight of the subjective. Our religion must, of course, be a personal thing, an "I" experience first of all. And our hymns should reflect its subjective nature. But our religion must not stop there. We must love our neighbors as a part of our loving God. So our thinking should move from "I" and "mine" in the direction of "we" and "ours," and then on to "they" and "theirs." Our hymns should increasingly express the same movement. We may still sing "He leadeth *me*, O blessed thought," but we should not neglect "Lead *us*, O Father, in the paths of peace." There is still a place for "Breathe on *me*, Breath of God, / Fill *me* with life anew," but we should also make a larger place for "O grant *us* light, that *we* may know / The wisdom Thou alone canst give."

"They" and "theirs" are still not often enough in our thoughts. Yes, we, "whose souls are lighted / With wisdom from on high," have sung our missionary hymns with some condescension about "men benighted." Yet we have had too little concern for those people near at hand who are the victims of the moral and social evils with which we are surrounded. Our light solicitude in this direction is reflected in the small number of hymns that deal with social wrong and injustice. Almost alone in our current hymnals stand the Frank Mason North hymn, "Where cross the crowded ways of life," written in 1903, and Harry Emerson Fosdick's "God of grace and God of glory," written in 1930. These should be sung more often, along with others in the same spirit which are not yet known.

3. The content of hymns should be Biblical and Christian, and should deal with experiences common to all Christians. In a hymnal of the Presbyterian Church there is a so-called hymn which begins "These things shall be: a loftier race . . ." Then follows a discussion of a new social order as it might be conceived by a sociologist, with peace, disarmament, brotherhood, and the flowering of new arts, but no sign of God! This is perhaps an extreme case, yet it is not alone. Our young people frequently sing "I would be true, for there are those who trust me." The two stanzas which are commonly printed lack any *direct* Christian motivation. If one examines gospel song literature, he will find other examples.

4. Music and words of a hymn should fit. This sounds basic, but we still continue to use words of one meter against music of another. This is probably for no better reason than that words and music got started together, and never became separated; an early divorce would have been wise. Here is Adelaide Proctor's hymn, usually sung to Maker's tune, WENTWORTH. This is how it is sung, with the musical accents indicated:

> "My/God, I thank Thee,/who hast made The/earth so/bright,
> So /full of splen-dor/and of joy, Beau-/ty and light;
> So/man- y glo-rious/things are here, No-/ble and/right."

In this one stanza, the poetic accent is displaced three times by the musical accent. Then there is the great Oliver Wendell Holmes hymn, usually sung to the tune LOUVAN:

> "Lord/of all/be- ing,/throned a-/far,
> Thy/glo- ry/flames from/sun and/star;
> Cen-/ter and/soul of/ev- ery/sphere,
> Yet/to each/lov- ing/heart how/near!"

Again, there are three misplaced poetic accents. Some of our newer hymnals are putting these lyrics to different tunes, or altering the rhythm of the old one. The enterprising minister or choir-master may, however, find a better tune merely by referring to his metrical index. "Lord of all being," for instance, will go better with any Long Meter (L. M.) tune that begins on a strong beat than it will with Louvan.

5. Hymn tunes should be singable. This means several things: There should usually be a note-for-syllable relationship between tune and words. Such a relationship is notably lacking in "The spacious firmament on high," usually sung to the tune Creation. No one would question its beauty, but the somewhat florid melodic pattern of several notes to one syllable makes a problem for the musical beginner. The very appearance of it on the page discourages him.

Hymn tunes should rarely cover a wider range than an octave. Most of the hymn tunes we sing come within that range, or go not more than one note beyond it. Many writers on church music believe that the congregation should not be encouraged to do part singing. Some even urge the printing of pew hymnals containing words and melody only. Then such a tune as Easter Hymn, to which we usually sing "Christ the Lord is risen today," offers real difficulty to men and women with lower voices. It is florid, part of it lies high, and its range is wide.

A controversy has been running for many years between the proponents of Coronation and those of Miles Lane as to which tune should be used for "All hail the power of Jesus' name." There is no doubt of the musical superiority of Miles Lane, but somehow it has never been able to supplant Coronation after more than a century and a half of appearing beside it in hymnals. The reason is largely that Miles Lane spans over one and a half octaves in its melody, the same range as our unsingable "Star-Spangled Banner"!

Wide, difficult melodic skips also make a tune difficult to sing. Christmas, the usual tune for "While shepherds watched their flocks by night" and "Awake, my soul, stretch every nerve," is one of them. Neither the carol nor the hymn are sung as much as they would be if the tune were vocally more manageable.

A less-than-obvious rhythm can also make a tune difficult. "Immortal Love, forever full," that beautiful Whittier hymn, is usually sung to SERENITY, a tune that presents rhythmic problems to the musical tyro. Let a minister try once or twice to get a less than adequate pianist and a congregation of musical novices to agree on how to sing this hymn rhythmically, and he is not to be blamed if he decides it is not for his church.

The Hymn Is Announced

When we speak of announcing a hymn, two different acts may be meant: the minister's preliminary statement of number, tune, or stanzas to be used, and the playing of the hymn or portion of it before the congregation sings it. Both call for some comment.

There is seldom any need for the minister to announce the hymns. In churches where a printed bulletin is not used, a hymn board should serve. There is no good reason why the minister should duplicate orally what is available otherwise. But in the summertime when some churches print only a general order, it may be necessary for the minister to announce the hymns.

Clarity and brevity are to be sought in such announcement. The minister should not say, "Let us sing to the glory of God hymn number 237." Unless he is prepared to indicate what parts of the service are *not* done to the glory of God, the inference should be that the whole service is so dedicated. Nor should the minister say, "Let us join heartily in singing hymn number 237." If a person sings at all, he must join something or somebody. It is no more appropriate for the minister to urge hearty hymn singing than it is for him to ask for lusty, enthusiastic participation in the responsive reading, or for careful attention to his prayers and sermon.

He will simply say, "Hymn number 237—'A charge to keep I have'—hymn number 237." He will repeat the number once since a large part of the congregation will be inattentive enough to miss it the first time. He will indicate the first line of the hymn to reassure the seeker that he has found the right number.

If the entire hymn is not to be sung, the time to indicate that fact is in the announcement, rather than by an interruption between stanzas. There is still a great confusion among ministers concerning the use of "verse" and "stanza" as applied to hymns. A verse of a hymn, like a verse of poetry, is one line. Once through a hymn is a *stanza*. Let the minister say, "We shall omit the last stanza."

The organist then makes his announcement. How should this be done? Some writers want it to be brief, perhaps no more than a line of the hymn. Others feel that the entire hymn should be played through. The argument of those who prefer the short introduction is plainly that they want to "get on" with the service, with no time wasted. For those who prefer the more deliberate approach (and I wish to be numbered among these) the full playing of the hymn before singing serves three purposes. First, it gives the congregation ample time to find the place in the hymnal. Next, it serves to remind the congregation of the music to be sung. Finally, it should set the exact speed at which it will be sung. An abbreviated introduction would not serve the first two purposes, and might not serve the last one. Yet all three have a definite bearing on good hymn singing.

There should be exceptions noted. If one stanza only of a hymn is called for, a shorter introduction would be appropriate. If a hymn is to be called for while the congregation is already standing, the same would be true, since the congregation should not normally be kept standing for any length of time without any task to be performed.

Whether the whole hymn or an abbreviation of it is played in advance, the choir should stand at the beginning of the last phrase or line of it. If the congregation knows it is to stand with the choir, no signal from the minister is either necessary or appropriate.

The Hymn Is Sung

The organist must be firmly in charge of all hymn singing. Show me a congregation that habitually sings unrhythmically and drags the tempo, and I will show you an organist who is not doing his job well. People in church do not want to sing badly; they probably do the best they can in view of their leadership.

The control lies with the organist. He must play the hymn at exactly the tempo at which he expects it to be sung, and then carry out his intention! He must keep in mind that his instrument is not essentially rhythmic, like the piano. To make his rhythm felt he must separate his chords sharply during singing, in order that the regular pulsations of tone can be heard. If he has practiced these hymns with the choir, and his singers are working with him, the hymns will maintain a steady speed throughout, unless his full organ is so small that it cannot be heard.

What is true of hymn tempo is also true of musical errors of other types. I have heard a whole congregation miss the melody of a hymn for the very good reason that the melody sung is that which has been played. Likewise I have heard congregations that have mutilated the rhythm of such hymns as "What a Friend we have in Jesus" or "Jesus, Saviour, pilot me" or "Immortal Love, forever full" correct their mistakes completely when the rhythm was finally made clear by the organist. (This is usually a different organist than the one who had been playing before!)

Organist and choir have the further responsibility of bringing meaning out of words when that meaning is otherwise smothered and lost in the mechanical process of singing. Most of us were taught as children to avoid sing-song reading of poetry, and to combine words according to meaning. When poetry is placed within the regular cadences of the hymn, these divisions by meaning tend to be obscured. The casual singer ploughs heedlessly through all hymns, breathing regularly every two or four measures, depending on the wind supply available, regardless of word meaning. It is also apparent that most singers actually do not think about the words they are singing as they sing them. This comes partially from absent-mindedness, and partially from preoccupation with the ordinary task of matching words to music. But how can these sung words be given the meaning that is in them? The best way is for the choir to sing them as they would read them, making a "break" at the end of logical divisions without, of course, interfering with the normal flow of rhythm. The organist will momentarily lift his hands also at each of these logical divisions, phrasing with the choir. This effort may have no effect for a period. But eventually members of the congregation will become aware of a method of singing different from their own,

and may even pattern their own singing accordingly, as they per-
ceive its purpose.

To show how such logical phrasing should displace the normal
breathing pattern, let us examine the George Croly hymn, usually
sung to MORECAMBE. The breathing or phrasing marks will be
indicated (/). To make the differences between the stanzas clear,
the words must be arranged in the same awkward way as they
usually appear between the music staves.

(1) Spir-it of God, /de-scend up-on my heart;/
(2) I ask no dream,/no proph-et ec-sta-sies,/
(3) Hast Thou not bid us love Thee,/God and King?/
(4) Teach me to feel that Thou art al-ways nigh;/
(5) Teach me to love Thee as Thine an-gels love,/

(1) Wean it from earth;/through all its puls-es move;/
(2) No sud-den rend-ing of the veil of clay,/
(3) All,/all Thine own,/soul, heart, and strength, and mind;/
(4) Teach me the strug-gles of the soul to bear,/
(5) One ho-ly pas-sion/fill-ing all my frame;/

(1) Stoop to my weak-ness,/might-y as Thou art,/
(2) No an-gel vis-it-ant,/no o-pening skies;/
(3) I see Thy cross—/there teach my heart to cling:/
(4) To check the ris-ing doubt,/the reb-el sigh;/
(5) The bap-tism of the heaven-de-scend-ed Dove,/

(1) And make me love Thee as I ought to love./
(2) But take the dim-ness of my soul a-way./
(3) O let me seek Thee,/and O let me find!/
(4) Teach me the pa-tience of un-an-swered prayer./
(5) My heart an al-tar,/ and Thy love the flame./

As has been indicated earlier, some writers in recent years have
urged that congregations not be encouraged to do part singing,
limiting the pew hymnals accordingly. This suggestion is folly,
harmless only because few are likely to act on this advice. First
there is that great number of people who sing parts because they
prefer to; they have the right to be considered. Then there are
those people who can sing the melody only with great difficulty.
The young, those others who are naturally sopranos or tenors, and
those with lower voices who have had vocal training can readily

sing all hymn melodies. But a great group of people with lower and untrained voices can never sing the higher notes of a melody with complete comfort, and cannot sing them at all as they get older. Fortunate are they, as well as the people who sit near them, if they can drop comfortably onto an alto or bass part. Those remaining either engage in that horrible practice of growling the melody an octave lower than it should be, or else join the too large party of those who remain silent during the singing of hymns.

It is usually agreed that the choir should sing parts on the hymns. A change from this pattern may keep the hymn from drooping as it is wont to do toward the end. Let the choir always sing in unison on the last stanza. This gives a certain lift toward the close that counteracts this "running down." This does not apply to the processional and recessional, which offer a different problem that will be discussed later.

The Amen

"Amen" is a word of great antiquity and varied usage. In recent years its use has become gradually restricted to the close of prayers and of hymns. In fact, its use after hymns is far from universal. In certain parts of the country, the degree of formality within a church may be measured by its use of "Amen" after the hymns. Some churches that use the "Amen" after morning hymns omit it at the evening service to indicate the relative informality of the later service.

It is true, however, that to a large segment of Protestantism the use of "Amen" after hymns lends a certain dignity and orderliness to worship. It has, of course, a solid precedent in the New Testament, and we continue to use it as a ratification of sentiments which have been expressed, although somewhat less than formerly.

Since the primary use of "Amen" is now one of closing prayer, there is a growing feeling that it becomes inappropriate in some worship situations. It seems incongruous after most Christmas carols, as in this situation:

> "She bore to men a Saviour,
> When half spent was the night. AMEN."

It is little better following this Passion hymn:

> " 'Tis midnight, and from heavenly plains
> Is borne the song that angels know;
> Unheard by mortals are the strains
> That sweetly soothe the Saviour's woe. AMEN."

It is not hard to see an objection to putting it after this hymn:

> "Help me to watch and pray,
> And on Thyself rely,
> Assured, if I my trust betray,
> I shall forever die. AMEN."

The practice of the Episcopal Church in putting the "Amen" after prayer hymns only is to be highly recommended. If a hymn is addressed to God, it properly ends with "Amen," but not otherwise. Such an agreement made in any church is wholly appropriate and feasible. There is little danger of confusion in this practice, since ordinarily neither choir nor congregation would start to sing the "Amen" unless or until the organist starts to play it.

It should be added that, when an "Amen" is used, it should not sound both melancholy and apologetic, as it so often does now, but should be sung with feeling and conviction.

Sing All the Stanzas?

In the churches where the only fare available was the metrical psalm, it was felt necessary to sing the entire psalm, since the Word of the Lord must not be tampered with in any way. There are still in the church people who feel the same way about hymns. If seven stanzas are printed, seven stanzas must be sung! But the two situations are quite different. It is understandable that the seventeenth-century churchman would refuse to shorten a Psalm of David, even though it had been changed by being put in what may be charitably called poetic form. But many of our hymns have already been reduced before they reach us. Examine Julian's *Hymnology* and you will find that many are mere excerpts from longer poems. If you want further proof, examine hymnals used in the nineteenth century and compare them with ours, and you will find that many of the hymns still in use had definitely more stanzas printed then than now.

Not only is it permissible to shorten a hymn, but there are advantages in doing so. If a portion of a hymn will give emphasis to a sermon, that emphasis may be weakened if the whole hymn is used.

But hymn abbreviation should be done with care. There are some hymns that cannot easily be shortened at all, since the words form a logical whole. Such a hymn is "Ancient of Days," the stanzas of which begin thus:

1. Ancient of Days, who sittest throned in glory,
2. O Holy Father, who hast led Thy children
3. O Holy Jesus, Prince of Peace and Saviour,
4. O Holy Ghost, the Lord and the Life Giver,
5. O Triune God, with heart and voice adoring . . .

The hymn forms a unity which can scarcely be broken. There are hymns, however, which have less logical connection between stanzas, and may be divided for a specific purpose.

A regular pattern for stanza choice should be avoided. Let us take, for instance, the heedless use of first and last stanzas of hymns. If the hymn happens to be "A mighty Fortress is our God," the first stanza ends with these words:

"And, armed with cruel hate,
On earth is not his equal."

The last stanza begins thus:

"That word above all earthly powers,
No thanks to them, abideth."

What word? The meaning of the last stanza is largely lost unless the third is sung. The moral is that as much thought should be given to stanza choice as to hymn choice. The stanza choice, once made, should be part of the bulletin information.

Problems of Rhythm and Speed

Many congregations tend to drag hymns. The problem is met by organists in various ways. Here is one who tries to compensate for the pulling back by robbing some time from the longer note at the end, starting the next phrase early. The congregation is jerked through each hymn, breathless and off balance, and never having a satisfactory rhythmic experience from the singing. Then there is another organist whose compensation comes from playing all the hymns which would be naturally slow somewhat too fast. The singing may be rhythmic, but the character of many of the hymns is destroyed because the speed quarrels with the meaning of the words and the style of the music.

There is a correct speed for a hymn, a speed that will vary but little between churches and organists. This speed is determined by the character of words and music, as well as by the category to which it belongs. For instance, an old metrical psalm in Long Meter or Common Meter will be sung at the deliberate pace befitting its age. OLD HUNDREDTH or ST. ANNE should not be hurried on any account. Then there are certain other hymns that should be slowed down to give them even a trace of dignity! Here are two hymns, popular and often used: "Love divine, all loves excelling," sung to BEECHER, and "Jesus calls us: o'er the tumult," sung to GALILEE. Neither hymn is very good musically, and both become altogether commonplace when they are done at a lively speed. But since they *will* be sung, let them be slowed down in order that their words may have a chance in spite of their music.

There is some confusion today about the use of the *pause* (sometimes called the *hold*) in hymn singing. It is a common device to lengthen the final note of phrases of certain hymns, particularly German chorales. There are today two somewhat different treatments of the pause. One group of organists make it a practice to hold the note bearing the pause long enough to complete a rhythmic pattern. Another group insist that there can be no uniform way of dealing with pauses, that musical sense calls for different treatment of different situations.

To see how complete is our confusion on this question, let us look at the ways a number of our hymnals deal with that best-known of all chorales, EIN' FESTE BURG. The *Common Service Book of the Lutheran Church* (Columbia, S. C.: Lutheran Board

of Publication, 1917) puts the first two phrases, without time
signature, in this form:

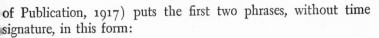

A might-y For - tress is our God,   A Bul-wark nev-er   fail - ing

The Hymnal of the Protestant Episcopal Church (New York:
The Church Pension Fund, 1940) does it in similar fashion, but
with longer notes at the ends of both phrases:

A might-y For - tress is our God,   A Bul-wark nev-er   fail - ing

*The Hymnal Authorized by the General Synod of the Evangelical
and Reformed Church* (Saint Louis: Eden Publishing House,
1941) uses pauses:

A might-y For - tress is our God,   A Bul-wark nev-er   fail - ing

The *Concordia Hymnal* (Minneapolis: Augsburg Press, 1933)
uses straight rhythm like the above, but without pauses. *The
Hymnbook* (Philadelphia: John Ribble, Publishing Agent, Wither-
spoon Building, 1955) compromises between the two preceding
versions:

A might-y For - tress is our God,   A Bul-wark nev-er   fail - ing

Pilgrim Hymnal (Boston: The Pilgrim Press, 1958) spells out part
of the rhythm, leaves part to the organist's discretion:

A might-y For - tress is our God,   A Bul-wark nev-er   fail - ing

All these hymnals present the same hymn, but no two versions
are the same! What, then, are we to conclude? Certainly we are

justified in saying that there is no one right way. The organist would do well to follow as nearly as possible the hymnal he is using; where a specific number of beats is asked for, that number of beats should be given. Thus one hymnal ends each phrase with a two-beat note, and another with a three-beat one. But what do we do with the pauses? If the organist chooses to end each phrase by giving the pauses either two or three beats, he will be following an established usage. This organist votes for the latter choice. In the interest of uniformity, it is well to have the pause complete a rhythmic pattern. If choir and congregation know that a pause will be performed in a certain way, there will result a smoothness in the hymn singing that would be hard to achieve if the organist were to vary his interpretation with the situation.

Applying this rule to EIN' FESTE BURG, we would end all phrases with a note of the same length:

> "A mighty Fortress is our *God*,
> (three beats)
> A Bulwark never fail*ing;*
> (three beats)
> Our Helper He amid the *flood*
> (three beats)
> Of mortal ills prevail*ing* . . ."
> (three beats)

The first four phrases, then, end with notes of the same length as those which end the later phrases, which are usually spelled out as three-beat notes.

Then there is the problem of performing the archaic rhythm of some of our old hymns, mostly in Common Meter. Let us look, for instance, at ST. AGNES, which appears with at least four sets of words, of which we choose one at random:

> "Jesus, the very thought of Thee (four measures)
> With sweetness fills my breast; (three measures)
> But sweeter far Thy face to see, (four measures)
> And in Thy presence rest." (three measures)

Although the Common Meter (C. M.) arrangement (in syllables 8 6 8 6) seems to fit the words perfectly, a three-measure phrase is not a normal one for our western rhythmic sense, which feels out of balance without some lengthening of the shorter phrase. But how much lengthening? Some organists say, "That depends . . ." Others say that as a rule a fourth measure should be added to the shorter phrase. In this case *breast* and *rest* should be doubled in length, adding an extra measure to the second and fourth phrases. This will produce a sixteen-measure hymn, instead of an irregular fourteen-measure one. In the interest of uniformity as well as agreement between organist and singers, this organist casts his vote on the side of uniformity.

There are not many of these unbalanced Common Meter hymns still in use. One other well-known one should be mentioned. It is "Joy to the world! the Lord is come," sung to Handel's tune, ANTIOCH. The second phrase, "Let earth receive her King," is usually printed with three measures only. Most knowing organists agree that this should be corrected by adding a full measure to the note that goes with the word *King*.

What shall we do with the liberties that are taken by some congregations with some hymns? I suppose the answer again should be, "That depends . . ." I have in mind such a hymn as "Beneath the cross of Jesus," in which some add a pause to the next to the last line: "From the burning of the noontide *heat* . . ." Some organists would say under their breaths at this point, "No, you don't!" and jerk the singers on to the scheduled stanza ending. Others would permit them to enjoy that pause, sentimental as it may be, as a harmless concession to congregational preference. In this case my vote would go to the latter group of organists.

Some organists fail to allow sufficient time between the stanzas of hymns. It should be remembered that for some worshipers hymn singing is strenuous business. At the end of a stanza they need time to get a big new breath, and a chance to fix their eyes firmly on the first word of the next stanza. If the organist does not allow sufficient time, some people just do not continue. This amount of time will vary somewhat, according to the speed of the hymn. Usually about one measure should be added to the end of a stanza before the next one is started. For about three-quarters of this added measure the organist should hold the final chord (enough to match those singers who like to "hang on"). The other quarter should be silent.

Variety in Hymn Performance?

In theory and practice efforts are being made to surround our hymn singing with devices designed to give the experience more interest and variety. One writer suggests that the organist change registration at the end of each stanza, letting the worshipers as they sing hear now the diapasons, now the reeds, now full organ. There are also being published new organ harmonizations of familiar hymns, and new choral descants to go above them.

One cannot visit many of the larger churches without hearing in action these attempts to enliven or to enrich hymn singing. Here the choir sopranos launch into a descant above the last stanza of NICAEA. There an organist will delay the progress of a hymn long enough to do a tasteful modulation at the end of the third stanza, in order that the last stanza may be sung on a higher pitch, with greater intensity. In another church the organist produces a new harmonization to a familiar hymn during its last stanza. (I found myself wondering what was happening to the altos, tenors, and basses in the congregation who were still trying to sing the parts in the hymnal.)

Hymn singing is an act of worship. It is one of the ways by which we commune with God, a communion that is most complete as our contemplation of Him is the least obscured. But it *is* obscured by any act of choir or organist that calls attention to itself, for at the same time it calls attention away from God.

This same idea is put mildly by Carl Halter:

> Organ and choir descants may be used at times for the purpose of securing variety and in order to heighten musical effectiveness. They are of doubtful value since the result, in the writer's experience at least, is that the congregation usually sings more softly in order to listen.[4]

Does this seem unduly harsh? Are we trying to take beauty out of worship, as did the Puritans? I believe not. When choir and organist act *in behalf of* the congregation, then their offering should be as perfect in beauty as they can make it. But when choir and organist are joined by the congregation in hymns, the first goal is not beauty but full, perfect participation, from which a beauty of simplicity will emerge unspoiled. Let organist and choir, then, perform altogether self-effacing tasks in their support of hymn singing. Does this mean that none of the indicated "varieties" may be used at all? No. But they would not appear on ordinary Sundays. They should be reserved for the festival occasion.

The First and Second Hymns

Protestants have never found a better model for worship than Isaiah 6: 1-8. The spiritual movement from initial adoration to final self-offering is the basis still for the building of most of our orders of worship.

It is agreed that early in the service there should be a hymn of praise. Most of our standard hymnals recognize this principle by putting near the beginning of the book those hymns which are appropriate to the beginning of worship. These are largely objective in character, including not only hymns of adoration and praise, but those appropriate to the Sabbath only, and those that deal with the power and majesty of God.

There is less clarity in regard to the place and function of the second hymn. "Subjective" is the word often used to describe it. It may be a prayer hymn, one of thanksgiving, or one of dedication or consecration, depending upon what the minister wants it to say. It is frequently used as a "sermon" hymn, to set the stage for the message.

Because of its versatility, the second hymn should be given a floating assignment. On one Sunday it may act to confirm the New Testament lesson; on another it may follow the pastoral prayer; when the minister has found just the one to prepare the way for the sermon, it should be just before the sermon. The service should be sufficiently flexible so that the second hymn and the anthem may be interchanged, according to which one seems to fit a particular situation more appropriately.

Most churches tend to get themselves into a patterned "regular" order of worship which is harder to change than the wording of the Lord's Prayer. The reason is probably not so much the momentum of tradition as it is the preoccupation of the minister. So busy is he with the many tasks that are his that he feels himself fortunate if his sermon is reasonably ready to present on Sunday. He seldom takes proper thought for the remainder of the service. However, so rewarding is the well-planned service that the minister who sets aside time for such planning will not fail to continue the practice.

Closing Hymn?

For many years the closing hymn has been under attack from both the pew and the pulpit. From the standpoint of many worshipers the reaction has been simple and understandable. When the sermon is finished they have received what they came to church for. Thinking about dinner, which is always late on Sunday, and the plans for the remainder of the day, they see no real reason to take the time to sing another hymn before they leave.

Some ministers have reached the same conclusion by different reasoning. Where the final hymn has not been an "invitation" hymn, it has traditionally served to "nail down" the final thought of the sermon, and further to involve the congregation actively in its ultimate meaning. Yet ministers have realized that often it has served neither purpose well. How seldom has the minister been able to find a hymn which will say exactly what he wants it to say! He is often forced, therefore, to substitute another hymn from the same general area of meaning, and then either to bend the sermon to meet the hymn, or to permit the hymn to remain somewhat irrelevant. It is not to be wondered at if such a minister will then listen readily to the suggestion made by some member of his congregation that the final hymn be omitted. If he is also a minister who has difficulty in saying what he wants to in the allotted twenty minutes, here is the gift of another three or four minutes without putting him beyond the legal limit of one hour!

There are, however, many churches that continue the final hymn for no other reason than that the practice is customary. The minister selects some devotional hymn for the purpose, not concerning himself too much about whether or not it goes with his sermon. Sometimes the hymn in this place may be deadly in effect.

I recall once hearing a sermon on the greatness, power, and majesty of God. He is not the fellow Rotarian whom we familiarly slap on the back. He is the Maker of us all. He rules with justice over the affairs of men; He is mighty and wise above our imagining. It was a good sermon. Then we arose and sang "What a Friend we have in Jesus." The question is not in regard to the truth of both the sermon and the hymn, but rather is whether or not we can keep the attributes of God's greatness and Jesus' lowliness before us at the same time. Certainly in this instance we could not. The hymn utterly destroyed the sermon.

On the other hand, there are distinct values coming from the quiet ending of the worship period. It is possible to carry for a long time the thought and mood of worship after one has left the sanctuary if the worshiper has not been disturbed by that which is irrelevant and unnecessary at the end of worship. This is particularly true if the preaching has been of high quality.

This last statement, however, points to the real objection to ending worship with only a prayer and benediction after the sermon: it tends to exaggerate the importance of the sermon. Dean Sperry expressed it this way some years ago: "The minister who insists upon concluding his sermon at once with a prayer and benediction overestimates his importance as a preacher and is lacking in charity."[5] Dean Sperry would use a closing hymn as a psychological bridge between the service and the world outside in which the worshiper soon finds himself. This bridge then presumably reduces the sermon in its importance.

The argument for the retention of the final hymn continues somewhat in this fashion: Another act of worship is needed after the sermon, an act of personal dedication, which requires congregational participation. This is appropriately a hymn. This hymn may or may not grow directly out of the sermon. But the final congregational act, just before the dismissal, should be a personal commitment to service in the world. It should not be an act of the minister, like a prayer, but one in which each worshiper participates. Incidentally, this congregational act presumably prevents the sermon from appearing to be the dominant act of worship.

At a glance, this is a plausible argument. But, in my opinion,

it fails when applied to worship itself. For the closing hymn ha
been just—the closing hymn. If it is an invitation hymn, it is
directed toward the unsaved, and is not general in its import
Otherwise, related vaguely to the sermon it follows, it in no way
reduces the importance of the sermon but may even do the op
posite. Nor would calling it the Hymn of Dedication give any
assurance that it would achieve the purpose for which it is devised
This act of self-offering, which might well be the culminating step
in worship, cannot be effectively performed so casually.

If a regular closing hymn fails to achieve any high purpose, an
occasional hymn after the sermon can be doubly effective. The
same may be said of a solo or anthem planned for this position
If a minister, perhaps with the aid of his choirmaster, finds in a
solo, anthem, or hymn exactly the message to give point to his
closing thought, he should not fail to use this help. That which
is unusual calls attention to itself and to its purpose because of its
very unusualness.

How, then, should a service end, if not with a hymn? Let us
agree with Dean Sperry that something more is required than a
closing prayer and benediction after the sermon. Let the sermon
be completed by a confirming prayer. Then there may well be a
closing liturgy, of the sort suggested by John Knox in his *Book of
Common Order*; he even placed the Lord's Prayer in this position
and I can think of no better place. Another plan offered by more
recent religious leaders is the placing of the offering, made as a
symbolic act of self-giving, at the end of the service. Either of
these alternatives is to be preferred to the traditional final hymn.

The New Hymn

One of the insistent problems in many churches is getting the
congregation to learn to sing new hymns. Like the proverbial horse
than can be led to water, congregations will not necessarily sing
hymns after being exposed to them. There are some people who
refuse to add to the hymn repertoire they learned as children, and
who resolutely close their lips whenever a new hymn is proposed

The "Hymn of the Month" is a method which has a certain
limited value in teaching new hymns. Reduced to its simplest

form, the plan would be to have the minister and choirmaster agree on a new hymn to be taught to the congregation, and then use this same hymn every Sunday for a month. If this is all that is done, probably the plan will not succeed. There are variations of it which may work or not, depending upon the type of church using them, and the diligence with which they are applied. The hymn may be introduced to the congregation by the junior choir on the first Sunday of a month, and then used by the whole congregation for three or four more Sundays. Another church may have the adult choir sing the hymn the first Sunday, perhaps asking the congregation to join the choir on the last stanza; on the second Sunday perhaps the choir will sing the first stanza, and then the congregation will join in. Neither plan recommends itself to me. The best way for a congregation to learn is to *try* to learn, right from the beginning. This cannot be done, of course, unless the congregation wants to learn new hymns. It becomes, then, a problem in motivation, which somehow must be supplied by the minister.

Many years ago I heard a minister preach a sermon on that noble Oliver Wendell Holmes hymn, "Lord of all being." I cannot remember a single statement he made on his topic, but to this day I feel a warm glow of appreciation for this hymn, a glow that began, I am sure, with the understanding he gave me of its meaning. I probably would like the hymn even if I had not heard this sermon, but it does have a beauty for me it would not possess otherwise.

It should not be inferred that a minister should always preach a sermon concerning a new hymn that is being undertaken. But he should at least give the pertinent facts concerning the history of the hymn and its significance. I do not mean the type of sentimental anecdote found in many books on favorite hymns, but rather statements on the position of the hymn in the life and thinking of the Church. Let us assume, for instance, that the hymn chosen for learning is "Christian, dost thou see them," written by St. Andrew of Crete well over a thousand years ago. Will not the "powers of darkness" to which the author refers take on added meaning for us if we see the hymn in its historical perspective?

Some may object to using a worship service for teaching either a hymn or the facts about it. There may be, of course, churches in which the discussion of a hymn would seem inappropriate. But in any church which would permit as much informality as a children's sermon, or the reading of a notice from the pulpit, such a presentation should offer no offense.

The church Family Night offers another opportunity to teach new hymns. The singing of hymns frequently forms a part of the program for such meetings. Why not devote at least a part of this period to the planned addition of hymns to the worship repertoire of the church? The church school may also serve as a place of hymn learning; let the Hymn of the Month that is being sung in church also be sung in the church school on the same day.

The Gospel Song*

Although the assault against it continues, the gospel song's position remains strong throughout much of Protestantism. The reasons for this are not hard to find. In the great period of mass evangelism, not completely behind us, this song literature was taught with a vigor and skill unique in music history. The special songbooks sold by enterprising evangelists found their way into the church school, and the songs learned during the "campaign" continued to be sung long afterward. Some found their way into respected hymnals, and many more continue in the smaller songbooks used in town and country churches.

Just what are gospel songs? They are hard to describe briefly, since they are several things.

1. All are very singable, having what should be called a tune rather than a melody. One may be expected to leave church whistling "Love lifted me" when it would be unthinkable to do the same with "Our God, our Help in ages past."

2. Many, but not all, have the vigorous beat of the dance band.

---

*Reference must be made here to the new use of the words "gospel song." There is a current epidemic of "concerts," radio and television performances, devoted to highly "jazzed up" versions of Negro spirituals and other religious songs, accompanied by exaggerated bodily movement and percussion instruments. It is an understatement to call such performances a sacrilege. "Gospel song" is used here in its traditional sense.

A person can keep step on a frosty morning to "Anywhere with Jesus" but "A mighty Fortress is our God" would not serve this purpose at all.

3. Some are frankly emotional summons to the sinner to accept salvation, such as "O Jesus, Thou art standing / Outside the fast-closed door" and "Jesus is tenderly calling thee home."

4. Most, but not all, are directed manward instead of Godward. They are frequently exhortations, such as "Rescue the perishing" and "Yield not to temptation."

5. Some substitute sentimentality for precise religious meaning. Just how does one "cling to the old rugged cross"?

6. Some try to put eternal verities in terms of merely human emotion, as in "He whispers His love to me" and "In the Garden."

7. Almost all are easy to play, even for a limited pianist. The chords are few and oft repeated.

Frequently someone will ask, "Why can't we sing more of the good old songs?" The songs to which he usually refers are neither good nor old, coming from the period near the turn of the century. Yet the love of this person for the gospel songs he learned as a child may be little less profound than his love for the Bible verses he learned then. To argue about this is only to offend.

Gospel songs will be with us for some time. In their present form most of them are unworthy of any place in our religious thinking and practice. But as long as young people enjoy singing them for sheer amusement, and older ones for nostalgic pleasure, there is no real point in our raising hand or voice against their singing. Nor can we be sure that out of the gospel song there might not some day grow some religious music that is worthy; but it has not yet plainly appeared. Until then, minister and choir-master should see that gospel songs do not invade the sphere of worship. In the sanctuary, gospel songs substitute the lower for the higher values in worship.

XI

PROCESSIONAL AND RECESSIONAL

Once the processional and the recessional belonged peculiarly to liturgical churches. Now they are becoming increasingly common throughout Protestantism. There are two definite values in the practice, one practical and the other psychological. The processional solves the problem of getting the choir into its place without awkwardness. Any entrance of the choir is sure to attract attention. If it happens during the prelude, it breaks into what should be an undisturbed period of meditation. But if a processional is used, the entrance becomes part of the worship itself, and not an interference with it.

When and Why?

In the non-liturgical church the processional and the recessional are not religious processions, since they have been given no symbolic meaning. They furnish an orderly method by which minister and choir may move from one place to another. They may be used, therefore, as much or as little as a church pleases. They are regular routines in some churches, and in others are reserved for festival occasions.

There are situations in which the processional and recessional are not appropriate. There is no good reason why a choir should proceed in formation to a rear balcony. Likewise it is questionable planning to have a choir move down the main aisle, then disappear into stairways in the front of the church, only to reappear in an elevated choir loft. The movement down the aisle has become a parade rather than a procession. Ill-conceived also is a processional made up of a solo quartet and minister. Five people can scarcely form a procession, and may appear slightly ridiculous trying to do so. In all of these situations the singers and minister should make their entrance as unobtrusively as possible, without ceremony.

Under what circumstances, then, are the processional and recessional desirable? The general answer may be that in all situations where the choir must enter and remain in full view of the congregation, the processional and recessional may provide an altogether fitting beginning and ending to worship. This is particularly true where the choir loft cannot be easily entered except through the congregation. It is equally true of every church containing a divided chancel, which almost seems to require this treatment.

To make our picture sharper, let us look briefly at the beginning of a typical church service without the processional. The organist enters and starts his prelude. Sometime later the choir members enter one at a time. Whether or not it is planned that they sit at the same time, it never quite happens. Some have to turn and remove hymnals from chairs before they sit. Then follows arranging of the music, and the scrutinizing of the congregation. Later the minister enters by another door. After Bible and notes are arranged on the pulpit, he also sits. Then there is another wait for the end of the prelude. No matter how the service begins, when it does begin there is an air of casualness about it that belies the high purpose it is meant to serve.

Let the same service in the same church begin with a processional and the feeling is different. The organ prelude serves no other purpose than that of preparing the minds and spirits of the faithful for what is to follow. There is no noise or movement at the front of the church. Then, by an act as definite and dramatic as the opening of the curtain on a stage, the first step of corporate worship takes place, as hearts and voices are joined at once in praise. It is effective and moving.

Where?

Speaking of processional and recessional hymns and their performance, Dr. Sperry writes, "To be fully real, however, they presuppose an actual point of departure and an actual point of arrival, and the line of march should be the shortest way between these two points."[1] Otherwise, he says, they become parades, which are not religiously impressive. Since Dr. Sperry's stated purpose is to achieve reality in worship, we are justified in supposing that here he is seeking to avoid pomposity and sham in our devotional practices. Indeed, here is a danger which should not be overlooked.

I once attended a very beautiful church with a long nave. Its shape was cruciform, with the choir room opening on one of the transepts. Yet the processional and recessional began and ended in the narthex, and covered the full length of the nave. It was, of course, common knowledge that the choir in the performance of its regular tasks, moving from robing room through the basement to the narthex to the chancel to the narthex through the basement to the robing room, traveled approximately four city blocks each Sunday within the church. Are we to suppose that the choir or the congregation acquired virtue by all this unnecessary travel? Or would the processional and recessional have been just as effective, and less ostentatious, had the choir moved from the transept into the chancel and back again directly? Is not the long-distance processional the parade that Sperry was speaking of?

It may be argued that at the end of the service the choir should escort the minister to the narthex, where he will stand to greet his parishioners. Without being drawn into the argument about whether or not this is the proper position for the minister at the end of the service, may we ask whether or not he requires such an escort from pulpit to narthex?

There is, in short, a fine line to be drawn between those religious acts which seem to be direct, sincere expressions of devotion, and those which seem to be pretentious and pompous. There are undoubtedly many places where this line can be drawn. Just where it is placed is ultimately not important. It is important that we give thought to its placing.

How?

There are churches in which it is planned that the processional and recessional hymns shall be done entirely by the choir, others in which they are partially choral and partially done with the congregation, and those in which the choir and congregation join throughout. Unfortunately, there are also those churches in which these hymns have become entirely choral merely because the congregation does not participate! Which way is best? The weight of logic is entirely on the side of full participation of congregation with choir throughout.

The compelling reason for this is the need of as complete sharing as possible of the congregation in active worship. At the center of Luther's thinking was the involving of the people in worship, and much of the effort of Protestantism since his day has been directed toward increasing that involvement. Today the most typical as well as the most satisfying act by which the congregation may join in worship is in hymn singing. If the processional and recessional, which *are* hymns, are removed in whole or in part from contact with the congregation, we have thereby impoverished our worship.

Two occasional practices should be mentioned here: One is to reserve to the choir the singing of the first stanza of the processional hymn, with the congregation joining on the second. The other is for the members of the congregation to cease singing on the recessional the moment the choir has passed on its way to the narthex. Both practices should be condemned, for the reason given above. But another valid reason for avoiding such "tricks" is that they may throw into embarrassed relief the stranger worshiping within the congregation. If he finds himself singing when everyone around him is silent, this awkward situation may destroy his worship, as well as keep him from returning to the same church again.

The processional and recessional should be planned, then, in such a way as to make congregational participation as easy and complete as possible. It is first necessary that the congregation be standing in preparation for singing by the end of the organ announcement. Since neither choir nor minister is in position to present a signal for rising, it is desirable to have in the congregation a number of bellwethers. These people, seated mostly toward the front of the sanctuary, will assume the responsibility of standing first; the rest of the congregation will follow.

The moment the organist begins his announcement of the processional hymn, the choir should begin its movement. By the end of this announcement all, or nearly all, of the choir members should be inside the sanctuary. At the time singing is begun, the choir will be in position to lead it vigorously. The congregation, feeling this support, should more readily join in the singing.

For the recessional hymn the opposite should apply. If the time required for the choir's leaving is less than that needed to sing the whole hymn, the choir should remain in its position for part of the hymn, beginning its movement with not much more than ample time left to get it out of the sanctuary by the end of the hymn. In this way the congregation will have the support of the choir for a longer period than otherwise. Of course, the same result may be achieved by omitting part of the recessional hymn, but this would require difficult advance planning. A larger or smaller choir than expected on a given Sunday could upset the advance timing.

Several basic suggestions may be offered here.

1. The correct space between pairs is about an arm's length. Perhaps this is more easily estimated as the distance between one pew and the next.

2. The distance between each partner in the line should be—within limits—as great as the width of the aisle or passage will permit. The appearance of the choir in movement should be of two separate files, rather than that of couples. Disparate height, length of step, and amount of sway will be less in evidence if the members march somewhat separated.

3. The leaders should keep the speed of advance very deliberate. If steps or turns have to be passed, the pace should be slow enough to prevent the end of the line from having to hurry to keep pace.

4. All processional and recessional hymns should be done *in unison*. As the choir passes through or near the congregation, there should not be the confusion of various vocal parts passing the people in succession.

To Walk or to March?

There is still a disagreement, particularly in this country, about whether the choir should keep step with the music of processional and recessional, or merely walk at a slow pace during both. There are many people, mostly men, who feel that keeping step is orderly and beautiful, and failure to keep step is ragged and chaotic. I have even heard a minister say that he finds beauty in the swaying of a choir from side to side as it tries to move at a slow regular cadence down the aisle. But I think it may be demonstrated that those who prefer walking to marching have all the best of the argument. Even if we ignore the telling point that keeping step is a military device that has no place in church, there are other valid reasons why it should not be done.

The most significant argument against marching is that all the hymns so used must be in march rhythm. This not only seriously narrows the number of hymns available, but also fixes the mood in which every service must both begin and end. There are numbers of hymns altogether suitable for the opening of service that must forever be banned because their rhythm is triple. Without searching far, we come upon such hymns as "O worship the King," whether it be sung to Lyons or Hanover, "Praise ye the Lord, the Almighty" (Lobe den Herren), and "Come, Thou Almighty King" (Trinity), none of which can be used. Then there are other hymns in the proper rhythm which, if played at the proper speed, just will not go with marching feet: one step to each beat is too fast, and one step to each two beats is too slow. Such hymns are "A mighty Fortress" (Ein' feste Burg) and "Ancient of Days." Others like them are easily found.

If the use of march rhythm presents a severe limitation on the choice of processional hymns, its imposition is worse for the recessional. Whether it grows directly out of the sermon, or follows a closing period of dedication, the vigorous recessional must be often incongruous with the motive of the end of the service.

Where minister and choirmaster have no rhythmic limitations placed on their choice of processional and recessional, great possibilities for enhancing the beauty and significance of worship are opened. For instance, in a large church giving a Lenten performance of a portion of the Bach *St. Matthew Passion*, the processional hymn, during which the choir entered quietly, was the Bach *Passion Chorale*, "O sacred Head, now wounded." One may search the hymnal without finding another hymn that could as fitly prepare the worshipers for what was to follow. Could any "marching" hymn have served the purpose at all?

This limitation on the hymn literature available for the purpose is not the only argument against the marching processional and recessional. It is also unnecessarily noisy. Unless the choir's movements are cushioned by rubber heels on thick carpet, the striking of those twenty to forty heels simultaneously on the floor during marching will make itself heard, and to no good purpose. I recall a conspicuous example of this in the performance of a choir, large and well trained, which entered the sanctuary before an oratorio performance singing "Onward, Christian soldiers." Its members took exactly three steps between the last note of one stanza and the first note of the next. As they reached the first refrain, this is how it sounded, rhythm-wise:

"On – ward, Chris – tian sol   –   diers,

March – ing as   to   war,"   CLUMP!

"With the cross of Je   –   sus

Go – ing on be – fore."   CLUMP!

CLUMP!   CLUMP!

"Like   a   might – y ar   –   my

Moves the Church of God;"   CLUMP!

"Broth – ers, we   are   tread   –   ing

Where the saints have trod."   CLUMP! . . . .

The choir's entrance, which should have been impressive, was merely disconcerting. However the saints may have trod, they surely did not tread in this manner.

Other difficulties come from the pure mechanics of the process. It is not easy to put words and music together, to maintain a uniform distance from the person before you and the one beside you, and to measure both the speed and the length of your step. It *can* be done with practice, but a fine organist I once knew added another handicap: he was quite insistent that the marching be very precise, yet he played processional and recessional so unrhythmically that it was impossible for the choir both to sing well and to march well at the same time.

Finally, there is no justification in religious tradition for the marched religious procession. Whether we trace the custom to Old Testament beginnings, or seek its roots in the Church of some 1500 years ago, we do not find the military manner a part of it. Nor should it enter the sanctuary now.

It is probable that the processional serves a more vital purpose in worship than does the recessional. As some feel the final hymn superfluous, so is the recessional. Some churches recognize this by using the one and omitting the other. That this is not done more often is perhaps because the two together seem to furnish an appropriate frame for the service. The one seems to call for the other.

As we end here the discussion of hymn singing, it should be clear that the attempt has not been to find one logical answer to each question, since no one answer may be generally applied. Perhaps all we can do is to set the direction toward which we should travel to seek the answers. Perhaps it is more important that we seek the answers than that we find them.

XII

CONGREGATIONAL SERVICE MUSIC

The Gloria Patri

Henry Sloane Coffin's discussion of the *Gloria Patri* can scarcely be improved upon:

> In the second and third centuries, when controversies arose in the Church as to whether the God of the Old Testament is the God manifest in Christ, and whether his self-revelation as Father, Son, and Spirit is continuous with his self-unveiling to Israel, it became customary to affirm the identity of the God of the Old with the God of the New Covenant by concluding the chanting or reading of a psalm or psalms with the Gloria Patri:
>
> "Glory be to the Father, and to the Son, and to the Holy Ghost;
>
> As it was in the beginning, is now, and ever shall be, world without end. Amen."
>
> This ancient canticle brings a selection from the Psalter to an appropriate climax. In view of the origin of the Gloria Patri, and its long historical association with the psalms, it is vandalism to tear it from its proper context and attach it to something else in the service.[1]

The Doxology

Although the word "Doxology" properly refers to a number of songs of praise, including the "Gloria in Excelsis" and the "Gloria Patri," to most Protestants it means only one thing: "Praise God from whom all blessings flow," sung to OLD HUNDREDTH.

The origin of the words is well known. They were written by the English bishop, Thomas Ken, sometime near 1670, to form the last stanza of three different hymns, a Morning Hymn, an Evening Hymn, and a Midnight Hymn. They are actually an ascription of praise. Removing them, as we have done, from their context, we have remaining a call to worship. In many churches, particularly those that do not use a processional, they signal appropriately the beginning of worship. There can be no question as to their fitness for this position in the service.

Because of the one clause, "from whom all blessings flow," the Doxology has acquired other surprising positions and functions in the order of worship. Some churches place it at the end of the service. The reason for this is a little hard to understand, unless some worshipers feel that the service should end on the same note of praise with which it began. However, it is a dubious practice if for no other reason than that it offers the inescapable implication that the people are praising God for the end of the service!

More attention should be given to the frequent position the Doxology has achieved in many churches at the end of the offertory. The argument for this design goes somewhat as follows: the giving of our offering should be the highest point in our worship, the one toward which the whole service moves. As we give our gifts, we are deeply aware of the manifold gifts God has given us. In expression of our gratitude, we rise and sing, "Praise God *from whom all blessings flow.*"

Let us freely agree that the offertory should mark a high point in our worship. It follows *not at all* that the highest expression or motivation of our giving should be in terms of gratitude. It should be definitely more than that. The gifts we give should be symbolic self-offering, with which should go self-dedication. It may be argued that this is what we *imply* in our use of the Doxology. However, the words themselves bear no such implication, nor do they even hint it. In fact, the Doxology is not even addressed to God!

If we have been using the Doxology after the offering because we can find nothing more suitable, we should seek further. But more appropriate responses for this purpose are available, if we choose to use them. At least we should not continue to use the

Doxology in a place it fills so imperfectly. Let us repeat: the Doxology is a call to worship.

The Offertory Response

If not the Doxology, then what response should follow the offering? Perhaps the answer to this question is not important so long as the offertory continues to occupy the lowly state to which it has fallen in many of our churches. It was once a significant act related to the Lord's Supper. This is the way Abba describes it:

> *The Offertory,* in which the people's gifts and more especially the elements of bread and wine are presented at the Lord's Table, corresponds to our Lord's first act: "He took bread." No other part of the Supper has been subject to more change. It was originally the solemn presentation of the people's free-will offerings, not of money but in kind—the fruits of the earth, the symbols of their toil and God's blessing—as a token of the consecration of themselves and all their possessions to the service of God.[2]

This once high experience in worship has been permitted in most of our churches to become little more than an absent-minded one during which the means for running the church are extracted from us. We attend to it only during that anxious moment when we have to pass the plate on. Otherwise we let our minds be occupied by whatever thoughts wander into them. Lest we be bored during this period, some solo or anthem is provided for our entertainment. Then the preacher "prays over the plates" and that is that. Perhaps he says the appropriate words at that time, but we cannot be sure.

Some churches have tried to improve this by having the choir provide an offertory response. Certainly this is an improvement, since the choir speaks for the congregation. Yet if this is to be the high point of symbolic self-offering it should be, does it not call for the active participation of the whole congregation?

A congregational response should be used here. As the offering is brought to the Table and presented, the congregation should stand. As the offering is placed on the Table, the congregation should express, in words sung or spoken, its own affirmation of the act of self-offering. (No thought need be given to those churches whose ushers merely carry the offering out and never "present" it; they do not receive an offering, but merely "take up the collection.")

The problem is to find the response that expresses just that idea of self-offering. The familiar Beethoven setting of "All things come of Thee, O Lord" does not express the idea perfectly, and it has, moreover, been sung so badly by so many choirs and congregations for so many years that it can scarcely do. The Bishop How poem is better, and comes close to expressing the full idea:

> "We give Thee but Thine own,
> Whate'er the gift may be:
> All that we have is Thine alone,
> A trust, O Lord, from Thee."

Another approach is that taken from the Lutheran service, and reproduced in some hymnals, a chant not too difficult to sing, from Psalm 51:

> "The sacrifices of God are a broken spirit.
> A broken and a contrite heart, O God,
> Thou wilt not despise."

While any or all of these suggested responses may lie closer to the true meaning of the offertory than does the Doxology, perhaps some seekers will still not find them entirely satisfactory. Should this be true, it may be necessary to leave the realm of music and use a unison prayer, such as this:

> Let us pray.
> Almighty God, from whom cometh down every good gift and every perfect gift; accept, we beseech Thee, the offerings which Thy people here present to Thee with willing and thankful hearts; and grant us so to consecrate ourselves to Thy service here, that we may glorify Thee hereafter in Thy heavenly kingdom. . . . . AMEN.[3]

or this:

> O Lord our God, send down upon us Thy Holy Spirit, we beseech Thee, to cleanse our hearts, to hallow our gifts, and to perfect the offering of ourselves to Thee; through Jesus Christ our Lord. AMEN.[4]

At this point we should remember that some leaders believe that the offertory should be placed at the end of the service. If the presentation of our gifts can really be made an act of self-giving and dedication, that is a good enough reason to make it our closing act at each service of worship.

The Benediction Response

The church that normally uses neither a closing hymn nor a recessional may find that a congregational response following the benediction adds a lasting and valuable meaning not covered by the pastoral benediction. Such a response should not be, of course, a repetition of the idea of the pastoral benediction. But an effective one for this position is, for instance, the second stanza of the Ellerton hymn, "Saviour, again to Thy dear name," usually sung to ELLERS:

> "Grant us Thy peace upon our homeward way;
> With Thee began, with Thee shall end the day:
> Guard Thou the lips from sin, the hearts from shame,
> That in this house have called upon Thy name."

XIII

THE ANTHEM

The anthem as we know it has grown out of a practice of the Church of England which, at a certain point in Morning and Evening Prayer, called for a number by choir or soloist. As often as not a hymn was used in this spot instead of the more elaborate anthem. Historically, then, we may say that the anthem has been interchangeable with a hymn.

We are fairly safe in saying that originally the anthem in the Anglican Church was an "added feature." To a degree, that is what it has remained ever since. All other items of our order of worship form parts of a pattern. Each part should fit neatly into the rhythm of worship. But into this otherwise ordered scheme is dropped this number by the choir, which sometimes seems to be as inappropriate in its place as the announcement of the coming rummage sale would be right after the pastoral prayer.

This difficulty arises because of the anthem's very versatility. In spite of the curious tendency among some ministers to speak of all singing in church as "praise," the anthem is not predominantly praise. Neither is it thanksgiving, confession, assurance, petition, consecration, or any other one thing. It is none of these because, at some time or other, it is all of them. Like a hymn, it may express any shade of religious meaning.

Yet in most of our churches where one anthem only is sung each Sunday, it is supposed to occupy one fixed position in the order. It may be after the New Testament lesson, after the pastoral prayer, or after the offertory. But wherever its place is, there it is supposed to remain. The careful choirmaster, however, would not want his choir always to be singing praise anthems, prayer anthems, or any other one type. Yet if he seeks any variety in theme, part of what his choir sings will be inappropriate in this fixed position on a given Sunday. A setting of the Charles Wesley hymn, "Jesus, the weary wanderer's Rest," would sound emotionally extravagant early in the service. On the other hand, the César Franck *One Hundred Fiftieth Psalm* would sound pompous after the offertory.

The solution of this problem, mentioned earlier, is quite simple. The position of the anthem, like the second hymn, should be movable. The weekly conference between minister and choirmaster should fix the position of both at points where their impact on worship will be the greatest. For this Sunday they may decide together to place the *One Hundred Fiftieth Psalm* early in the service, immediately following the prayer of adoration. The anthem for next Sunday may be at its best after the pastoral prayer. "Jesus, the weary wanderer's Rest" the minister may place after the sermon, using the anthem as the point toward which he will work.

The anthem, then, should not be an "added feature." Like the tugboat that is present to help berth the ocean liner, it should be there always to exert its pressure where it will do the most good. Its place should be chosen with care, and there should be no hesitation in moving it to that place. An anthem wrongly placed confuses and dissipates the worship near where it is offered. An anthem rightly placed fits into, and becomes a part of, the rhythm of worship, enhancing and intensifying that portion to which it belongs.

The Second Anthem?

If one anthem is good, are not two anthems better? Many churches apparently think so. Back in the days of the solo quartet it was the custom for the quartet to sing an anthem earlier in the service, and then the soloists would take turns singing during the offering, with sometimes a duet for variety. This gave the ultimate in diversity from four voices, and overworked nobody. Of course, the solo was frequently unsuitable for its position, and did not prepare the congregation for the sermon to follow, but nobody seemed to care.

Although the chorus choir is replacing the quartet, the same offertory custom has persisted in some churches. But as religious writers have assailed the use of soloists in church, and the emphasis has swung toward choral performance, the soloist is giving way to a new phenomenon, the *offertory anthem*. I do not mean an anthem sung after the offering has been taken and presented, but rather one sung *during* the taking of the offering. This is not the usual device of the smaller church. It is rather to be found in the larger city churches, and in a rather generous portion of them.

I may only surmise the reasons for the emergence of this practice. It is apparent first that these churches are not concerned with the high spiritual significance of the offertory. It seems just the usual and accepted way to collect the money by which the work of the church is carried on. If it takes five minutes to do the job, it is up to the church to fill those five minutes as pleasantly as possible. The organist could, of course, play during this period, but other churches are using an offertory anthem each Sunday, and this church should not do less. Besides, we are paying enough for our church music to get this second anthem, so we should certainly get it.

Whether or not this is a fair representation of the thinking of these churches on this subject, I cannot say. Perhaps they have done very little thinking on the subject, and have merely adopted a practice because others were doing it. One writer has described our offertory as an "interlude" in the service. If that is all it is, its continuance cannot be justified. A sixty-minute service does not require it. Let us just omit the interlude, and let the ushers "wait on" the congregation with the plates at all exits after the service has ended.

But the offertory is and must be more than an interlude. From the days of the early Christian Church, it has been a significant part of the Lord's Supper, and remains so in the Roman Catholic Mass to this day. As has been pointed out earlier, it was the occasion for the presentation of free-will offerings in kind, rather than in money, by the people as a token of their consecration of themselves and all their possessions in the service of God. But when money replaced these offerings in kind, something was lost that has never been regained. If it has become no more than the negligent dropping of an envelope into a carved plate, something needs to be done to restore its rich symbolic meaning. But what can be done?

First we need to divest the offertory period of all unnecessary distractions. Certainly there should be neither anthem nor solo during it. Dr. Archibald Davison and others would not even permit any organ music. Then whatever prayers or statements are made before and whatever prayers or responses are offered after the taking of the offering, they should direct our thinking toward that more important giving, of which the gift on the plate is merely the symbol. Various of our denominational books on ordered worship give help in this direction.

Where, then, should we place the second anthem? We should place it back in its folder to be used another Sunday. One well-placed anthem, plus several choir responses, is sufficient choral music for one service of worship. To add more is to invite the entrance of an entertainment factor which should have no place in worship.

Some Criteria for Choir Music

Very little will be said here concerning the criteria for good anthems. For readers who would like to know more than is offered here, Dr. Archibald Davison's recent book[1] will prove stimulating. For the rest, here is a summary of general ideas:

Obviously the first consideration in the choice of anthems is the *words*. Are they appropriate to the worship situation? In general, those that have proved their worth throughout the years are more to be trusted. Those taken from the Bible, from a standard hymnal, or from *The Book of Common Prayer* are the established sources. Other words found acceptable should have literary merit, dignity, and intelligibility. They should not be too sentimental on the one hand, or too theologically involved on the other.

It is a truism to suggest that the *music* of anthems should be sacred. Yet it would be difficult within the next hundred pages to define the word "sacred" accurately. Perhaps it would do just as well to suggest a too simple rule of thumb: Music may be sacred or other-worldly if it does not suggest in its style or content the experiences or moods of the secular world. Is this too nebulous? If it is, it at least enables us to ban completely the use of any secular music with sacred words. No matter how well the words seem to fit the music, no Chopin "Nocturne," no quartette from a Verdi opera, no movement from a Beethoven symphony, should ever find their way into church hidden under the clothing of sacred words. Harder to discover by the musical amateur are those melodies which turn out to be sentimental tunes, vigorous march rhythms, or any other music that reminds one of something outside of church. None of this is sacred, no matter what name it bears.

Also to be avoided in church is music which is pompous, too complex, too showy. On the other hand, no choir should be permitted to sing dull music, no matter how above reproach are the words.

Is this not another place where consultation between pastor and choirmaster may be productive? The minister tends to look at the words first, and the choirmaster first examines the music. Then let them compare notes. If the anthem does not meet the standards of both minister and choirmaster, let it be put aside.

XIV

THE CHORAL RESPONSE

Not long ago I attended a worship service in a large city church. It was a beautiful service. There was a quiet reverence throughout. I was aware of a feeling of expectancy on the part of both minister and congregation, as though all were waiting, not for the minister to speak but for the Lord to speak in and through every act of worship. The whole experience was rewarding. Not until after the benediction was over and I had left the church did I realize that not a single choral response had been sung throughout the service.

Choral responses are so generally accepted as a regular part of Protestant worship that their absence from a service in which they would normally appear becomes noteworthy. Yet I cannot forget services in country churches where, with no choir and a poor piano, the worship brought a sense of God's presence in reality and power that sometimes seems to be weak in churches with ample musical resources. As we have examined other musical practices in our churches, it would seem wise to seek to discover the intrinsic value of the choral response, and what we expect it to achieve.

Let us start with S. Arthur Devan's statement that "music stimulates and reinforces the ideas and emotions with which it is associated."[1] This idea is too generally accepted to require supporting evidence. But if some music in worship is good, much music is not necessarily better. Devan expresses this well when he suggests that "music is a powerful auxiliary, but a bad master." Protestantism in general accepts a limitation beyond which we should not go. There is no widespread effort to institute within our fellowship what would correspond to the Roman Catholic High Mass. (We do not, of course, include in this discussion High Church Episcopalianism, which is not characteristically Protestant.)

Yet there are Protestant churches which are tempted in this direction. There is, for instance, the "free" church whose minister some years ago developed a liturgical service made up of beautiful and effective dialogue between minister and choir, with an occasional unison prayer or litany thrown in. Its congregation was quiet and attentive, but seemed rather like an audience, participating in the service little more than the Roman Catholic does as he observes the unfolding of the drama of the Mass. The service tended to become, as one minister put it, "worshiping the order of worship."

Each one of us has attached himself to a Christian fellowship, whose worship is determined by its history, its basic convictions, and the influences currently brought to bear upon it. Worship should be a combination of fixed tradition and change, with neither one being supreme. Its broad framework we may not easily alter, but within this framework we should constantly study to improve its content.

Worship is a blend of acts communal and individual, of words said and words sung, of phrases formal and extempore, of sound and silence. It should be a careful division of functions among minister, congregation, choir, and organist. The proper choice and assignment of these functions and the balance between them form the foundation for satisfying worship.

What words are better sung than spoken? What belongs appropriately to minister, to choir, to congregation? Let us examine a typical order of worship, admitting that it is highly variable among different churches:

Prelude
Call to Worship (1)
Prayer of Adoration (2)
Prayer of Confession
Assurance of Pardon
Old Testament Lesson (Responsive Reading)
Gloria Patri
New Testament Lesson

Response to Scripture (3)
Hymn
Creed (4)
Call to Prayer (5)
Prayers of Thanksgiving, Supplication, Intercession, and Communion
Response to Prayer (6) or Lord's Prayer (7)
Offertory (8)
Response to Offertory (9)
Anthem
Sermon
Hymn
Closing Prayer and Benediction (10)
Benediction Response (11)

We leave without comment those items on the order which are plainly assigned. We shall discuss only the eleven numbered items, all of which at some time or other have been done by the choir. It should be understood that in no one service would the choir do *all* of them. In fact, three or four responses in a service are ample. It is desirable that these several responses be spread throughout the order, and not bunched together. The rhythm of the service will be more smooth if musical items are not placed side by side. Probably the choir should not perform two responses in connection with one act of worship, such as singing both a call and a response to prayer. It should also be obvious that congregational participation should be spread in the same manner.

1. If the call to worship is to be sung, there is nothing more appropriate than the Doxology. It is also proper that the choir, which shares with the minister the leading of the congregation in worship, should call the congregation to that worship. The words "choral introit" as applied to the opening sentence have caused some confusion, since they have been used indiscriminately to denote both the call to worship and the following introductory prayer. The two are quite different. One is addressed to the congregation, and is an invitation, expressed or implied. The other is addressed to God. The two acts should be clearly differentiated.

2. The prayer of adoration is a better way of describing what has been called the invocation. To invoke God's presence in the traditional sense is to imply that He is absent from His house

until we send for Him. But in a prayer of adoration we humble ourselves in the presence of Him who is always there waiting for us to recognize Him. From the standpoint of rhythm in worship, items (1) and (2) should not both be choral, or even musical. If choir or congregation sings the call to worship, the minister should deliver the prayer of adoration. If the service has begun with, say, a processional hymn, the minister may well deliver the call to worship and the choir follow with a choral prayer of adoration. It would be well to point out here that there are authorities on worship who feel that the opening prayer, like the benediction, should be done by the minister only; for those the prayer of adoration would be said and never sung.

3. A response to Scripture can be a meaningful act of worship as the choir, speaking for the congregation, sings some such sentence as

> "Teach me, O Lord, the way of Thy statutes, and I will keep it unto the end."

or

> "Thy Word is a lamp unto my feet, and a light unto my pathway."

This becomes the identification of each worshiper with that which has been read.

4. The use of the Creed as a chant is practiced in some churches, but this is not a widespread Protestant practice in this country. If a creed is to be used, there is good reason to have it affirmed positively by the whole congregation. To assign it to the choir is to weaken it.

5. "The Lord is nigh unto them that call upon Him in truth" is the type of sentence that may be sung by the choir before the pastoral prayer. Responses normally used after the prayer also are appropriate here, although they serve a slightly different function. In general, a call to prayer loses some of its importance in those churches in which there is a tendency to reduce the relative importance of the pastoral prayer. More and more the whole service is being regarded as a succession of prayers—of adoration, confession, thanksgiving, intercession, and so on—rather than an

order in which there is one large prayer. Such a concept makes less significant the preparation for one prayer which may be different only because it is longer. But in churches which still use *the* pastoral prayer, the choral preparation for it is less effective only because the best preparation for prayer at this point is complete silence.

6. The response to prayer continues to have general use and acceptance. It varies from an "Amen" response to an elaborate extension of the prayer. Especially helpful are those which seek to add a thought and a sense of personal involvement to what has gone before. Though it has been often used, "May the words of my mouth" remains effective for this place. In case the Lord's Prayer is being recited at the end of the pastoral prayer, any choral response thereafter would be superfluous.

7. In some churches the choir chants the Lord's Prayer following the pastoral prayer. Although this practice has won favor in some places, it is still somewhat questionable. The choir has a dual role: it leads the congregation in worship, and it sometimes speaks for the congregation. In the anthem and in the responses it clearly speaks for the congregation in a way the congregation cannot easily speak for itself. But when an act of worship that the congregation could well perform for itself is taken from it and given to the choir, the change is hard to justify. I have heard the Lord's Prayer chanted beautifully by a fine choir. It was for me a fine musical experience, but was I praying the prayer or listening to the music? If it was for others as it was for me more an aesthetic experience than a religious one, it has no place in worship. Since the Lord's Prayer was given as a model for the people, it should be done by the people. If its repetition by the people has become perfunctory, it should be removed from the order of worship for a season.

8. The offertory should be the occasion of self-giving through the symbolic gift that is offered at the Lord's Table. It should be a period of meditation, unbroken by any distractions. If any music at all is heard during this period, it should be organ music of unobtrusive character. Any vocal music is clearly inappropriate. An anthem may, however, *follow* the presentation of the gifts.

9. If the offertory is to be a high point of worship, the congregation needs to be involved in a way beyond the mechanical act of giving. There should be a response to the offertory, and it should be something involving the whole congregation; a choral response is scarcely adequate.

10. The benediction belongs exclusively to the minister, and under no circumstances should the choir assume this task.

11. Unless the congregation itself responds to the benediction, the choir's best contribution here is an "Amen" response. Above all, the choir should not offer any duplication of the benediction, such as the John Newton words, "May the grace of Christ our Saviour," or anything as formal as the "Nunc Dimittis." The "Amens" are clearly sufficient.

While it is important that the choir in no way duplicate or displace that which is the minister's, it is also important that the minister give thought to refraining from infringing on that which has been committed to choir or to congregation. Just as the minister should avoid reading aloud the "congregational" portion of the responsive reading, so he should also not trespass on that which is the choir's. I have in mind a certain minister who has a great and fine choir behind him, but who sings a response to his own pastoral prayer, accompanied by the choir's humming! That minister not only lacks humility, but also a proper appreciation of the place of other believers in the house of the Lord. The same minister who insists on ordering, by gesture or command, every act of worship in his church is likely to be the one who insists on saying "Amen" after every prayer, whether or not a choir response follows. He also lacks humility.

The "Ordinary" and the "Proper" Items in Worship

Whether or not we so plan it, our orders of worship, like the Mass, are divided between the fixed or ordinary and the variable or proper items. The obviously fixed ones are such things as the Doxology, the Gloria Patri, the Apostles' Creed, the Lord's Prayer. The variable ones include the hymns, the Scripture lessons, the pastoral prayer. Are the order itself and the responses that go with it also fixed? In many of our churches they seem to be so. The minister arrives at an order that seems to agree with him, his congregation, and his choir. If it is good, why should it ever be changed? If comfort and ease are all we seek in worship, then we are right in resisting change. It seems wise, however, that once or twice a year at least some minor shift be made in the general order. Change will not necessarily bring improvement, but there can be little improvement without change. Perhaps the only difference will be the position of one hymn, or the omission of the Creed. Whether or not improvement in worship results, for a period the worshipers will be more alert, will follow the order with more intentness.

If an occasional change may do something to improve worship, it is more important applied specifically to choir responses. If a certain response goes well, and the people seem to like it, it is a temptation to continue to use it indefinitely. I recall a beautiful benediction response which had been sung by a fine choir for a number of years. Its words had been written by its pastor, its music by its choirmaster, and it was greatly loved by the congregation. On one Sunday a little old lady came to the choirmaster and asked him to lend her a copy of this response. When he, not a little pleased at her request, complied, she commented, "I have always loved this response so much I have wanted to find out just what the words are." The choirmaster, a very wise man, drew at least two morals from the incident.

The repetition of any response over a long period of time is deadly in church, both to worship and to choir efficiency. It breeds woolgathering, in choir and in congregation. Obviously, the choir's interest in any given number will languish when its performance has become automatic. The congregation also will cease to attend to anything it has heard too often.

In general, no response should be used beyond a certain fixed limit of, say, six consecutive weeks. It is therefore important that the choirmaster keep on hand a sufficient variety of responses covering each required category so that the supply will always seem to be fresh and unused. There is a fairly adequate reservoir of good responses for the choirmaster who keeps searching.

XV

ORGAN MUSIC

It would be generally agreed that the organ music heard in church should be sacred. But we are in difficulty the moment we attempt a precise definition of sacred music, since so much thinking and writing on the subject has been anything but precise. There is, for instance, the popular idea that the eighteenth-century style of Bach and Handel is the truest sacred style possible. As an example, we find Blackwood writing, in his excellent book on worship, "No secular music has ever surpassed the spiritual harmonies of Bach."[1] But musical scholars would largely agree that Bach's sacred and secular styles are virtually undistinguishable. A person who knows no German would be unable to tell his sacred from his secular cantatas. Likewise, we know that some of the themes used by Handel in his sacred works were used earlier by him in works that are far from sacred. But since we hear normally more of the sacred vocal works of Bach and Handel than we do of their secular, some of us have arrived at the belief that their style is essentially sacred.

In general, music, like people, develops a reputation by the company it keeps and the associations it forms, and this reputation can change. We have a good example of this at hand. Some years ago Mr. Edwin H. Lemare composed an organ piece called "Andantino in D-flat." Although it was tuneful, and had an easy, flowing rhythm, it was accepted by many organists as being sacred, and was often heard in church. Then the popular tunesmiths discovered it, dressed it in words, and surrounded it with luscious orchestration; its new name was "Moonlight and Roses." Although its original form is still clearly recognizable, it is now thoroughly secular, and may no longer appear in church. It may be argued by musical purists that the Lemare "Andantino" never was sacred in style, but the fact remains that by many of the musically unwary organists it was so accepted.

There is no doubt that today we are at the mercy of Tin Pan Alley. At any time someone in the business of making tunes popular may discover a great opportunity in something we now universally accept as sacred, and will ruin it for church use forever. In fact, a start has been made in this direction. Is it just a strange coincidence that the popular hit of some few years ago, "Yes, We Have No Bananas," begins with the same four chords melodically, harmonically, and rhythmically identical to those that start the Handel "Hallelujah Chorus"? I shudder to think of what would happen if someone in that business found possibilities in, say, "He was despised," from the *Messiah*. The only reason I dare to mention such a possibility here is that I am quite certain that no one in Tin Pan Alley will ever read this.

For those readers who would like to know more about the differences between sacred and secular music, the best present sources of information are Davison's two books on church music.[2] For the rest, the broad suggestion of association will have to do: a piece of music may be sacred if in its content and style there is no suggestion of the music of the world outside the church.

The great body of organ transcriptions is at once suspect. In the catalogues of music publishers, particularly in this country, there is a wide choice of arrangements for organ of keyboard pieces— from Bach's *Well-Tempered Clavichord* to the piano pieces of Debussy, classic Italian songs, operatic instrumental and vocal material, movements from symphonies and other symphonic material. These have been handy potboilers for music arrangers, and have helped keep music publishing profitable. But it must be remembered that every single organ transcription has first been something else, most belonging outside the church. Unless what it had been is utterly forgotten, it does not belong in church now.

But while the musical pots have been merrily boiling, worthy church organ literature has also been growing. The organist who is not too easily discouraged may find many good choral preludes

on well-known hymns, and many other pieces suitable for the
service of worship.

Writers have warned before—and the warning is worth repeating—that worship is not intended to teach the arts. Although the
organist, like the choirmaster, should not give much effort toward
trying to please the congregation, he still should not be completely
indifferent to its likes. Organists have been heard repeating a silly
adage: "When in doubt, play Bach." Bach is no more the solution
to the organist's problem than is any other composer. Variety in
organ music is as desirable as variety in diet. The purpose of the
organist is to make available music that helps to create a worship-
ful environment.

The Prelude

The first requirement of a prelude is that it *be* a prelude. The
preparation for this service which is dedicated to God needs to be
done with care and order. It will not be like a family picnic that
starts after everybody has arrived. It will be timed to end at the
appointed hour for the service. I am not sure that I would go as
far as those ministers who insist that their organists play eleven
notes on the chimes precisely on the hour. The people who are
in their seats do not need this information; those who are not
here will not be helped by chimes they do not hear. I have also
wondered what horrible thing would happen if the organist should
some day lose count and play either ten or twelve strokes!

The organist's task is to provide a bridge between the outside
world and the sanctuary. As the seeker becomes aware of the quiet
environment, and beholds the sacred symbols, he should be led by
the music into the world of the spirit. Unless it is based on a sacred
theme, it must be unfamiliar music. The organist must not permit
himself to play the normal "request." And his repertoire needs to
be broad enough so that he is not forced to repeat often; his
listeners should not follow his music as an act of memory.

How long should the prelude be? Ideally, it should be going on
during the time that the major part of the congregation is entering.
Therefore, ten minutes is better than five, and fifteen is better than
ten. Of course, if the organist must be at a pre-service rehearsal,

he cannot start the prelude until after that. It is desirable that he start as early as possible, in order that there be no break in the middle of what should be a period of quiet meditation.

Should the organ prelude always consist of quiet, meditative music? Certainly the period should be no occasion for any brilliant technical display on the part of the organist. On the other hand, there is no good reason why the mood should always be subdued. The power and majesty of God may speak effectively through a full organ, which should have its place now and then in the prelude. But the prelude should end quietly as a rule, since from this mood may more easily come the air of expectancy which should begin every service of worship.

The Offertory

If the offertory is to be considered a high point in divine worship, how can music help make it so? Dr. Archibald Davison believes that music can add nothing: the offering should be taken, he writes, in absolute silence. Others object that absolute silence is not easy to achieve. Our churches are not soundproofed from the world. During any quiet period the noise of a passing bus, a police siren, or just a child's cry on the street, can bring the world at once into the church. Even within the church, the very process of taking the offering can bring distractions; the dropping of silver into wooden or metal plates or just one usher's squeaking shoes may be sufficient. A little unintended sound against silence may seem quite emphatic. But if against these sounds outside and within the church, the organist can weave a fine fabric of ordered sound, at least the smaller distractions may disappear.

Reference has been made earlier to the suggestion of some writers that the offering may take on added significance if it is moved to the climactic end of the service.[3] We need not consider this further at this point since any change in the location of the offertory need not change what happens during it. Wherever it is placed, it should be a period of meditation on the theme of self giving. Whatever happens at this time should make meditation easy, and interfere with it not at all. A solo or anthem at this

ime is out of the question. If the organist does play during this
period, his playing should be soft, and formless and indefinite to
 degree. Such music as the Benoit *Elevations* is suitable for the
purpose. Above all, the organist should do nothing to call atten-
ion to himself unnecessarily.

The Postlude?

As the processional and recessional form an inner frame to the
order of worship, the prelude and postlude have formed the outer
one. Can we have the one without the other? Many churches
pparently feel that we cannot.

I can remember well the postludes I played as a young organist.
Certainly no more than one second after the minister had pro-
nounced his closing "Amen" I took off on a brilliant, loud piece
nown variously as Toccata, Marche Brilliante, Sortie, or just
Postlude in some key or other. The waves of greetings and other
onversation rose in the congregation, necessarily also loud because
otherwise the people could not hear each other above the organ.
Then, in order to make myself heard, I had to add a few stops.
Therefore the people in the church had to speak even louder.
n this manner the contest continued until I had reached the
nd of the piece. Then I withdrew and permitted the sociability
o continue unhampered. This is, I suspect, a fairly accurate de-
cription of the postlude as it is still delivered in many of our
hurches.

Perhaps throughout the years the postlude has acted as a safety
alve for the organist. He has had to play quietly during the
ervice, and has not heard his full organ even during the hymns.
The postlude is the only vehicle in which he can let himself go.
But in this release, he has also shattered the feeling of worship
hat should remain at the end of the service.

Increasingly, as we tend to call the place of worship the sanctuary,
here is an urge to treat it as a holy place from which all thought-
ess, casual acts are shut out. As the sanctuary is entered in silence
before worship, so should it be left in silence at the end. I do not
mean to say that there should be no opportunity offered for

Christian fellowship, but that fellowship should be at the prope time and place. Increasingly ministers are meeting those who wis to see them after church, not at the entrance to the church, nc at the front below the pulpit, but in a social parlor or othe suitable place removed from the sanctuary. The after-church Coffe Hour is a growing institution, particularly in the city church.

Not only should worshipers leave the sanctuary in silence, bu it should also be possible for those who so desire to leave *the churc* in silence. The church should make every allowance for individua differences. Let the person who wishes to greet his pastor an friends after church go to the room designated for this purpos Here the stranger should find himself a stranger no longer. Like wise the person who would like to leave the church quietly shoul find this possible. He should not be required to run the gauntle of greeters at the door; he should not be compelled to shake th minister's hand. He should be able to return to the world in silenc if that is his desire.

What has this to do with the organ postlude? Just this: Obv ously the traditional postlude makes a quiet ending to the servic impossible. It is a sharp signal that the service is over. So is a meditation. It reminds the worshiper at once of the world t which he is returning, and shoves him abruptly into it. If he wan to ponder the service, he must say to himself, "I must recall th later. I cannot do it now." But the opportunity may never retur

How then should worship end? After the sermon the closin service, perhaps including the offertory, should follow quietl Then comes the benediction, with the congregation seated. Afte whatever choral response follows, the congregation rises and move toward the exits, while the organist plays softly for a short tim

Then, like the chord that Sir Arthur Sullivan lost, the orga will tremble away into silence, so that few will even be aware c when the music actually stops. Whatever the mood is at the en of the service, it will continue unbroken. The silence will not er courage conversation. But it will not be an oppressive silence, sinc it grows directly out of the service of which it forms a part.

Let the organ postlude, then, be quietly dropped and forgotter

The Interludes

Besides the regular "voluntaries" the organist contributes a certain amount of what might be called incidental music. This varies in amount and character from short improvisations during the stated periods when late comers are seated to the almost continuous playing throughout the earlier parts of the service, common to some musical services. In some churches the organist may play an "Amen" response; in some others the organ serves as a guide to thinking as it sounds a hymn softly during a period otherwise silent.

If a little soft organ music is good, is much of it better? Should the organist be encouraged to fill every unoccupied interval with music? Does the use of an organ "background" heighten or dissipate the atmosphere of worship? What ultimately is the purpose of "background" music? These and other questions growing out of them need to be answered. The question of purpose should come first.

As the organ prelude serves as the bridge between the outside world and this world apart, and prepares the spirit of the seeker for the experiences to follow, so the incidental organ music within the service should help to maintain the atmosphere of worship. To serve this purpose best, it must not call attention to itself. If it does, it destroys what it seeks to strengthen. The organist must work out his task within this limitation.

First, the organist should "cover" those movements and sounds within the church that have no relationship to worship itself. The seating of late comers will seem less like the suspension of activity during a manifest interruption if the time is filled by quiet music. The return of the ushers to the rear of the church after the presentation of the offering should likewise be made easier.

A second task, similar to the first, is the organist's maintenance of movement between different parts of the service. If worship is to be beautiful, within its framework should be no abrupt changes of direction. There should also be no period in which nothing at all seems to happen. The smooth flow of the order may be dependent upon the skill of the organist in linking one step with the next. Let us suppose, for instance, that the first hymn of the service is followed by the Old Testament lesson, read responsively. A certain amount of time is required at the end of the hymn for the congregation to find its new location in the hymnal. Silence at this point would serve no purpose; the service has come to an apparent stop. But if the organist continues to play for a short time after the end of the hymn, the movement of the service continues, and the hymn is led directly into the following reading.

Such a musical bridge is particularly needed when two musical items occur consecutively in the service. If the response to prayer is followed by an anthem, or if the offertory is followed by the "sermon" hymn, the organist should not only modulate with care between any key changes that are involved, but should see to it that the two elements are smoothly linked together. If the organist does not improvise readily, he should carefully plan in advance the steps he expects to use to obtain continuity in the service.

The organist should seldom make a contribution beyond this point. Particularly subject to suspicion should be all efforts to draw from the organ meaning which is not appropriate to it. The organ "Amen" is one example. A minister's "Amen" is the formal closing of a prayer, while the congregation's is the affirmation of that prayer. If the choir sings it, the choir speaks for the congregation. But the organ can neither say nor sing "Amen." The organ therefore should not be put in the position of representing the congregation, and should not be called out of the background in which it properly belongs after the beginning of the service.

Particularly objectionable is the use of the organ during "silent" prayer. It is highly desirable that there be at least one period set aside during worship for the individual petitions of worshipers. This period may be, and often is, placed at or near the beginning of the pastoral prayer. Unaccountably in many of our churches the organist regularly breaks this silence. The pastor will call for a period of silent prayer. Promptly the organist will begin playing "My faith looks up to Thee" or "O Love that wilt not let me go," or some other prayer hymn. At the conclusion of one stanza of the hymn, the demands of "silence" having been met, the minister proceeds with his prayer in behalf of the people.

What is wrong with this procedure? First of all, there are many people who cannot be in the presence of music without listening to it. For such people it is difficult or impossible to maintain their concentration within themselves while music is going on. Even though they may desire to make their own prayers, they are drawn helplessly through "More love to Thee, O Christ," in spite of themselves, and their own petitions go unsaid.

In defense of this procedure, ministers have argued that many worshipers do not know how to pray for themselves, and would find themselves unoccupied during a period of complete silence. The music of a hymn, then, is offered to direct their thoughts. To such ministers it should be pointed out that perhaps worshipers do not know how to use silence because they are so unaccustomed to it. If Christians cannot pray in silence, we may be sure that they are lacking in a basic religious experience, and need to be taught. Let the minister teach them, first of all by the use of directed or "bidding" prayers. We certainly need to learn to pray no less than did Christ's disciples, and they sought Christ's help in the matter. The organist has less right to invade my thoughts during a period of silent prayer than does the person in the pew beside me who chooses to whisper to me at this time. The person who whispers to me may disturb me alone, while the organist breaks the meditation of the whole congregation!

One other thought needs to be added here. There are churches on busy highways or in other locations where outside noise is frequently a disturbing factor. In such churches it may be felt that the organist should add a background of soft music during a period where there would be complete silence in a different environment. The organ then becomes a shield between the worshipers and the outside world. Here, but here only, where a period of silent prayer might be interrupted by the noise of traffic, the organist may properly weave a soft sound arabesque about the sanctuary at this time. But he must use care not only that he plays very softly, but that what he plays be indefinite and entirely *without specific meaning;* no hymn or other recognizable music should be used.

The Ministry of Silence

A Protestant believes that he may speak directly to God, and that God may also speak directly to him. Because he believes he can hear God's voice more clearly within the sanctuary, he attends church. Yet in many of our worship services we do not give God a chance to speak! We sing to God and pray to Him, and the minister reads and talks about Him at some length. But when do we stop our singing and praying and preaching and give Him the opportunity to bless, strengthen, and guide us? I have never heard of a Protestant minister who claims that his own voice *is* the voice of God, yet many ministers so fill the service with their own words that God, if He speaks at all, *must* speak through them.

Man's experience has been, however, that God frequently speaks most clearly through silence. Many modern writers on worship have called attention to this. Evelyn Underhill, for instance, stresses the use of "corporate silence" and regrets that we have let this ancient custom go into comparative disuse.[4] George Walter Fiske blames the jazz age for our abhorrence of pause, our speeded-up tempo, which does not give the Lord a chance to speak.[5]

Yet strangely enough there is some confusion about just what silence is. Heimsath in his fine book devotes a chapter to the "voice of silence" and urges that there be more than one period of silence in each order of worship.[6] But he sees no reason not to use organ music throughout these periods. To him as to many others silence is merely the cessation of speaking. So organists have been encouraged to play through all periods not otherwise filled, no matter what significance these periods may have.

But *organ music is not silence!* Why should we think that it is? From childhood we have been taught that the proper attitude for prayer is the bowed head and closed eyes. Why do we close our eyes during prayer? Simply to shut out all those distractions of sight which would cloud our contemplation of God. But there is no polite way a person may shut out the distractions of sound.

When a period of silent prayer is called for, and music promptly invades first the ear and then the mind of the worshiper, that perfect focus of thought and feeling on God will be dissipated. If silence at this time is *real* silence, this period of prayer may be the most precious moment within the whole period of worship.

When, then, should the organist play, and when should he refrain from playing? It is hard to do more than state a general principle: let the organist play during those intervals in the service when no important act of worship is happening. But let the organist's silence intensify the significance of every significant act. Such acts may be the presentation of the offering, the movement of minister to table in preparation for the Lord's Supper, all ceremonies, and, of course, all periods of silent prayer.

XVI

THE SOLO

"It must be said that solos are in general undesirable in common worship, because they direct attention to the voice of the singer, and only occasionally utter congregational aspiration."[1] So writes Dr. Coffin, and he has ample support among writers on worship. Some would even go so far as to ban incidental solos in anthems, turning them over to a whole section. In fact, the solo and soloist in church have few apologists among religious writers. Reference has already been made to a remark once made in a lecture by Dr. Peter Lutkin that the professional quartet is a baneful medium for the glorification of four people. If this is true, how much more is the solo the occasion for the glorification of one singer! Yet from its nature it can scarcely be otherwise. Choral work is a co-operative enterprise, from which the individual need not emerge. The soloist, on the other hand, can scarcely avoid the center of the stage. The result is so often manifestly unfortunate that there is little left to recommend it.

Yet for a condemned practice in corporate worship the solo shows a remarkable vitality. It is a convenience the choirmaster is reluctant to sacrifice. On those "off" days after Christmas and Easter, and during the dog days of summer, there seem to be times when it is just too difficult to get an anthem ready. Here is another Sunday when nearly all the sopranos are out of town. What do we do under these circumstances? Why not just ask Mrs. A. to do a solo? Little or no practice is needed, and the requirements are met in a minimum sort of way. The solo is the salvation of the indolent choirmaster.

It would be unfair, however, to end the discussion here, as some writers have done, with a round condemnation of all solos in church. It is not hard for us to recall occasions when a solo has been at least a part of a rare religious experience. Perhaps by accident, or perhaps by design, a solo has prepared the way for an unforgettable sermon, or has provided the memorable climax to a spoken thought. Since we know these rewarding experiences have happened, should we not seek to recapture them and make them work for us again?

Let us agree, then, not to use the solo in a routine way, nor in an emergency way either. If the choir is short on ammunition for this Sunday, there does not *have* to be a "special" number! In many situations, blessed silence is to be preferred. Let us rather use the solo only in that situation in which it can uniquely serve the spoken word. It should be used rarely, since its frequent use would dull its effectiveness. It should be planned carefully in conference between minister and choirmaster. Only solos of tried merit and churchly character should have a place in this situation.

Some illustrations may make the effective use of solos clear. Some churches make much of a Maundy Thursday communion service. Coming as it does at a time when we think of the Crucifixion, this service should seek to bring worshipers closer to the events of the first Holy Week than would be possible at any other time of year. This sense of "being there" can be no better achieved than by the singing of the Negro spiritual, "Were you there when they crucified my Lord?" just before the words of institution. Of at least equal impact for the same use is the Handel aria, "He was despised."

For the close of the Easter service, churches would do well to consider the substitution of Handel's "I know that my Redeemer liveth" for the more commonly used Hallelujah Chorus. The latter has an Easter message only by implication and association, while the solo gets directly to the heart of the matter. It should not be sung, however, by anyone less than an adequate, effective soprano.

A number of "situation" solos can be readily suggested. The works of Mendelssohn offer several good examples. A minister may wish to preach on the power of God to sustain His servants against fear, defeat, and discouragement, and may use as his text the story of Elijah's flight from Jezebel, and his sojourn in the wilderness, where the angel ministered to him, as told in First Kings 19. The solo that Mendelssohn wrote in his *Elijah* to comment on this incident, "O rest in the Lord," may effectively begin or end the sermon on this text.

If the minister would preach on the power of God to intervene decisively in the lives of men, and would illustrate this by the story of the conversion of Paul, he may well introduce this sermon by an excerpt from Mendelssohn's *St. Paul*: the recitative "And he journeyed with companions toward Damascus," and the following aria, "But the Lord is mindful of His own." And we should not forget that other solo from Mendelssohn's *Elijah*: "If with all your hearts." It is a supremely beautiful expression of our yearning for God, and the sureness of our satisfaction if we continue to seek Him.

Solos suitable for the purpose indicated do not necessarily come from oratorios. There are others to be found for the seeking, several of which may be mentioned. The setting of the Ninety-first Psalm by James MacDermid could well introduce a sermon on God's protection of His own people. In a different vein is the powerful solo on that striking poem by Harry Lee, "My Master was so very poor," made by Francis Frank; it would set the mood well for a Lenten sermon on the mystery of Christ's humanity and divinity. To prepare the way for sermons on the parables, two solos by Beardsley Van de Water should be mentioned: "The Publican" dramatically contrasts the prayers of the Pharisee and the Publican; "The Penitent" tells the story of the Prodigal Son.

We should return for a moment to the statement made early in this chapter that solos used in the church service should be of churchly character. It is easy to overstep here. It is not unusual, for instance, for a singer to bring the Mozart "Alleluia" into the sanctuary. Granting that "Alleluia" is an ancient Hebrew religious formula, Mozart's vocalization demonstrates not so much Jehovah's praise as it does the skill of the singer. But why should not a sermon on world peace be introduced by "Why do the nations" from Handel's *Messiah*? No one will question its musical merit.

But its character is bombastic, and the pyrotechnical display necessary to its effective performance will overshadow whatever religious significance it has. The same may be said to a lesser degree of "O thou that tellest good tidings to Zion," also from the *Messiah*. All these belong in the concert hall rather than in church. Such a work as "It is enough. O Lord, now take away my life" from Mendelssohn's *Elijah* is too dramatic for the worship situation.

Two conditions must obtain to give the solo a valid place in worship: The first is that its performance must be vocally and musically adequate. A solo poorly sung just before the sermon will start the minister with a handicap he may not be able to overcome in the course of his message. Likewise an ineffective solo at the end of the sermon may utterly destroy what has gone before. The second condition is that the soloist sing with complete humility. If by his appearance or manner or projection of himself through his solo he calls attention to himself rather than to what he is singing, what he does may do more harm than good to the spirit of worship. Unless the minister finds that the solos used make an unquestionable contribution to the religious significance of his service, he should firmly shut the door to all solos in his church.

XVII

THE OCCASIONAL SERVICE

Communion

It is not our purpose to discuss the various rituals connected with the sacrament of the Lord's Supper. We are interested in that portion of the service concerning which church rules have little to say: What should happen during the actual distribution of the bread and wine? In the absence of definite instructions, various churches have largely chosen to add music. The materials are usually Communion hymns, hymns of the Cross, and those of personal commitment. Sometimes these hymns are shared by choir and organ, and sometimes the organ alone performs all the music. The tendency of recent years is to use the organ more and the choir less during the distribution of the elements. This has been the time-tested method of a large proportion of our non-liturgical churches. Does it remain the best procedure?

"The important matter in sacraments is not what we say or do, but what God says to us and does for us and in us,"[1] says Dr. Henry Sloane Coffin. His suggestion, then, would be that we give God every opportunity to speak to us through the sacraments. Dr. Coffin continues: "In the Sacraments God is Himself both the Giver and the Gift." In a very real way Christ gives Himself to us in our observance of the Feast He has ordained. As we share with the Twelve the Loaf and Cup that He has blessed, so may we at that moment listen to His voice.

But we fear that He will not speak, or that we will not be able to listen. The Psalmist says, "Be still before the Lord, and wait patiently for him." (Psalm 37:7, R.S.V.) But we do not like stillness, and we have no time to wait, patiently or otherwise. Therefore, lest this waiting time be wasted and we face the possibility of going home from worship empty-handed, let our thoughts be led into the proper channels. Let the minister read helpful passages from the Bible, or let the organist play hymns that will suggest the direction our thoughts should take.

Yet are we not lacking in humility if we feel we know best how our thoughts should be guided at this time? Is this not the time when we should permit God to speak, without standing in His way? We have met in this sacred place, and have spread the Feast at His Table in remembrance of Him. Now, if ever, we should be silent and listen for His voice. No words should be said, or music played, which will at this time substitute our thoughts and words for His.

Yet silence in this service cannot be absolute, since it is dissipated by the movement and sound that are a necessary part of the serving of Communion. There is less movement, and for a shorter period, when the worshipers take Communion seated in the pews; only the elders move, and twice only, through the congregation. When the communicants kneel at the rail, there is more movement and attendant sound over a longer period, since the whole congregation must move forward and back in the course of the service. The movement itself makes meditation more difficult. As in the case of the period of the offering, music may serve as a cover for the necessary disturbance.

But, except where the church rubrics or strong custom suggest it, the music during the distribution of the elements should not be a remembered hymn tune, since it should in no way lead the thinking of the communicants. It should be soft, so that it may touch only the fringe of attention. It should be tenuous and indefinite in character, never making itself felt by any striking characteristics of melody, harmony, or rhythm. It should make the way smooth but without making its presence felt.

The Funeral Service

When a death occurs the focus of thought and feeling of everyone concerned should be on the enhancement of life's values for the living.[2]

This statement by Leroy Bowman is eminently reasonable, and it is essentially the position of the Church. The purpose of the funeral is not to honor the dead, nor to demonstrate to the world the esteem held for him by his relatives and friends. It is rather, first of all, the Church's ministry of comfort and hope to those who have sustained this loss. It is also the opportunity for the Church again to state to the world, perhaps through the record of the life that has passed, its own convictions concerning man's worth and his eternal destiny.

Yet a number of influences conspire to make the funeral something quite different from what it should be. Perhaps the most powerful of these is the sense of guilt so easily felt by bereaved families: somehow those who remain nurse the idea that they might have done more for the departed than they ever did. Now they feel an urge to compensate for their apparent shortcomings by excessive spending on casket, funeral, flowers, and monument. In general, those who supply these professional services are quite willing to fill these requests, and to encourage them further. The result of all this is to exaggerate the importance of "the remains" and the honors paid to it. This cannot fail to add an emotionalism to funeral services which is to be deplored.

Because music speaks directly and immediately to the emotions, it has a direct bearing on this evident emotionalism. The singing of hymns by soloist, quartet, or choir, although a diminishing custom, is still practiced in many parts of our country. The songs chosen, if they are not from that lugubrious category on separation, sorrow, and eternal rest, are hymns selected because they were the favorites of the deceased. Those of us who have attended funerals of this sort will recall that the "mourners," who have conducted themselves with a certain dignity and reserve earlier in the service, have almost invariably dissolved into paroxysms of uncontrolled grief when the singing began.

Although these customs are changing, they do change slowly. Each bereaved family wants the same honors paid to its dead as were paid to others who went before him. Therefore, if the quartet sang two numbers for Mrs. A's funeral last week, no less should be done for our loved one. However, hymns that were once sung are more and more being played on piano or organ. But the hymns tend to remain, in some form or other.

The greatest change of recent years has been the tendency to move the funeral from the church to the funeral parlor. Where the church, designed first as a place of worship, only imperfectly seemed to serve the needs of the funeral, the funeral parlor is designed with nothing else in mind. The perfect stage setting for viewing "the remains," the flickering candles, the heavy odor of flowers, the unearthly light coming from the latest devices of indirect illumination, and the soft enveloping music coming from hidden sources, all combine to create an effect, to say the least. The music has gone electronic. It may be an organ, played with full tremolo from several concealed speakers. It may be high-fidelity recorded music for chimes and harp. But the purpose and effect are the same: they tend to raise the emotional tone of all who are present.

But all of these trappings of grief seem somehow out of place. Christians, who believe in the resurrection, should not publicly mourn as though they live without hope. To the degree that music has been responsible for exhibitions of grief—and its guilt has been great—it should be curtailed within the service. There should be no solemn hymns sung by soloist, quartet, or choir, nor should they be played by piano, organ, or hi-fi record player. Does this mean that there should be no music at all? No. As long as we have the processions surrounding the "earthly remains" into and out of churches or funeral parlors, accompanied by the sounds of hushed but audible movement, just so long will the fabric of music rising above the whole, reducing by a little its awkward painfulness, be welcome. This should not be formal funeral music, but merely an arabesque of soft sound, without definite meaning or character. At other periods in the service, we should not fear silence, which is more precious by far than ill-chosen music.

Since less movement is necessary at the service in a funeral parlor, there is less need for music. Yet it is often harder to control. At great cost has the "mortician" installed all this electronic equipment! He is uncomprehending and a little hurt if you do not permit him to give you the Full Treatment. Besides, he cannot afford to let anyone think that his competitors give more service than he does. Yet blessed silence is worth striving for in this situation.

Have we not made a mistake in permitting the funeral service to leave the church and go to the funeral parlor? Would not the Christian Church do well to bring it back within the sanctuary? But let us not bring back what we used to have. Let us leave outside the church all the more forbidding details of the traditional funeral: the casket, the bank of flowers, the parade of the pallbearers, the reserved section of "mourners." We may still have what is the essential part of the funeral service: the Scripture, the prayers, and finally, the greatest boon music can bring to the funeral: the congregational hymn. Hymns cannot be sung by those attending at a funeral parlor; the atmosphere of the place just does not encourage the practice. But in God's house, as believers stand together in memory of a friend, and sing a great hymn of faith, the hope and confidence of all the living are lifted. The story is told of the singing of "A mighty Fortress is our God" by the congregation at the funeral of a great Christian leader. Those who were there will never forget the feeling of elation that came over them as they sang together:

> "Let goods and kindred go,
> This mortal life also;
> The body they may kill:
> God's truth abideth still;
> His Kingdom is forever."

The Wedding

> No married person should attend a wedding without giving thanks to God for his own marriage, and renewing in his heart the vows that are being taken for the first time by others.[3]

The wedding service is a religious rite. This fact we in this country tend to forget. Because normally we do not participate in the wedding ceremony we attend, we tend to become merely observers. To many of us who attend weddings, I suspect that Miss Fryxell's suggestion that we at the same time renew for ourselves the vows we hear would be a novel suggestion; the same would be true of her further suggestion that we pray actively for those who are being married. For the guest at a wedding is also the guest of the church, as well as a fellow worshiper.

But through the years we have permitted the religious element in our weddings to be pushed into the background. Indulgent parents and other relatives of the bride have urged willing decorators, florists, dressmakers, caterers, and musicians on toward more spectacular creations. The church looks less like a church than a woodland bower. The wedding party, in a state of exhaustion from the press of social events and other "arrangements," arrives at the church in too agitated a state really to be aware of what follows. The long procession of beautiful maidens resembles more a fashion show than the solemn movement toward the altar. Sentimental music is played and love songs are sung. Incidentally, there is a short religious observance. But the newspapers of the following day discuss it as a social event.

There is, of course, nothing intrinsically wrong with much of this celebration. Why should not a decorated sanctuary and beautiful clothing grace this joyous occasion? These are not of themselves incompatible with the religious ceremony. But if they are part of a ceremony that has become largely secularized, they cannot escape their share of the blame. Ultimately, the sacred or secular character of the wedding will be determined by its music. Certainly the songs of courtship have no place where the union of two people is being consecrated and blessed by the Church. Certainly instrumental music that is associated with the everyday world should not be heard here. The purely secular is as out of place at this time as it is in divine worship.

Then let ministers and church musicians agree to oppose the use of secular music at the wedding. First to go must be "At Dawning," "I Love You Truly," and all other songs of this type. Next to go would be "To a Wild Rose," "Liebestraum," and all other transcriptions of secular connotation.

What, then, shall we do with our traditional marches? They are certainly secular. The Wagner March from *Lohengrin* was preceded in the opera by a betrothal based on something less than complete trust and honesty, and was followed soon by tragic misunderstanding and separation. It is likewise true that the Mendelssohn *Midsummer-Night's Dream* music, from which the wedding march is taken, was composed to go with a play concerned with fairies and pagan love potions. A growing number of churches are banning both traditional marches for use at the wedding service. This is as it should be. For these marches are in a real way associated with all the sentimental secular influences that have been brought to bear on weddings in recent years.

If not the traditional marches, then what? It is not very profitable to look for other marches, since none seem to fit the situation. But why look for a march at all? During these years when the two traditional marches have been used in this country, it is obvious that very rarely has any bridal party succeeded in keeping step; there is no reason to believe that a change of marches would achieve this. Indeed, why *should* a bride march to her wedding? Increasingly we are coming to the conclusion that the bride and her party should never march and never hurry. The movement to and from the altar should be made with great deliberation.

Various suggestions have been made concerning what music should be used during the wedding procession. Here are some of them, picked at random from books on wedding music: the "Sinfonia" to Bach's Wedding Cantata No. 196; the first movement to the Franck "Fantasie in C"; Marcello's "Psalm XIX"; Purcell's "Trumpet Voluntary"; Karg-Elert's "Nun Danket." This list can be extended indefinitely. But why should not hymns, played or sung, be used for this purpose? The present Queen of England entered during "Praise, my soul, the King of Heaven." Any of the several wedding hymns may be used for the purpose. Also appropriate, particularly for the Recessional, is the great Lutheran hymn, "Now thank we all our God." As to whether these hymns should be played, or sung by the congregation, there is a growing feeling that they should be sung. From the standpoint of the congregation, there should be a great and satisfying sense of personal identification as its members move from their role as inactive observers and become active participants in the service. The bride and groom should also experience a support and encouragement from their friends and relatives which they could not have felt otherwise.

The pre-ceremony music should be standard, not too familiar, service and recital music. Such numbers for organ as the Bonnet "Romance sans Paroles," the Franck "Cantabile in B," the Bach "Sheep May Safely Graze," the Bossi "Siciliana," and Sowerby's "Carillon" are safe choices. If other instruments are to be used, the choices should be comparable. Again, any transcriptions of music belonging to the secular world should be avoided.

The choice of good vocal music for the wedding is somewhat limited. The very difficulty of getting a choir to sing at the odd hours chosen for most weddings has made choral music rare in this situation. This leaves available to us a small number of vocal solos; fortunately a large variety is not needed. One solo should be normally sufficient, sung not long before the ceremony. Not much may be sung in the course of the ceremony, since to do so would leave the wedding party poised awkwardly, with the movement of the ceremony apparently brought to a halt.

There is not much good vocal music designed for wedding use. There are, first of all, the several wedding hymns appearing in our hymnals, the best-known being "O perfect Love." There is also the benediction hymn of John Newton, "May the grace of Christ our Saviour." There are a few solos written for the purpose. Probably the best of them are two more settings of "O perfect Love," one by Joseph Clokey and the other by Leo Sowerby.

A more fertile field are those solos borrowed and, by a stretch of meaning, pushed into the wedding environment with varying appropriateness. We may mention the several settings of such Scripture as "Though I speak with the tongues of men and of angels," "Beloved, let us love one another," and "Love never faileth." Everyone knows that the Scriptural references are to love of the brethren, and not love between the sexes—*agape* as against *eros*—but not many lyrics have been written that will serve better. An even greater strain on logic comes with the occasional use of a musical setting of the words of Ruth: "Entreat me not to leave thee." It takes some imagination to see how these words uttered by a woman to her mother-in-law can apply to man and maid. I should not, however, leave this topic without mentioning two great vocal masterpieces, whose pure beauty makes them particularly suitable for the wedding: one of the Brahms Serious Songs, "Though I speak with the tongues," and one of the Dvořák Biblical Songs, "I will sing new songs of gladness."

At least two hymns have been similarly borrowed. "Love divine, all loves excelling" obviously speaks of divine love. But if it is to be used in this environment, let it be sung to such tunes as HYFRYDOL or LOVE DIVINE, rather than the more common jingly tune, BEECHER. A happier choice is "Blest be the tie that binds," the words of which seem to come close indeed to the proper sentiment for the wedding:

> "Blest be the tie that binds
> Our hearts in Christian love . . .
>
> "Before our Father's throne
> We pour our ardent prayers . . .
>
> "We share our mutual woes,
> Our mutual burdens bear . . ."

Let those stanzas beginning "From sorrow, toil, and pain" and "When we asunder part" be omitted here. This hymn is probably best used at the end of the service, just before the benediction.

A comment should be added here concerning the singing of the Lord's Prayer toward the end of the ceremony. If it must be sung, I wish to register my vote against the too familiar setting by Malotte. It is plainly music of a secular character attached to the sacred words. There are other settings which may be sung. But the same objection should be raised against the Lord's Prayer sung during the wedding service as against its use in this way for Sunday worship. The Lord's Prayer is for the people, and should be done by them. Why should it not be another item for congregational participation at the wedding?

Almost as evil as the use of love songs preceding the ceremony is the use of soft music during it. There is no more reason to have soft music at this time than there is to have it during a sermon on Sunday. During these few highly solemn moments when the vows are said and the Church through its ministry seals the marriage, nothing should be permitted to dissipate the centrality of the words then said and the acts then performed.

How, it may be asked, are these ideals to be achieved? How are we to change local customs that have been virtually hallowed by use? Certainly the choirmaster should not be expected to refuse flatly the requests of engaged couples who come to him with choices which do not meet the standard. The first step needs to be a regulation passed by the governing board of the church. Its form is not important if its intent is understood. It can be a part of general legislation on the use of the whole church. It need say no more than this: *The use of secular music in this church is not permitted*. It may be a set of special regulations in regard to the conduct of weddings. It would be prudent for the board or session to avoid passing such a code immediately following one wedding, or soon before another! But once there is such an impersonal code on the books of the church, the organist's problem is simplified. He cannot do what the young couple requests, for the church will not permit it.

Almost every minister of discrimination today requires one or more conferences with each engaged couple before he will perform the marriage ceremony. A part of these conferences may well be given to explaining to the couple the place and significance of music in the wedding. The result of this explanation should be not only a more beautiful wedding, but one for which the young couple will have a deepened appreciation.

XVIII

THE SMALL CHURCH

Too often when we discuss the problems of the Church we see them in terms of our larger organizations. We forget that the country is full of small churches, in the small towns and rural areas and in the crowded slums of our large cities. A large proportion of these have little more than one room, part of one minister, one piano, no choir, no choir loft. It is easier to remember our "pivotal" churches in "strategic" areas. But we should frequently remind ourselves that a great proportion of the members now in the larger churches were once boys and girls in these smaller churches. To neglect the smaller churches is to harm the whole Church.

Because its physical resources are so limited, it is not easy for the small church to worship with the propriety and dignity that seem desirable. It should be easier to worship in a stately sanctuary containing a beautiful organ and a well-trained choir. But how may we achieve the same result with none of these things? The same room must serve for church school and for the worship service. The heating system is inefficient. The piano has deteriorated. Merely getting out a weekly bulletin presents a major problem. Is a minister to be blamed too much if, in the face of these difficulties, he puts his major efforts on his pastoral duties and on preaching, and lets worship take care of itself?

Yet those who assemble weekly in the one-room church have the same desire for orderly worship as those who attend the city church. The men and women, for instance, who delight in the ceremonials of the lodge during the week will take no less pride in appropriate worship on Sunday. Once the minister decides to give leadership in this direction, his church will work with him to overcome the handicaps of environment, equipment, and training, against which they must work together.

What are the musical needs of many of these small churches? Almost every need that can be imagined! The piano needs repair. The pianist is inadequately trained. The hymnbooks are small and poor. The hymns sung are few in number, and largely of the wrong type. The singing is bad in quality, if not in quantity. Because of all these imperfections, the worship service tends to be reduced to a series of items which are little more than the apologetic preliminaries to the sermon. Yet these needs may be met and these problems solved if patience and persistence prevail, and if immediate results are not demanded and expected.

The Pianist

Assuming that the minister has had sufficient training and experience to know his musical needs, probably his first and greatest difficulty in the average small church will be to get adequate service from his pianist. Rare indeed is the church that has a good one. The new minister may find that he has inherited a pianist who plays by ear only; therefore his church's hymns are limited to those the pianist has heard often enough to be able to reproduce them after a fashion. Or he may have a pianist whose musical study ended before she (it is usually "she") learned the bass clef; the soprano and alto parts may be passable, but the sounds made by the left hand purporting to be the tenor and bass parts may have little relationship to the other two, harmonically speaking. Or the pianist may never have developed a sense of rhythm. But the fact we may never forget is that whatever the pianist's deficiencies are, they become the deficiencies of the whole congregation. If the pianist can play only twelve hymns, then the congregation may sing only twelve hymns!

The pianist, then, may offer a new minister the first and most urgent problem he needs to solve. Certainly the pianist, of whatever age or circumstances, should be given every encouragement to study his job. If no teacher is close at hand, the person should be helped to travel as often as possible to wherever he may be taught. He need not go, sometimes should not go, to a professional teacher. He needs rather to find a person willing to work at the practical level. If hymns are needed, hymns should be studied. If the pianist is unable to pay for his instruction, there are few places the church can put some money more profitably than in improving the skill of its own pianist.

No matter how busy the minister is, he should arrange to meet with his pianist weekly. He, or his wife, should with great patience encourage the learning of new hymns, or correct matters of speed and accuracy in old ones, and in every other way attempt to improve the skill of the pianist. As has been pointed out earlier, many gospel songs are used instead of better hymns because they are what the pianist can play. They are not easier to sing, but repeated harmonies make them easier to play. The Doxology, for instance, offers to the beginning pianist more problems than a good share of gospel song literature. But the Doxology and hymns of comparable difficulty are needed in worship, and the minister should labor until he can get them. All his efforts to improve his pianist may be very rewarding in worship values.

A church does well to look to its musical future. If among its young people there is a boy or girl who exhibits an interest in music, the church would do well to encourage that interest. If the child does not have a piano at home, the church instrument should be offered, and other needed help to make study possible. Even if the church has to wait some years to earn dividends on its investment, that investment may pay well, both in the development of a life and in the worship of the church.

The Instrument

The old reed pump organ is a thing of the past. The piano that has replaced it has not been an unmixed blessing. At its best, it is not a churchly instrument. Its emphatic rhythm serves for playing hymns, but for little else in church. Its care has always been a problem. Because most small churches remain unheated between Sundays, the piano swells with moisture, and expands or contracts with heat or cold. If its keys do not stick, its action rattles, and it seldom sounds in tune. Rare is the church that will willingly expend both the effort and the money necessary to keep it in good condition.

The church that misses its old reed organ may now buy one with electric power. It is built by the Estey Organ Corporation (Brattleboro, Vermont) which built so many famous reed organs of many years ago. It sounds like its Estey forbears, and may satisfy many churches at comparatively low cost.

Many others of our small churches are buying electronic organs. Even the poorest of these can sound more churchly than a piano. They also have the advantage of being less subject to pitch and mechanical difficulties resulting from changes in temperature and humidity than is the piano. But in the hands of the unwary organist, it can be perhaps the worst of all instruments for a church. Most electronic organs are equipped with a vigorous tremulant, which can make their tone quiver and shake. Unfortunately, many beginning players enjoy this effect, and use it excessively. An electronic organ so used produces music more like that heard between innings at a baseball game, or as the interlude music for a radio soap opera, than like sacred music. A piano is infinitely better than an electronic organ used in this manner. After all, one does not hear a piano at a baseball game, nor as the usual radio "background." Moral: if an electronic organ is installed in your church, forbid all use of the tremulant, except for rare, brief occasions.

One other warning: If you buy an electronic organ, and your organist is your old pianist put to new use, do not expect him at once to sound better on the new instrument than he did on the old. The organ is certainly no easier to play than the piano. In fact, three problems promptly present themselves to the person changing from the one to the other. First, he must learn a new finger technique, *legato* or connected. Second, he must discover the secrets of registration. Finally, he must use those fascinating pedals. Therefore, if he was not a skillful pianist, he may well be a less skillful organist. There is also less opportunity to study organ than there is piano. Again, the minister is wise who works regularly with his new organist until as satisfactory results as possible are obtained.

The Children

As is always true, the minister's biggest single challenge is the training of the children in his church. It is a fertile field. The adults of the church may be inflexible in habit and thought, but not the children! Unlike their city cousins, whose lives are complicated by excessive school and community activities, the small-town and country boys and girls live comparatively simple lives; they have more time for, and may take more interest in, the life of the church.

Here, first of all, is where hymns should be taught. A part of every Sunday school period may properly be devoted to singing new hymns. This may well be continued in the young people's vesper group, if there is one. Whether or not the children are organized in a junior choir, they will enjoy learning new hymns, and there is no reason why these hymns should not be good ones. Here should be found no insistence on the old, no prejudice against the new. And what they learn, their parents may learn later.

The vacation church school has an even higher function in this respect. Let this be first of all the training school for worship. Without neglecting the usual fun songs, handiwork, games, and Bible stories, let part of the day be given to planning and practicing for worship. Included in rehearsal should be responsive reading, the Lord's Prayer, the Doxology, the Gloria Patri, processional and recessional, the Creed where it is used, and perhaps several congregational responses. Then, the details having been practiced, let them be put together into a worship service, done as adults should do it, with reverence and with dignity.

What we have described, of course, is a junior church service, but a junior church in an environment where it does not usually appear. It could not easily appear in the small church except during vacation church school. Should the experience end at this point, it would still be worth all the effort that had gone into it. However, this should not be the end, but just the beginning, for the junior church could now move into the "grown-up" church, and the children could share with their parents what they had previously shared with each other.

There is no requirement that the children of such a church be organized into a choir. The church does not greatly need a choir loft, but it is good that the children be seated together at the front of the church, near the piano (or organ). It is helpful to have the minister exemplify the interest of this church in its children by his preaching to them each Sunday a carefully prepared children's sermon. (Incidentally, it should be remembered that some adults get more help from the children's sermon than from the one designed for the more mature in the congregation.) But if the children are also made to feel their responsibility for leading the church in worship and in the learning of new hymns, their church should be a healthy church, and they should be growing in Christian faith and experience.

Worship: The Hymn and the Response

The small church tends to have a very limited repertoire of hymns, and these are heavily weighted with gospel songs. Whether the reason for this lies in a poor hymnal, a limited pianist, or lack of leadership, the result is bound to be impoverished worship. Of high priority, then, should be the teaching of the standard hymns of the Church to the congregation. All the suggestions made earlier in this book for teaching hymns should be used on the small church, plus the use of more repetition. Where the Sunday night service and the Family Night are available, they should be used liberally for this purpose. In short, if the minister is willing to make the effort, he may have a church in which hymn singing is effective.

It is also possible for a church without a choir or choir loft to develop a service with musical responses by the use of the full congregational response. It need not be a very full service, but it can be a rewarding one. Single stanzas of hymns and other available responses from the hymnal may be used in any of the positions in the order of worship in which the choral response may appear. How many responses should be sung? Certainly not many. Three is about the right number.

The three responses chosen in a certain order may be a call to worship, an offertory response, and a benediction response, all done with the congregation standing. The best of the calls to worship is, of course, the Doxology. For an offertory response use either "We give Thee but Thine own," or "All things come of Thee, O Lord," whichever is available. For a benediction response the second stanza of "Saviour, again to Thy dear name we raise," which begins with "Grant us Thy peace upon our homeward way," is good music and appropriate. I once heard a rural congregation sing the stanza only (eight measures) of the familiar "God be with you till we meet again" after the benediction; it was effective and beautiful.

Other hymn stanzas are readily available as congregational responses for other parts of the service. Either stanza of "Break Thou the bread of life" may be used before or after the New Testament lesson. In fact, both stanzas may be used: "Break Thou the bread of life" may be sung just before the lesson, and "Bless Thou the truth, dear Lord" just after it. Before the pastoral prayer, a stanza of "Breathe on me, Breath of God" may be sung. After the prayer, the final stanza of "Immortal Love, forever full" makes a good response: "O Lord and Master of us all." Not all of these should be used in any one service. A total of three for the whole service is sufficient. But the choice and pattern should change from time to time, lest the performance become perfunctory.

The order of worship should make the offering of these responses as easy as possible by giving in the bulletin explicit information about where they are to be found in the hymnal and whether the congregation is to do them seated or standing. The membership will take pride in following the order exactly. The minister should therefore refrain from ordering the service by either spoken word or gesture. If the children sitting near the piano know their task, a chord from the piano will be sufficient to set each response into motion.

Finally this question may be fairly asked: Of what real value are these congregational responses? I believe that the answer is that they are particularly needed in the small church which lacks in beauty of sanctuary and musical appointments the conditions which would make worship natural and easy. By involving the people directly in more of the acts of worship, these acts lend a certain sense of God's presence to the service. When a worshiper sits in a larger church, and hears the choir offer a response, it takes a conscious effort on his part to appropriate the choir's act to himself. But when he himself offers his response to an act of worship, that act becomes his simply and immediately. In fact, the response of the whole congregation is the only true and complete response.

The Inner-City Church

Are the musical problems of the small church in the large city similar to those of the rural or small-town church? When one reads of the excesses that seem to be characteristic of "store-front" religion, he might feel that quite different aims would be desirable, and quite different methods needed. In a very limited way, I have sought the answer to the question I have stated.

In 1948 a group of Protestant ministers in New York City, feeling that the historic churches of their city were not doing what they could to meet the needs of *all* the people, decided to begin a work where they felt it was most needed: in the center of Harlem. As their field they took the small area bounded by 99th and 106th Streets on the south and north, and East River Drive and Lexington Avenue on the east and west, an area in which live about 40,000 people who are the victims of all the evils known in this overcrowded section of an overcrowded city. Here are four small churches, the membership of which now totals about five hundred, churches which offer, besides worship, a variety of community services which meet vital needs of many people. This is the East Harlem Protestant Parish.

My particular interest was in the worship and music of these small churches. Since the parish draws a large part of its financial support from eight national denominational boards, and its staff is also interdenominational, the worship of the four churches, although similar, does not bear the stamp of any one sect. Let us take a typical service in one of these, the 100th Street Church: The "church" is a small one-room store space, with curtains across the store windows as well as the opposite end of the room; it is only large enough to hold a piano, a simple altar, a pulpit, and about fifty folding chairs. The piano is on one side, the pulpit on the other side of the altar, on which rests an open Bible; there is no room for a choir. The Hymnal of the Presbyterian Church is used. The congregation, which occupies every chair, is interracial but mostly Negro. The "prelude" is a number of hymns played on the piano. The service begins with the ceremonial lighting of candles on the altar. What follows is done with dignity and reverence: call to worship, the usual prayers, Scripture, four hymns, and sermon. There are some unusual features, including the gathering from the congregation of the names of those who, for one reason or another, have special need for prayer, and the mention of each of these by name in the prayer of intercession. The offertory follows the sermon. The closing hymn becomes one of fellowship as, during the singing, those who lead move through the congregation, shaking the hand of each person, and then each worshiper shakes the hand of those near him. After the closing response, the service closes with the extinguishing of the candles.

Space forbids taking time here to discuss the service in detail, but its music requires comment. The hymns that were sung were all good hymns, and were well sung by everybody I could see. Also, two or three responses were sung beautifully and reverently by the whole congregation. After the service I left the friendly group with a deeper sense of having worshiped than I had experienced in many larger, richer churches.

I also found there the answer to the question with which this discussion started: Are the musical problems of the small church in the large city similar to those of the rural or small-town church? They are essentially the same, and can be met in much the same way. The store-front and the country churches have much in common.

XIX

FINALLY

It is, I suppose, inescapable that in the presence of anything concerning which there may be a difference of opinion, men divide to the right and to the left. We are conservatives, proposing to keep unchanged what we have. Or we are progressives, seeking to move on to something we believe will be better. But in our worship practices we should be neither—or both. Our religion rests on the foundations of the past, foundations that are unchanged and unchanging. Yet, because we are led by the Holy Spirit into all truth, we must never be content with what we have raised above these foundations. The Church, Christ's Body, which we are, must always seek to improve in understanding, in love, and in service.

Dean Sperry points to the thousand years of trial and error that have produced worship as we now know it.[1] There is no need, he says, to study bizarre orders of worship. Let us rather study what we have in our own tradition. His point is well made. Our future, to be steady, must be anchored in our past. But are we forever alone with trial and error? Is there any one point in our history where we have a right to say that we can find no new ways of worshiping our God?

On our place in history, A. G. Hebert has this to say:

> The judgments that we make on history are conditioned by the fact that we are not outside observers pronouncing a fully objective verdict, but are ourselves part of the whole movement of history, some particular episode of which is the immediate matter of our study. So it is with all study of Christian worship; the judgments which any observer makes will inevitably

reflect the position in which he himself stands, within a Christendom that is broken and divided. . . . None of us is, therefore, in a position to pronounce magisterial judgments, or to draw up ideal forms of worship, or to decide finally what is right.[2]

Father Hebert's statement appears to be reasonable. Yet is it possible to avoid pronouncing what appear to be "magisterial judgments"? Is not anyone who takes a position at all trying "to decide finally what is right"?

The answer is that he who opposes all change is the only one who is deciding *finally* what is right. The most magisterial of all judgments is that which stands irrevocably for what "was in the beginning, is now, and ever shall be." He who thinks of change at all must avoid the use of the word *finally*. His only concern is that each step be an onward one.

Not long ago a very wise urban pastor asked my opinion of the "Jazz" Mass. Rather rashly I answered that I was really not interested in it. His response was terse: "You should be!" He said further that, although this particular work had not received present acceptance, it or something like it would return and would find its legitimate place in our worship. I at once studied the "Jazz" Mass, more correctly known as the *20th Century Folk Mass*, by Father Geoffrey Beaumont.[3] Is this the sacred music of the future? I do not believe so, but I realize that in my doubt I must not express "magisterial judgments." During the waning years of the twentieth century and the succeeding twenty-first century let the worshipers decide what music best expresses their praise and adoration of God.

A congregation should not expect much spiritual stimulation from that minister who decides that his own preaching is good enough, and needs no improvement. In the same way, if we are content with our worship as it is, is it not in danger of becoming "vain repetition"? It is to be hoped that the whole worship team of every church will never rest with what seems to be good enough, but will constantly seek to improve both the content and manner of worship.

A few years ago, when I was discussing music in its relationship to worship with a group of seminary students, more than once in the course of my talks a very wise minister who was present reminded me, "You are speaking of the ideal situation, of course." Of course I was! I believed then as now that Christians should never cease pressing toward the ideal. But I recognize now, as I did not then, the significance of his statement. We must never forget to follow the injunction of the writer of the Epistle to the Hebrews: "Let us run *with patience* the race that is set before us."

I have reason to know of a minister who once had an ideal of what he wanted worship to be in his church. It called for great changes, including the dropping of quartet and organist, and the hiring of a new choirmaster. A new choir was started, and a different order of worship instituted. The minister had planned well the realization of his ideal, except for one detail: he had failed to "sell" his congregation on his program. The predictable result was the congregation's rejection not only of the changes that had come to them, but of the minister, the choirmaster, and the choir as well. The latter state of that church was worse than the earlier one, for the strife within it ended for a season that congregation's witness to Christian love.

Those who have anything to do with music in the Protestant Church should keep steady eyes on goals that are far away. The pace toward these goals should be steady, and probably will be slow. If we attempt to cover difficult ground rapidly, there is a good chance that we shall stumble. We already know that we cannot train a skillful organist or build a beautiful choir in a few days. We must also remind ourselves that with the advancement of our physical resources and abilities in worship must come also growth of the resources within the human spirit. Within neither the physical nor the spiritual realm should we seek to rush unwisely the growth we desire.

Appendixes

ELECTRONIC ORGANS

ORGAN BUILDERS

CHOIR ROBES

CHURCH ORGAN MUSIC

Bibliography

Notes and Acknowledgments

Index

Appendix A

ELECTRONIC ORGANS

Of the approximately ten builders of electronic organs in this country, only two produce what may properly be called custom-built organs. Both of these companies, selling almost exclusively to churches, may be regarded as the quality leaders in the field. They are the Allen Organ Company of Macungie, Pennsylvania, and the Haygren Organ Company of Chicago.

ALLEN ORGANS (Allen Organ Company, Inc., Macungie, Penna.) are the aristocrats among electronic organs. The firm takes pride in publicly pitting its product against all comers in the field, and invites comparison between it and pipe organs. A true electronic organ, using vacuum tubes from the beginning, it has recently replaced all tubes, except those in the amplification circuits, with long-wearing transistors. All Allens use the Gyrophonic Projector, a series of slowly rotating speakers which create a "dispersion of tone" which minimizes speaker blast and at the same time simulates the "nervous quality" which Allen claims is characteristic of pipe organs. In all models "stereophonic sound" is suggested, causing certain stops to sound from one speaker, and certain others from another some distance from the first.

Allen offers three acceptable standard models. The C-1, selling for under $4,000, is a two-manual, twenty-six-stop instrument with full-sized pedal board and one expression pedal. Model C-3, slightly larger and more complete, sells for around $6,000. Model C-4, selling for about $7,500, is the one recommended by Dr. Barnes as being equal to any $15,000 organ.

Allen's chief fame comes from its Advanced Custom Series, large three- and four-manual organs, especially designed for the rooms in which they are placed, and priced in general between $30,000 and $60,000. Allen is the unquestioned leader in the large electronic field, and continues to improve its product by intensive research.

HAYGREN ORGANS (Haygren Organ Company, 2212 East 75th St., Chicago 49, Ill.) are not well known, since the company is not large and its advertising budget is modest. The firm states its purpose simply: "The primary intent of Haygren is to build an instrument with resources fitting for the service of the church." Believing that tone qualities should be mixed, not in the tone chambers, but in the air outside, Haygren uses multiple speakers, well separated, each one voicing different stops. Its smallest complete organ, the Regal, sells for about $5,000. Between this amount and $15,000 Haygren custom-builds organs to occupy particular churches. Their instruments have richly varied stop qualities and an imposing full organ.

All the remaining electronic organ firms in this country turn out primarily standard models, most of them small and fairly inexpensive. Four of them produce at least one larger model each, with full-sized pedal board, and tonal facilities adequate for the small church. These companies are Baldwin, Conn, Hammond, and Wurlitzer.

BALDWIN ELECTRONIC ORGANS (The Baldwin Piano Company, 1801 Gilbert Ave., Cincinnati 2, Ohio) produce their tone by means of the vacuum tube, and have a record of largely trouble-free service. The company stresses expert installation of its speakers, which are preferably mounted on baffle boards in well-designed chambers. Recent improvements in its product include its Chora-tone Projector, which enhances the full organ ensemble, and separate amplification systems which it recommends for the various divisions of the organ.

Baldwin offers two models that are adequate for church. Its 5A has two full manuals and a complete pedal board, with twenty-six stops and six couplers, as well as two expression pedals. Its price, including the Chora-tone Cabinet, is around $3,500, f. o. b. factory. Model 10A is larger, more complete, with a full set of couplers, adequate pistons, two expression pedals, and a crescendo pedal. Its price starts at a little over $6,500.

CONN ORGANS (Conn Organ Corporation, Elkhart, Ind.) are built by a firm long famous as makers of band instruments. For years this company called its organs Connsonatas. It has been particularly successful in producing a full organ of good quality. Its one model adequate for church is its "Classic," Series 800, with nineteen stops, fourteen couplers, full pedal board, and two expression pedals. Its stated price is $3,610. It now has in preparation a more "de luxe" version of the Classic.

HAMMOND ORGANS (Hammond Organ Company, 4200 Diversey Ave., Chicago 39, Ill.) are not, strictly speaking, electronic instruments, since their tone is activated by rotating notched discs, but they are considered in the electronic class since their tone comes through speakers. Because it is the original of the mass-produced, nationally distributed electronic organs, backed by a massive advertising campaign, it was at home in hundreds of churches, theaters, night clubs, mortuaries, radio stations, and baseball parks almost before its competitors got under way. Because of its versatility in performing its highly varied tasks the company has kept largely unchanged its original design, adding a few refinements only recently. The new Hammond, like that of twenty years ago, has no stops like other organs, but series of pre-set keys for each manual, and five sets of adjustable "harmonic drawbars" by which the organist may "mix" what qualities he may desire on either manual or pedal. A Chorus Control simulates the slight pitch variation associated with pipe organ tone. Two more recent additions should be mentioned, one built in and one optional: a Pedal Solo System, added to correct the basic pedal deficiency, and a Reverberation Control, to enliven the acoustics of a "dead" room. Because it retains the percussive "pop" that other electronics have eliminated, because all Hammonds may produce bizarre effects that are the opposite of churchly, and because the company continues to be so successful in selling its product to churches that deserve better instruments, Hammond organs today remain the most controversial of all electronics, heartily despised by most trained organists.

In spite of what has been said here, Hammond's Concert Model

(RT-3 Console) can do an effective job in a small church. The console sells for just above $3,000, to which must be added $450 to $600 for one of five Tone Cabinets.

WURLITZER ORGANS (The Wurlitzer Company, Dekalb, Ill.), or at least the larger of them, have as their tone source a metal reed from which the various desired qualities are picked up by patented tone selectors, furnishing a rich choice of timbres. The company has managed to build a standard console, with full pedal board and built-in speakers, for about $2,700; this is its Model 4602, the least expensive of what we may call complete electronic organs on the market. The Concert Model 4800 has more stops and a crescendo pedal, and its price is between $3,400 and $3,800; again, the speakers are built in, so this is the complete cost. Either of these models will bring the possibility of beautiful music into any small church that does not seek a large tone for hymn singing. If a church wants to augment the tone of one of these models, three different speakers of the plug-in variety are offered at prices from $273 to $605.

Two other electronic organ firms should be mentioned at this point. Both are old firms, but young in the electronic organ field. Both now build smaller organs, but have indicated plans shortly to release models with complete consoles and full pedal boards. GULBRANSEN TRANSISTOR ORGANS (Gulbranson Company, 2050 North Ruby Street, Melrose Park, Ill.) are a new departure for an established firm of piano builders. The smaller Gulbransens are beautiful little instruments with a good tone and fine flexibility. The larger model, the data on which has not yet been released, should be worth examining. KIMBALL ELECTRIC ORGANS (W. W. Kimball Company, Cornell Avenue at Armitage, Melrose Park, Ill.) are a rather recent development of a firm which for many years built superior pipe organs. Using the somewhat unusual device of the photo-electric cell and scanning disc as the means of producing its tone, Kimball is also experimenting with an electronic transistor organ. Two larger models, intended for church use, are presumably about ready for public release. Although data on Kimball organs cannot easily be obtained at the present time, the company's integrity is such that its products should be worth examining as they become known and available.

Two other reputable firms of electronic organ builders serve to complete the list. Both firms have for some time produced successful smaller models, their largest making use of twenty-five-note pedal boards. When these companies build organs with full-sized pedal boards, their instruments will merit examination. These are the Lowrey Organ Company, 7373 North Cicero Avenue, Lincolnwood, Chicago 30, Illinois, and the Minshall Organ Inc., Brattleboro, Vermont.

"Do It Yourself" with Electronic Organs

In a church that contains some interested mechanics and electricians, the do-it-yourself electronic organ is a distinct possibility. At least one firm sells all the components of electronic organs of any desired size at prices well below those of assembled instruments.* A group of men with patience, time, some electronic knowledge, mechanical skill, and some musical knowledge, can custom-build an electronic organ for a church, and then add to it as further needs or musical appetites arise. In this period of increasing leisure, such a project may prove stimulating and desirable to the men of a church.

---

*Eby, Robert L., *Organ Builders Manual*, a Complete Assembling Instruction Manual and Parts Catalogue (Third Edition). Los Angeles: Electronic Organ Arts, 1958.

Appendix B

ORGAN BUILDERS

Here are the names of sixteen American organ manufacturers. The list is my own, drawn from the pages of *The Diapason*, the official magazine of the American Guild of Organists. The basis for the list is the present activity of these firms in making installations in American churches. There are doubtless other firms unwittingly omitted. No attempt will be made here to discuss any of these companies or their products. Few general statements could be made without being challenged by somebody. What one organist would call a preference another would name a prejudice. Certain companies at a given time lean in certain directions toward certain types of organs with various degrees of firmness. But since the good old profit motive presumably enters into the thinking of all of them, most of them will give the buyer what he desires, within limits.

There are other firms engaged in organ maintenance and repair that are also prepared to build new organs of any size. Since these are not primarily organ builders, they are not included in this list.

Aeolian-Skinner Co., Inc., Boston 27, Mass.

Austin Organs, Inc., Hartford 1, Conn.

Casavant Brothers, Limited, Saint Hyacinthe, Quebec, Canada

Estey Organ Corporation, Brattleboro, Vermont

Hillgreen, Lane & Co., Alliance, Ohio

Holtkamp Organs, Cleveland 9, Ohio

Kilgen Organ Co., 4632 W. Florrisant Ave., St. Louis, Missouri

M. P. Moller, Inc., Hagerstown, Maryland

J. H. & C. S. Odell & Co., 82 Morningside Ave., Yonkers, N. Y.

Pels Organ Co., Grand Rapids, Mich.

The Reuter Organ Co., Lawrence, Kansas

Schantz Organ Co., Orrville, Ohio

Schlicker Organ Co., Inc., Buffalo 17, N. Y.
Tellers Organ Co., 2419 Holland St., Erie, Penna.
Wicks Organ Co., Highland, Ill.

Appendix C

CHOIR ROBES

This list makes no pretensions of being complete. It consists of those firms with which this writer has had dealings, and those that have reached his attention through their national advertising.*

Bentley and Simon, Inc., 7 W. 36th St., New York 18, N.Y.
Collegiate Cap and Gown Co., 366 Fifth Ave., New York 1, N.Y.
Cotrell & Leonard, Albany, N.Y.
Cox Sons & Vining, Inc., 131 E. 23rd St., New York 10, N.Y.
Ireland Needlecraft, 3661 San Fernando Road, Glendale 4, Cal.
E. R. Moore Co., Chicago 13, Ill.
National Church Goods Supply Co., 821 Arch St., Philadelphia 7, Penna.
C. E. Ward Co., New London, Ohio.

---

* Choir robes from reliable firms may be ordered also through most denominational book stores.

Appendix D

CHURCH ORGAN MUSIC

This is not a standard list of church organ music. We take for granted the organist's knowledge of the works of such composers as Bach, Mendelssohn, Brahms, Franck, Rheinberger, Widor. It is our hope to suggest here at least a few lesser known works. They vary in difficulty from easy to rather difficult. I consider all of them acceptable music. Particular attention is given to chorale preludes, which are easily appropriate for the church service.

Andriessen, Hendrick
Sonata Da Chiesa (Theme, Variations, Finale) (Edward B. Marks)
Benoit, Paul
Fifty Elevations on Modal Themes (J. Fischer)
Four Preludes (J. Fischer)
Biggs, Richard Key
Religious Suite (McLaughlin & Reilly)
Star of Hope (J. Fischer)
Bingham, Seth
36 Hymn and Carol Canons (H. W. Gray)
12 Hymn Preludes, Sets I and II (H. W. Gray)
Bristol, Lee H.
Variations on *Old Hundredth* (J. Fischer)
Brown, Allanson G. Y.
Improvisation on Two Chorales (H. W. Gray)
Busch, Adolf
Eight Chorale Preludes (G. Schirmer)
Butcher, Vernon
Two Improvisations on Anglican Chants (Peters)
Buxtehude, Dietrich
6 Chorale Preludes (J. Fischer)
Candlyn, T. Frederick H.
Prelude on "Divinum Mysterium" (A. P. Schmidt)
Clokey, Joseph W.
Ten Meditations (J. Fischer)

DeLamarter, Eric
  Chorale Prelude, "Ach bleib bei uns, Herr Jesu Christ" (Witmark)
Elmore, Robert
  Two Chorale Preludes (Elkan-Vogel)
Edmundson, Garth
  Seven Classic Preludes (J. Fischer)
France, William E.
  Miniature Suite for Organ (O. Ditson)
Freed, Isadore
  Invocation (Transcontinental Music Corporation, N.Y.)
  Praise to the Lord (Transcontinental Music Corporation, N.Y.)
  Pastorale (Transcontinental Music Corporation, N.Y.)
  Meditation (Transcontinental Music Corporation, N.Y.)
  The Lord of All (Transcontinental Music Corporation, N.Y.)
Jacobi
  Three Quiet Preludes (H. W. Gray)
Jongen
  Choral (Durand)
  Priere (Durand)
Karg-Elert, Sigfrid
  Six Volumes of Chorale Improvisations (Edward B. Marks)
  Sempre Semplice in two books (Paxton)
  Sursum Corda (A. P. Schmidt)
  A Cycle of Eight Short Pieces (A. P. Schmidt)
Kee
  Een Vaste Burg (A Mighty Fortress) (Ars Nova)
Langlais
  Mors et Resurrectio (Peters)
Lee, John
  Four Improvisations (Gregorian Institute)
Lucas, Clarence
  Seven Short Pieces
Macfarlane, Will C.
  Ad Ecclesiae Gloriam (G. Schirmer)
McGrath, Joseph J.
  Twenty-Four Divertimenti (J. Fischer)
McKay
  Benedictions (Carl Fischer)
McKinley, Carl
  Ten Hymn Tune Fantasies (H. W. Gray)
Matthews, H. Alexander
  Twelve Organ Pieces in Varied Styles (Elkan-Vogel)
Mead, Edward
  Prelude on *Duke Street* (H. W. Gray)

Mueller, Carl
   Chorale Prelude on "A mighty Fortress" (G. Schirmer)
Noble, T. Tertius
   Seven Choral Preludes (A. P. Schmidt)
Niles, John Jacob
   Four American Carols (G. Schirmer)
Oldroyd
   Three Liturgical Pieces (Oxford University Press)
Parrish, Carl
   Chorale Prelude on *St. Denio* (Witmark)
Parry, C. H. H.
   Seven Chorale Preludes (Novello)
Peeters, Flor
   Morning Hymn (H. W. Gray)
   Sixty Short Pieces (H. W. Gray)
   Ten Chorale Preludes, Op. 68 (Peters)
   Ten Chorale Preludes, Op. 69 (Peters)
   Ten Chorale Preludes, Op. 70 (Peters)
   Thirty-five Miniatures (McLaughlin-Reilly)
Penick
   Three Preludes on Welsh Tunes (H. W. Gray)
Phillips
   Six Chorale Preludes (Oxford University Press)
Piche
   Rhapsody on Four Noels (H. W. Gray)
Purvis, Richard
   Carol Rhapsody (Leeds)
   Communion (Leeds)
   Divinum Mysterium (Leeds)
   Four Carol Preludes (Leeds)
   Four Prayers in Tone (Witmark)
   Seven Chorale Preludes on Tunes Found in American Hymnals
     (Carl Fischer)
   Vexilla Regis (Leeds)
Reger, Max
   Thirty Short Chorale Preludes (Peters)
Rowley, Alec
   Five Improvisations (Novello)
   Pavane (H. W. Gray)
   Soliloquy (Novello)
Sowerby, Leo
   Prelude on *St. Dunstan's* (H. W. Gray)
   Prelude on "Were you there?" (H. W. Gray)
Thiman, Eric
   Improvisation on *Crimond* (Novello)

Preludes and Voluntaries in three books (Curwen)
Three Pieces (Novello)
Titcomb, Everett
Adoro te Devote (B. F. Wood)
Cibavit Eos (B. F. Wood)
Gaudeamus (B. F. Wood)
Van Hulse
Joyeux Noel! (Fitzsimons)
Vaughan Williams, Ralph
Carol and Musette (Oxford University Press)
Greensleeves (Oxford University Press)
Three Preludes on Welsh Hymn Tunes (Stainer & Bell)
Walton
Christmas Rhapsody (Leeds)
Warner
Ten Short Preludes on Hymn Tunes and Carols (Carl Fischer)
Wesley, S. S.
Choral Song (H. W. Gray)
Whitford, Homer
Five Choral Paraphrases in two sets (H. W. Gray)
Whitney, Maurice
Aberystwyth (Jesus, Lover of my soul) (Mercury)
Improvisation on *St. Agnes* (H. W. Gray)
Wood, Charles
Sixteen Preludes in two volumes (Stainer & Bell)
Zechiel, Ernest
Six Chorale Preludes (G. Schirmer)

Bibliography

ON WORSHIP IN GENERAL

Abba, Raymond, *Principles of Christian Worship*. New York: Oxford University Press, 1957.

Blackwood, Andrew W., *The Fine Art of Public Worship*. Nashville: Cokesbury Press, 1939.

Bowman, Clarice, *Restoring Worship*. Nashville: Abingdon-Cokesbury Press, 1951.

Coffin, Henry Sloane, *The Public Worship of God*. Philadelphia: The Westminster Press, 1946.

Hedley, George, *Christian Worship*. New York: The Macmillan Company, 1953.

McDormand, Thomas Bruce, *The Art of Building Worship Services*. Nashville: Broadman Press, 1958 (revised).

McNutt, William Roy, *Worship in the Churches*. Philadelphia: The Judson Press, 1941.

Maxwell, William D., *A History of Worship in the Church of Scotland*. London: Oxford University Press, 1955.

Maxwell, William D., *An Outline of Christian Worship*. London: Oxford University Press, 1939.

Christian Worship, by Members of Mansfield College, edited by Nathaniel Micklem. London: Oxford University Press, 1936.

Palmer, Albert Wentworth, *The Art of Conducting Public Worship*. New York: The Macmillan Company, 1939.

Underhill, Evelyn, *Worship*. New York: Harper & Brothers, 1937, 1957.

ON BUILDING THE CHURCH

Mills, Edward D., *The Modern Church*. New York: Frederick A. Praeger, 1956.

ON THE PIPE ORGAN

Barnes, William Harrison, *The Contemporary American Organ*. New York: J. Fischer & Bro., Seventh Edition, 1959.

Blanton, Joseph Edwin, *The Organ in Church Design*. Albany, Texas: Venture Press, 1957.

Sumner, William Leslie, *The Organ*. London: Macdonald & Co. Ltd., 1952; New York: Philosophical Library, 1952.

ON THE ELECTRONIC ORGAN

Eby, Robert L., *Electronic Organs*, a Complete Catalogue, Textbook and Manual. Wheaton, Ill.: Van Kampen Press, 1953.

Eby, Robert L., *Organ Builders Manual*, a Complete Assembling Instruction Manual and Parts Catalogue. Los Angeles: Electronic Organ Arts, Third Edition, 1958.

ON MUSIC IN WORSHIP

Ashton, Joseph N., *Music in Worship*. Boston: The Pilgrim Press, 1943.

Bacon, Allan, *The True Function of Church Music*. Stockton, Calif.: Printwell Press, 1953.

Davison, Archibald T., *Church Music: Illusion and Reality*. Cambridge: Harvard University Press, 1952.

Dickinson, Edward, *Music in the History of the Western Church*. New York: Charles Scribner's Sons, 1902.

Douglas, Winfred, *Church Music in History and Practice*. New York: Charles Scribner's Sons, 1937.

Gardner, George, and Nicholson, Sydney H., *A Manual of English Church Music*. London: Society for Promoting Christian Knowledge, 1923. New York: The Macmillan Company.

Halter, Carl, *The Practice of Sacred Music*. St. Louis: Concordia Publishing House, 1955.

Lovelace, Austin C., and Rice, William C., *Music and Worship in the Church*. New York: Abingdon Press, 1960.

Soule, William E., *Music in the Town and Country Church*. New York: The National Council, Protestant Episcopal Church, Division of Town and Country Work, 1958.

Sowerby, Leo, *Ideals in Church Music*. Greenwich, Conn.: The Seabury Press, 1956.

ON CHOIRS, CHOIR MUSIC, AND CHORAL CONDUCTING

Clokey, Joseph Waddell, *In Every Corner Sing*. New York: Morehouse-Gorham Co., 1945.

Davison, Archibald T., *Choral Conducting*. Cambridge: Harvard University Press, 1940, 1956.

Ehret, Walter, *The Choral Conductor's Handbook*. New York: Edward B. Marks Music Corp., 1959.

Jacobs, Ruth Krehbiel, *The Children's Choir*. Rock Island, Ill.: Augustana Press, 1958.

Jones, Archie Neff, *Techniques in Choral Conducting*. New York: Carl Fischer, Inc., 1948.

Kettring, Donald D., *Steps Toward a Singing Church*. Philadelphia: The Westminster Press, 1948.

Steere, Dwight, *Music for the Protestant Church Choir*. Richmond: John Knox Press, 1955.

Whittlesey, Federal Lee, *A Comprehensive Program of Church Music*. Philadelphia: The Westminster Press, 1957.

Wilson, Harry Robert, and Lyall, Jack Lawrence, *Building a Church Choir*. Minneapolis: Schmitt, Hall & McCreary, 1957.

ON MUSIC IN CHRISTIAN EDUCATION

Morsch, Vivian Sharp, *The Use of Music in Christian Education*. Philadelphia: The Westminster Press, 1956.

Shields, Elizabeth McE., *Music in the Religious Growth of Children*. Nashville: Abingdon Press, 1953.

Thomas, Edith Lovell, *Music in Christian Education*. Nashville: Abingdon Press, 1953.

ON THE SPEECH CHOIR

de Banke, Cécile, *The Art of Choral Speaking*. Boston: Baker's Plays, 1937.
Gullan, Marjorie, *Choral Speaking*. Boston: Baker's Plays, 1931.
Swann, Mona, *An Approach to Choral Speaking*. London: Macmillan and Co. Ltd., 1946.

ON HYMNS

Benson, Louis F., *The Hymnody of the Christian Church*. Richmond: John Knox Press, 1956. (Reprint of 1927 edition.)
Haeussler, Armin, *The Story of Our Hymns*. St. Louis: Eden Publishing House, 1952.
Julian, John, *A Dictionary of Hymnology*. New York: Dover Publications, 1957. (Reprint of the 1907 revision.)
McCutchan, Robert Guy, *Our Hymnody: A Manual of the Methodist Hymnal*. Nashville: Abingdon Press, 1937.
Tufts, John, 1689-1750, *An Introduction to the Singing of Psalm-Tunes*. Boston: Printed for Samuel Gerrish, 1738; Philadelphia: Printed for *Musical Americana* by A. Saifer, Publisher, 1954.

ON THE FUNERAL

Bowman, Leroy, *The American Funeral*. Washington, D. C.: Public Affairs Press, 1959.

ON THE WEDDING

Fryxell, Regina H., *Wedding Music*. Rock Island, Ill.: The Augustana Press, 1956.
Music for Church Weddings, The Joint Commission on Church Music. Greenwich, Conn.: The Seabury Press, 1952.
Pickett, Wilberta Naden, *Music for the Christian Wedding Service*. Master's Thesis at the School of Sacred Music of Union Theological Seminary, New York City, 1952.

Notes and Acknowledgments

Introduction

1. Charles H. Heimsath, *The Genius of Public Worship*, p. 176. New York: Charles Scribner's Sons, 1945. Used by permission.

2. John Calvin, *Institutes of the Christian Religion*, translated by John Allen, Book IV, Chapter X, p. 375. Philadelphia: Presbyterian Board of Publication.

3. *Recovery of Worship*, by George Walter Fiske. New York: The Macmillan Company, 1931.

Restoring Worship, by Clarice Bowman. Nashville: Abingdon-Cokesbury Press, 1951.

Reality in Worship, by Willard L. Sperry. New York: The Macmillan Company, 1925.

4. Albert W. Palmer, *The Art of Conducting Public Worship*, p. 1. New York: The Macmillan Company, 1939. Used by permission.

5. Members of Mansfield College, edited by Nathaniel Micklem, *Christian Worship*, Chapter XIV, "Prayer and Praise," by K. L. Parry, p. 242. New York: Oxford University Press, 1936. Used by permission.

6. Earl Enyeart Harper, *Church Music and Worship*, p. 42. New York: Abingdon Press, 1924.

7. *Christian Worship*, op. cit., p. 239.

8. S. Arthur Devan, *Ascent to Zion*, p. 150. New York: The Macmillan Company, 1942. Used by permission of Mrs. S. Arthur Devan.

9. Oswald B. Milligan, *The Ministry of Worship*, p. 9. London: Oxford University Press, 1941. By permission.

PART ONE—WE BUILD A CHURCH

I. The Place of Worship

1. Henry Sloane Coffin, *The Public Worship of God*, p. 58. Copyright, 1946, by W. L. Jenkins, The Westminster Press. Used by permission.

2. *Ibid.*, p. 61.

3. George Hedley, *Christian Worship*, p. 40. New York: The Macmillan Company, 1953. Used by permission.

4. S. Arthur Devan, *Ascent to Zion*, pp. 131-132. New York: The Macmillan Company, 1942. Used by permission of Mrs. S. Arthur Devan.

5. Devan, *ibid.*, pp. 132-133.

6. Hedley, *op. cit.*, p. 44. By permission.

7. Von Ogden Vogt, *Modern Worship*, p. 115. New Haven: Yale University Press, 1927. Used by permission.

8. Scott Francis Brenner, *The Way of Worship*, p. 105. New York: The Macmillan Company, 1944. By permission of the author.

9. Coffin, *op. cit.*, p. 59. By permission.

10. Devan, *op. cit.*, pp. 133, 134. By permission.

11. Also consult Albert W. Palmer's *The Art of Conducting Public Worship*, Chapter VI (New York: The Macmillan Company, 1939), and George Fiske's *Recovery of Worship*, Chapter X (New York: The Macmillan Company, 1931).

II. The Choir

1. *Ye Olde New-England Psalm-Tunes 1620-1820*, with Historical Sketch by William Arms Fisher, p. vii. Boston and New York: Oliver Ditson Company, 1930. Used by permission.
2. Archibald T. Davison, *Protestant Church Music in America*, p. 47. Boston: E. C. Schirmer Music Company, 1933. Used by permission.

III. The Organ

1. Leo Sowerby, *Ideals in Church Music*, p. 16. Greenwich, Conn.: The Seabury Press, 1956. Used by permission.
2. William Leslie Sumner, *The Organ*, pp. 237-238. New York: Philosophical Library, 1952. Used by permission of Macdonald & Co. Ltd., London.
3. William Harrison Barnes, *The Contemporary American Organ*, pp. 356, 358. Glen Rock, N. J.: J. Fischer & Bro., 1959. (Quoted from Barnes' full report on the four-manual Allen electronic organ in Stamford, published in *The Diapason*, April 1958.) By permission of the author.
4. Allan Bacon, *The True Function of Church Music*, p. 50. Stockton, Cal.: Printwell Press, 1953. By permission of the author.
5. Barnes, *op. cit.*, pp. 361-362.
6. Leslie Norman Leet, *An Introduction to the Organ*, p. 84. Cranford, N. J.: Allen Printing and Publishing Company, 1940.
7. Barnes, *op. cit.*, p. 331.
8. Barnes, *op. cit.*, p. 331.
9. Barnes, *op. cit.*, chapter 18.

IV. Musical Accessories

1. Robert Alexander Stewart Macalister, *Ecclesiastical Vestments*, p. 139. London: E. Stock, 1896. Used by permission.
2. *The Ministry in Historical Perspectives*, edited by H. Richard Niebuhr and Daniel D. Williams. Chapter V, "The Ministry in the Time of the Continental Reformation," by Wilhelm Pauck, p. 147. New York: Harper & Brothers, 1956. Used by permission.
3. Dwight Steere, *Music for the Protestant Church Choir*. Richmond: John Knox Press, 1955.

PART TWO—WE BELONG TO A CHURCH

V. The Minister

1. Von Ogden Vogt, *Modern Worship*, p. 134. New Haven: Yale University Press, 1927. Used by permission.

VII. The Multiple Choir System

1. Federal Lee Whittlesey, *A Comprehensive Program of Church Music*, pp. 23-24. Copyright, 1957, by W. L. Jenkins, The Westminster Press. Used by permission.

2. *Ibid.*, p. 25.

3. *Ibid.*, pp. 29-30.

4. *Ibid.*, p. 25.

5. Donald D. Kettring, *Steps Toward a Singing Church*. Philadelphia: The Westminster Press, 1948.

PART THREE—WE GO TO CHURCH

X. The Hymn

1. See Henry Sloane Coffin, *The Public Worship of God*, Chapter VI. Philadelphia: The Westminster Press, 1946.

2. Andrew W. Blackwood, *The Fine Art of Public Worship*, Chapter VI. Nashville: Cokesbury Press, 1939.

3. Archibald T. Davison, *Protestant Church Music in America*. Boston: E. C. Schirmer Music Company, 1933.

4. Carl Halter, *The Practice of Sacred Music*, pp. 35-36. St. Louis: Concordia Publishing House, 1955. Reprinted by permission.

5. Willard L. Sperry, *Reality in Worship*, p. 302. New York: The Macmillan Company, 1925. Used by permission.

XI. Processional and Recessional

1. Willard L. Sperry, *Reality in Worship*, p. 219. New York: The Macmillan Company, 1925. Used by permission.

XII. Congregational Service Music

1. Henry Sloane Coffin, *The Public Worship of God*, p. 101. Copyright, 1946, by W. L. Jenkins, The Westminster Press. Used by permission.

2. Raymond Abba, *Principles of Christian Worship*, p. 159. London and New York: Oxford University Press, 1957. Used by permission.

3. From *Book of Common Order*, p. 17, by permission of the Church of Scotland Committee on Public Worship and Aids to Devotion.

4. *Ibid.*, p. 28. (Slightly adapted.)

XIII. The Anthem

1. Archibald T. Davison, *Church Music, Illusion and Reality*. Cambridge: Harvard University Press, 1952.

XIV. The Choral Response

1. S. Arthur Devan, *Ascent to Zion*, p. 150. New York: The Macmillan Company, 1942. Used by permission of Mrs. S. Arthur Devan.

XV. Organ Music

1. Andrew W. Blackwood, *The Fine Art of Public Worship*, p. 95. Nashville: Cokesbury Press, 1939. Used by permission.

2. Archibald T. Davison, *Protestant Church Music in America* (Boston: E. C. Schirmer Music Company, 1933) and *Church Music, Illusion and Reality* (Cambridge: Harvard University Press, 1952).

3. See Albert W. Palmer, *Come, Let Us Worship*, p. 52. New York: The Macmillan Company, 1941.

4. Evelyn Underhill, *Worship*, pp. 93-96. New York: Harper & Brothers, 1937.

5. George Walter Fiske, *Recovery of Worship*, Chapter XI, "The Religious Use of Silence." New York: The Macmillan Company, 1931.

6. Charles H. Heimsath, *The Genius of Public Worship*, Chapter XVII, "The Voice of Silence." New York: Charles Scribner's Sons, 1945.

XVI. The Solo

1. Henry Sloane Coffin, *The Public Worship of God*, p. 119. Copyright, 1946, by W. L. Jenkins, The Westminster Press. Used by permission.

XVII. The Occasional Service

1. Henry Sloane Coffin, *The Public Worship of God*, p. 136. Copyright, 1946, by W. L. Jenkins, The Westminster Press. Used by permission.

2. Leroy Bowman, *The American Funeral*, p. 147. Washington, D. C.: Public Affairs Press, 1959. Used by permission.

3. Regina H. Fryxell, *Wedding Music*, p. 7. Rock Island, Ill.: Augustana Press, 1956. Used by permission.

XIX. Finally

1. See Chapter XIV, "The Order of Service," in Willard L. Sperry's *Reality in Worship*. New York: The Macmillan Company, 1925.

2. A. G. Hebert, in *Ways of Worship*, edited by Pehr Edwall, Eric Hayman, and William D. Maxwell, Chapter III, p. 66. New York: Harper & Brothers, 1951. Used by permission of SCM Press Ltd., London.

3. Fiêsta Record FLP-25000.

Index